D0207840

Liberalism Against Populism

To my students and colleagues
past and present

Liberalism Against Populism

A Confrontation Between the Theory of Democracy and the Theory of Social Choice

William H. Riker
University of Rochester

W. H. Freeman and Company
San Francisco

Project Editor: Judith Wilson
Copy Editor: Patricia Herbst
Designer: Nancy Benedict
Production Coordinator: Linda Jupiter
Illustration Coordinator: Richard Quinones
Artist: Catherine Brandel
Compositor: Allservice Phototypesetting Company
Printer and Binder: The Maple-Vail Book Manufacturing Group

Library of Congress Cataloging in Publication Data

Riker, William H.
 Liberalism against populism.

 Bibliography: p.
 Includes index.
 1. Democracy. 2. Populism. 3. Social choice. 4. Voting. I. Title.
JC423.R5   320'.01'1   81-12458
ISBN 0-7167-1245-8   AACR2
ISBN 0-7167-1246-6 (pbk.)

1 2 3 4 5 6 7 8 9 0 MP 0 8 9 8 7 6 5 4 3 2

Contents

4

Voting Methods with Three
or More Alternatives 65

Preface

In this book I have used social choice theory to explicate the theory of democracy. In particular, I have examined the feasibility of the political ideal of democracy in terms of the practical constraints that the social choice analysis reveals concerning various democratic aspirations. Therefore, this book is written for three kinds of readers: political philosophers, students of political institutions, and beginning students of social choice theory.

For political philosophers, I hope it will demonstrate the inescapable relevance of the social choice analysis to the normative concerns of political philosophy. Unfortunately very few political philosophers have heretofore recognized this relevance, possibly because social choice theory has usually been cast in mathematical form, thereby suggesting that it is merely a technical exercise. By showing that important themes from the social choice literature necessarily enter into philosophic discourse and by presenting these themes wholly in nonmathematical terms, I show the importance of the theory of social choice.

For students of political institutions, this book will demonstrate that analytic theory can help in the interpretation of events. One central question of political description—a question much disputed but little understood—is the problem of explaining why some issues are politically salient and others not. This problem has usually been investigated by reducing politics to something else—to economics, for example, as in Marxism, or to psychology, as in psychoanalytic visualizations—thereby producing an economic (or psychological) interpretation of politics. However, in Chapters 8 and 9, I offer a political interpretation of politics, a theory about the rise and decline of the salience of issues that derives directly from social choice theory and is entirely political in form. This theory is an extension into political description of the rational choice model of individual decision that underlies social choice theory. At the same time, my theory utilizes some of the main discoveries of social choice theory to describe politics generally.

For beginning students of social choice theory—a category that should, I believe, include most beginning students of political science— this book will serve to introduce both the main topics of inquiry and the main conclusions so far arrived at in this theory. Since, as I have already noted, it has usually been presented in a fairly formidable mathematical form, many college freshmen and sophomores have probably not understood the intellectual motivation for the theory. I have summarized the main topics and related them to political philosophy and the description of politics. This will help beginning students to appreciate the importance— and even the elegance—of the theory of social choice.

• • •

I began to think about the theme of this book when I was a Fairchild Fellow at the California Institute of Technology, and I was given the opportunity to write it by the Scaife Family Charitable Trust. I deeply appreciate the support from both these endowments. So many friends have helped me to understand the topics in this book that I cannot thank them all. But I must single out for public appreciation Duncan Black, Gerald Kramer, Steven Brams, Richard McKelvey, Peter Ordeshook, John Ferejohn, Richard Kronick, Darrell Dobbs, James Enelow, Gideon Doron, Raymond Jean, and especially Kenneth Shepsle, whose criticisms of the first formulation of the theme of this book (at a conference in 1976 sponsored by the Mathematical Social Science Board) have been a constant warning and whose comments on the final formulation have clarified many a paragraph, Jeffrey Richelson, whose dissertation "A Comparative Analysis of Social Choice Functions" (University of Rochester, 1975) provided one main point of departure, Charles Plott, whose seminar at Cal Tech gave me a chance to converse with him and others about most of these issues, both analytic and normative, and Richard Niemi, whose incisive criticisms of every page have greatly benefited both me and my readers.

At various stages in the writing of this book, Janice Brown, Donna French, Hilda Porter, Doris Smith, and Claire Sundeen have helped me with typing, and Mary Riker with the drawings, more than I can adequately thank them.

July 1981   William H. Riker

Analytical Table of Contents

In the liberal view, the outcome of voting is morally neutral; in the populist view, it is morally right. By reason of this difference, populists can, on moral grounds, justify tyranny by supposed embodiments of the popular will such as socialist dictators.

1.G The Vitality of the Liberal and
Populist Interpretations of Voting   14
Although these views involve old philosophical issues, they are central to current political debate, as illustrated in two polemical books.

1.H The Paradox of Voting   16
Reflection on this paradox raises questions about whether either interpretation can be sustained and hence about whether democratic means (and the democratic ideal) are socially feasible.

2

Different Choices from Identical Values   21

To illustrate the practical immediacy of these questions, evidence is presented from several real events that identical preferences (votes), aggregated (counted) by different methods, produce different social choices.

2.A Evidence from Elections   22

2.B Evidence from Experiment   29

3

Simple Majority Decision   41

Different social choices from identical sets of individual values need not cast doubt on the feasibility of democracy, provided that one method of aggregating preferences is clearly superior to all others. Simple majority voting on two alternatives is one possibly superior method, the desirable properties of which are analyzed in this chapter. It is shown in conclusion, however, that binary choices occur rarely in nature and can be artificially generated only by violating fundamental notions of fairness.

3.A Introductory Definitions   42

3.B Properties of Simple Majority Decision: Monotonicity   45
A monotonic method of counting votes is such that, when individual valuations of an alternative increase, the social valuation also increases. Since voting is intended to relate preferences to social choice, monotonicity is an elementary criterion of fairness that is clearly satisfied by simple majority voting.

3.C Violations of Monotonicity   47

3.D Properties of Simple Majority Decision:
Undifferentiatedness (Anonymity)   51
Another criterion of fairness, not always appropriate but satisfied by simple majority voting, is that the vote-counting rule not differentiate among the voters in order to count them differently.

A third criterion of fairness, again only sometimes appropriate but satisfied by simple majority decision, is that the rule for vote-counting be neutral—that is, not treat alternatives differently.

Only the rule of simple majority decision on two alternatives satisfies these three criteria simultaneously. Consequently many theorists of democracy have been entranced with the rule and have sought to institutionalize it by providing only binary choices, as in the notion of the system of two "responsible" parties. To enforce binary choice is itself undemocratic, however, because it unfairly deprives proponents of third and other alternatives of a chance to win.

4

Voting Methods with Three or More Alternatives 65

Fairness requires that the decision rule operate on more than two alternatives. Unfortunately no such rule satisfies reasonable criteria of fairness. Since there is no deeper ethical system of judging among criteria, there is no way to show that one decision method is superior to another.

The method of majority rule, when extended to more than two alternatives, is usually regarded as adequate if it satisfies the Condorcet criterion that the winner beat (or tie) all other alternatives. When, however, no Condorcet winner exists, majority rule is theoretically confused and practically inadequate.

Majoritarian methods are based on binary comparisons, but with three or more alternatives n-ary comparisons are possible by considering the position of alternatives in all the individual orderings. Positional methods thus often produce different winners from majoritarian methods.

Taking utility as a measure of preference, cardinal utility is a measure of degrees of preference, and methods of aggregating cardinal utility thereby incorporate the intensity of individual valuations. The transformation of an initially ordinal measure into a cardinal measure is difficult to justify.

In addition to the criteria of Chapter 4, reasonable and widely accepted standards are the Condorcet criterion (embodying the majoritarian ideal), the consistency criterion (embodying the positional ideal), and the criterion of independence from irrelevant alternatives (embodying a concern for consistent application of a rule).

5

The Meaning of Social Choices 115

Although individuals can order alternatives, no method of aggregating preferences can simultaneously satisfy elementary conditions of fairness and an elementary condition of logicality. Hence, not only may the results of voting be unfair, they may also fail to make sense.

6

The Manipulation of Social Choices:
Strategic Voting   137

probably occurs frequently. Since, however, it can never be positively identified, we can never know whether a particular outcome is a true aggregation of preferences or a product of both preferences and manipulation.

7

The Manipulation of Social Choices:
Control of the Agenda 169

Leaders can control agendas by establishing the sequence and content of business. Everyone can control agendas by inventing new alternatives and new dimensions of judgment.

7.A The Universality of Agenda Control 170
At the most abstract level, equilibria in voting rarely exist, and if they do, are fragile. In the absence of equilibrium, any voting situation is vulnerable to manipulation of the agenda.

7.B Examples of Agenda Control 173

7.C The Paucity of Equilibria 181
If alternatives are continuous and located by two or more dimensions and if utility is differentiable, then the conditions for equilibria are highly restrictive (Plott's theorem). Furthermore, without equilibrium, every possible alternative is in the cycle of best outcomes (McKelvey's theorem).

7.D Practical Stability and Theoretical Instability 188
Consequently, what stability of outcomes is observed must depend on institutional constraints, not on voters' preferences.

7.E The Fragility of Equilibria: An Example of the Introduction
of New Alternatives to Generate Disequilibrium 192
Given that equilibria are rare and fragile and dependent on institutions, voting can usually be manipulated by introducing new alternatives or changing the dimensions of the space in which they are evaluated, as illustrated by an elegant maneuver by Chauncey DePew.

8

The Natural Selection of Political Issues:
An Interpretation of
Political Disequilibrium 197

The general possibility of manipulation and the typical absence of equilibria account for and explain political evolution or the perpetual flux of politics. Losers generate new issues in the hope of becoming winners, though which issues are successful is a matter of a natural selection we do not yet understand.

8.A Disappointments with Disequilibria 198
The revelation in social choice theory of the fundamental disequilibrium of politics forces a reassessment of the nature of politics, which is undertaken in this and the next chapter.

Political situations typically do not admit of outcomes in which all participants are minimally content. Hence, there exist losers who are worse off for having participated, especially when universal values, detested by losers, are imposed by victors—a kind of political scarcity.

Even if outcomes are in equilibrium, there are dissatisfied losers—especially dissatisfied if the issue at stake involves political or moral scarcity. If outcomes are not in equilibrium so that under majority rule, the outcome actually adopted would lose to another potential majority, a majority of participants—often a large majority—is dissatisfied.

Given widespread dissatisfaction, the content of politics is the invention and promotion of new alternatives in support of which the dissatisfied can unite to win. By reason of the fact of disequilibrium, it is known that such alternatives potentially exist, and the art of politics is to find them.

Political entrepreneurs thus constantly promote new alternatives, some of which ultimately succeed in a social world somewhat like that world within which biological evolution by natural selection occurs.

Although the generation and acceptance of new issues may appear to be a random process, doubtless structural and procedural regularities exist about which a political science can be centered.

9

Manipulation and the Natural Selection
of Issues: The Development of the
Issue of Slavery as a Prelude to the
American Civil War   213

In the new view of politics as the propagation of new issues in a world without equilibrium, an important illustration is the rise of the slavery issue in American politics from quiescence prior to 1819 to the central concern after 1846. This new and wholly political interpretation differs sharply from economic interpretations, interpretations in terms of ideology, and such ad hoc interpretations as the notion of critical elections.

In 1819 the status quo on slavery, incorporated in the Constitution, was its exclusion from national politics as a matter of local concern. This status quo especially suited the dominant intersectional coalition of agrarian expansionists (Jefferson Republicanism and Jacksonian Democracy) that governed most of the time from 1800 to 1860. The slavery issue threatened this dominant coalition and ultimately disrupted it. Therein lay the opportunity for the losers, the commercial

guarantees of the integrity of elections, the two interpretations are probably incompatible.

10.E The Preservation of Liberal Democracy   249

The constitutional limitations intended to preserve the limited tenure and regular elections of liberal democracy are multicameralism, the separation of powers, multipartyism, federalism, and an independent judiciary. These reinforce the political pattern of shifting coalitions characteristic of the liberal kind of voting. And together these institutions will, it is hoped, guarantee the circulation of leadership and hence the maintenance of the instrument and ideals of democracy.

Liberalism Against Populism

1

The Connection Between
the Theory of Social Choice
and the Theory of Democracy

The theory of social choice is a theory about the way the tastes, preferences, or values of individual persons are amalgamated and summarized into the choice of a collective group or society. Because voting is one method of aggregating values, social choice theory must include, among other elements, a theory of voting. Voting is in turn an indispensable feature of democracy because, however the goals of democracy are defined, its method involves some kind of popular participation in government. Although participation can take many forms, historically—and probably logically—it invariably includes voting. Therefore, the theory of social choice is highly relevant to the theory of democracy.

Only recently, however, has this relevance been recognized. One reason recognition has come slowly is that students of democracy have tended to regard the mechanism of voting and counting votes as a trivial subject. There has, it is true, been a century-long controversy over proportional representation, but that controversy has centered more on fairness than on the operating characteristics of alternative mechanisms. Otherwise, political philosophers, engaged in the pursuit of justice, have ignored and neglected the theory of voting methods as something best left to the attention of municipal employees.

To some degree, the philosophers have been right: The theory of voting has barely existed until this generation, and one cannot attribute much relevance to a theory that barely exists. Only in the 1940s did Duncan Black, then an unknown lecturer on economics in Glasgow, rediscover the paradox of voting (see section 1.H) and recognize the full significance of a theory of social choice.

The paradox of voting is the coexistence of coherent individual valuations and a collectively incoherent choice by majority rule. In an election with three or more alternatives (candidates, motions, etc.) and three or more voters, it may happen that when the alternatives are placed against each other in a series of paired comparisons, no alternative emerges victorious over each of the others: Voting fails to produce a clear-cut winner. This paradox was originally discovered by Condorcet in the late eighteenth century, just at the time that voting was becoming a much more frequently used method of social decision. Condorcet's discovery made little impression on his contemporaries, and neither did the rediscoveries in the late nineteenth and early twentieth centuries by Lewis Carroll (Charles Dodgson) and E. J. Nanson make much impression on their contemporaries. Duncan Black, however, in a series of essays begun in the 1940s and culminating in his *Theory of Committees and Elections,* effectively communicated the profound significance of the rediscovered paradox to other scholars.[1] One was Kenneth Arrow, who proved in *Social Choice and Individual Values* that the paradox may occur in any reasonably fair system of counting votes.[2] Another was Robin Farquharson, who showed in *Theory of Voting* that political strategy and dissimulation about tastes were ineradicable parts of the process of voting.[3]

The work of Black, Arrow, and Farquharson launched the theory of social choice and connected it logically with the theory of democracy. But, though the connection is now made, it is on the whole still true that political scientists and political philosophers have not worked out the significance of the connection. Most writers simply ignore the problem, and those who recognize it tend to sweep it under the rug.[4] Robert Dahl did try to work out some connection between the two theories.[5] But social choice theory, at the time he wrote, was not yet mature. Consequently, the full significance of the connection was not visible to him.

Now, however, that significance can be specified more easily: Democracy is an ideal of both justice and political life, and it is a method of realizing that ideal in ordinary politics. The ideal is individual self-realization (that is, the achievement of the human potential for good qualities of character and behavior) and individual self-respect (that is, a sense of one's worthiness as a person and a pride in one's self-realization). The method is, for each person, free and equal participation in the political life of the community, engaging thus in whatever control of the social environment is possible. Both parts, the ideal and the method, are necessary for democracy. They can exist separately in other contexts—the ideal in, for example, an ethical system and the method in, say, a religious society. But what makes democracy unique is that the democratic means and the democratic ends are joined. Indeed, they are the same things viewed ideally and instrumentally. According to democratic theory, democratic ends can be achieved by democratic means. Now, of course, that assertion may or may not be true. If it is true, then the notion of democracy makes sense. But if it is not true, if the method cannot realize the ideal, then, however lofty the ideal may be, the notion of democracy is meaningless. Thus, a profoundly important question about democracy is whether the means are capable of achieving the ends.

The theory of social choice permits us to approach, and perhaps even partially to answer, that question. The ideal of democracy is set forth in a normative statement of what we want the natural world of human interaction to yield for us. The theory of social choice is an analytic theory about the way that natural world can work and what kinds of outputs that world can yield. By means of this analytic theory, we can discover whether pursuit of the ideal is promising or futile.

What we hope to have is always conditional on what we can have. To seek what we know, a priori, we cannot get is about like trying to square the circle. But to search for an algorithm to compute a result that we know is, at least in principle, computable is a sensible task. This then is the connection between the theory of democracy and the theory of social choice: By use of the latter it is possible to assess, at least in part, whether it is sensible to pursue democratic ends by democratic means.

1.A. The Attainability of Justice

In the study of justice the need to investigate whether the specified means can be used to achieve the specified ends recurs frequently. It is exactly such investigation that has heretofore been neglected by students of democracy.

Such neglect is common enough in contemporary political thought, and many recent interpreters of nondemocratic notions of justice have been equally guilty of neglecting the study of institutions by which their versions of justice might be attained. Witness, for example, John Rawls' utilitarianism with a Kantian overlay or Herbert Marcuse's improbable combination of humanism and violence. Both of them have been presented as definitions of goals, but they lack any consideration at all of whether the goals are physically attainable by any imaginable means.

It does not really make sense to ignore the question of attainability, and in the long history of the study of justice such questions have typically been a central part of the inquiry. In the *Republic,* the earliest-recorded well-articulated theory of justice, Plato defines justice as a condition in which everyone is doing the job best fitted to his or her talents. This definition is only the beginning of a discussion of whether that particular goal can be achieved by various devices, such as an appropriate ideology (the so-called noble lie), an educational system for rulers, the generation of wisdom-loving kings, and even divine intervention in history. Similarly, in the modern world, the Marxian definition of justice as the distribution of material goods according to needs was proposed along with a concrete method of achieving it—namely, the dictatorship of the proletariat led by its vanguard, the Communist party. Marx himself devoted much thought to concrete steps in the revolution (for example, in the *Critique of the Gotha Program*), and his successors Lenin and Mao equated philosophy with a theory of party organization and a theory of propaganda.

In the interpretation of both the Platonic and the Marxian theories, it is certainly appropriate and in fact customary to inquire whether the means are efficient for attaining the ends. Very few people have seriously considered attempting to achieve Platonic justice, not primarily because Platonic justice is rather uninspiring, but because the education and the institution of a philosopher-king seem internally contradictory and quite unlikely to achieve the intended effects even if they could be carried through. Similarly, although the materialism of Marxist goals has a wide appeal, it is far from clear that the dictatorship of the Communist party has promoted distribution according to need. Many observers believe that Communist bureaucracies, multiplying disincentives for production and satiating themselves with perquisites, have produced distributions even less in accord with stated Marxist goals than was achieved under the systems they replaced. If so, then Marxist means may well have *prevented* the achievement of Marxist ends.

As these two examples indicate, the question of whether particular goals are achievable by specified means (or indeed by any means at all) is an elementary and unavoidable question about *any* theory of justice. Yet up to this time it has not been asked about democracy. The main reason it has not been asked is, I believe, that we have lacked an appropriate base for questioning. But now that we have an analytic theory about the main institution of democracy—namely, voting—we do have an appropriate base. Consequently, it seems both possible and worthwhile to study the relation of democratic means to democratic ends, and that is the purpose of this book.

1.B. The Elements of Democracy

To begin the investigation we need some agreed-upon notion of what democracy is. Unfortunately we cannot go to a unique authoritative source for a definition. Democracies have existed in the ancient Mediterranean world, in late-medieval central European cities, and in many nations of the modern world. Their social and cultural circumstances have been extremely diverse, and their goals and methods have been defined in many constitutions and in a vast body of judicial, philosophical, didactic, and popular commentary. Since the literature celebrating democracy— even authoritatively explicating it—is far too much for one person to read, it is difficult to set forth a fair and inclusive definition.

On another occasion I attempted to by-pass this difficulty by the statistician's device of selecting a sample. I compared five representative documents, looking for the elements they had in common.[6] Without repeating that analysis here, I will list the properties found in those documents. They are participation, liberty, and equality. Most recent writers attribute those properties to democracy; I will explain how they fit together coherently.

To anticipate my conclusion, and to indicate the direction of the argument, I want to point out that the coherence depends on the fact that all democratic ideas are focused on the mechanism of voting. All the elements of the democratic method are means to render voting practically effective and politically significant, and all the elements of the democratic ideal are moral extensions and elaborations of the features of the method that make voting work. Voting, therefore, is the central act of democracy, and this fact makes apparent the immediate relevance of the theory of social choice.

Participation

The crucial attribute of democracy is popular participation in government. This is what the root of the word originally meant in Greek. Although the institutions of participation have been many and varied, they have always revolved around the simple act of voting. Even recent theories, such as those from Dahl and his followers, that equate democracy with the free interplay of groups and the existence of an opposition cannot avoid an emphasis on voting as the ultimate way groups and oppositions make themselves felt. Voting, however, is not equivalent to democracy. Only voting that facilitates popular choice is democratic. This condition excludes voting both in oligarchic bodies and in plebiscites in communist and military tyrannies, where voting is no more than forced approbation. Thus one can say that democracy implies voting but voting does not imply democracy. Or, voting is a necessary, but not sufficient, condition of democracy. To render them equivalent, voting must be surrounded with numerous institutions like political parties and free speech, which organize voting into genuine choice.

The purpose of participation is twofold. In most cases it has been instituted to restrain oppressive rule by subjecting rulers to popular judgment. But, in addition, it has been invested with a positive value of its own. Ruling and being ruled in turn is, said Aristotle, the essence of good citizenship; and good citizenship he equated with the good life. To take, thereby, full responsibility for oneself—both by internal discipline and by cooperative management of the physical and social environment—is to achieve as much self-control as one can. And self-control is a necessary instrument of that human dignity and self-respect that moral philosophers of almost all persuasions have regarded as the best human achievement. To facilitate that achievement is the goal of democracy and its ideal of justice. Hence, participation is an end in itself as well as a practical method.

Liberty

A second feature of democracy is liberty to pursue one's goals. This notion has been variously expressed. In the tradition of Locke, which has dominated Anglo-American thought, liberty has been described as the natural rights inherent in human life and independent even of citizenship. Many of the great democratic declarations are tabulations of rights such as free speech, religious liberty, fair legal procedure, property ownership, and economic security. But the connection between democratic liberty and natural rights is not necessary. In the ancient world there was no notion of natural rights, yet Pericles praised freedom as one of the main features of Athenian democracy. And in the tradition of Rousseau, liberty resides in participation in government, not in rights distinct from government.

Nevertheless, however expressed, there is a close connection between liberty and democracy. How can the persistence of this association be explained? Historically, at least, the association is instrumental because liberty is necessary to organize participation in government. In the English tradition, limited government originated in claims of freedoms against the Crown. The earliest such claim was that members of Parliament not be prosecuted for speeches in Parliament. The claim protected politicians temporarily in office and not certain of staying there and thereby enabled them to form factions and organize voting against the government. Ultimately this freedom was extended to everybody, but it has never lost its association with political opposition and the nourishment of faction. Almost everything else that we think of as civil liberties (the rights of a speedy trial, habeas corpus, and security against unreasonable search and seizure, for example) originated to protect politicians who feared prosecution if and when they lost office. Thus the historic purpose of these fundamental democratic liberties has been not to provide freedom as an end in itself, but to render effective both political participation and the process of choice in voting.

Freedom, however, has also become an end in itself because, like participation, it generates self-control and facilitates self-respect. Hence it is not only an instrument for, but also a part of, justice. Civil liberties are now thought to be good for everybody, not just politicians. Religious liberty, which religious factions—uncertain of victory in the wars of religion—devised to protect themselves, is now thought to be part of self-control and the good life itself. Economic liberty—that is, the free markets and free entrepreneurship of modern capitalism—originally protected a faction, namely, merchants, in conflict with the Crown and the feudal order. Although it has been fashionable in this century to deride economic freedom, capitalism remains essential for faction: No government that has eliminated economic freedom has been able to attain or keep democracy, probably because, when all economic life is absorbed into government, there is no conceivable financial base for opposition. But economic liberty is also an end in itself because capitalism is the driving force for the increased efficiency and technological innovation that has produced in two centuries both a vast increase in the wealth of capitalist nations and a doubling of the average life span of their citizens. These practical achievements also facilitate self-control and are therefore important features of democratic justice.

Altogether, therefore, democratic liberty (whether civil, religious, or economic) originates as an instrument to organize voting and popular participation in government. Once in existence, however, it has always been found good in itself as a part of self-control and human dignity. So, like participation, democratic liberty—originally an instrument—became a part of the democratic ideal.

Equality

A third feature of democracy is equality, which like liberty and participation, originated in some rough sense as an instrument of voting. Voting would not mean much if each person's vote were not counted in the same way. So equality at the ballot box, by some measure, is necessary to make voting and participation work.

But the claim of equality usually involves much more. Sometimes it means equality before the law, which prevents powerful persons from using the law to take advantage of weaker persons. Sometimes it means equal educational or economic opportunity or even equal shares of the wealth of the world. Whatever form the claim takes, its moral significance is clear: To permit serious inequality means to deny to some people the chance to the self-control and cooperative management involved in democratic justice. Equality thus becomes an instrument facilitating self-respect and self-realization, although like the other elements of the democratic ideal its logical base lies in the instrumental value of making voting work.

1.C. The Meaning of Democracy

Democracy is both an ideal and a method. Now, having catalogued its features, I can explain how the ideal and the method are assumed to cohere, though, as will be seen, there may be profound philosophical difficulties beneath this assumed coherence. The ultimate moral ideal of democracy is the self-respect and self-realization that are made possible by self-control and the concomitant cooperative control of the environment. Whether that ideal is achieved depends on how individuals view themselves and what they themselves do to realize their potentials. The function of political justice is to facilitate that achievement by creating appropriate social conditions. In a society characterized by democratic justice, people are free (by reason of democratic liberty) and have the chance (by reason of democratic equality) to seek self-respect and self-control (through some kind of democratic participation). The democratic method that is supposed to achieve this ideal is, of course, the same three features viewed as means rather than as ends: The method is the process of participation, specifically through voting, in the management of society, where voting is understood to include all the ancillary institutions (like parties and pressure groups) and social principles (like freedom and equality) that are necessary to render it significant.

Consequently, we can say that voting, which is a main subject in the theory of social choice, is at the heart of both the method and the ideal of democracy. Clearly, therefore, the theory of democracy must be intimately involved with the theory of social choice.

1.D. The Liberal Interpretation of Voting

Democrats of all persuasions would probably agree that participation built on the act of voting is the focus of democracy. But they certainly interpret voting in different ways. What does it accomplish? What does it mean? The sharp dispute on these questions can be summarized in two views—one of which I call *liberal* or Madisonian, the other *populist* or Rousseauistic.[7]

In the liberal view, the function of voting is to control officials, *and no more*. Madison, who is the original American spokesman for liberal democracy (or republicanism, as he called it) defined a republic as "a government that derives all its powers directly or indirectly from the great body of the people, and is administered by people holding their offices during pleasure, for a limited period, as during good behavior."[8] The first requirement, popularness, he called essential (that is, *necessary*); the second, election and limited tenure, he called *sufficient*. Thus his definition is *logically* complete, and there is nothing to add. Madison said nothing about the quality of popular decision, whether good or bad.

Since all democrats would accept the necessary condition, it is the sufficient condition that is distinctive and hence deserving of detailed explication. Why is election and limited tenure sufficient? Popularness, the necessary condition, ensures participation and equality. The sufficient condition is intended to ensure liberty. In Madison's view, the danger for liberty lies in government officials who might deprive citizens of liberty or fail as agents of citizens' participation. In either case, the liberal remedy is the next election. That is all that is needed to protect liberty; so election and limited tenure are sufficient.

To consider first the protection of citizens' liberty: The replacement of officials is, in the liberal view, the only available instrument. The liberal fear is that the force of government can easily be deployed against citizens to make them support unpopular policies that officials believe necessary. The liberal hope is that officials will be restrained from such behavior out of fear of the next election. It is true that Madison and other framers of the Constitution provided the separation of powers as auxiliary protection, but Madison regarded that protection as distinctly secondary to "a dependence on the people." And the contemporary liberal agrees with Madison that the defense of liberty lies in the discipline of elections.

In the twentieth century it has sometimes (but not lately) been fashionable for populists to dismiss the liberal fear of oppression as an anachronism. Populists believe that, by reason of popular participation, democratic governments embody the will of the people and cannot therefore oppress. Only in the eighteenth century, they say, when executives were officers of the Crown was this danger real; now that elected executives supposedly embody the popular will, they cannot oppress. In *Roosevelt and Hopkins,* Robert Sherwood, for example, disputed Lord Acton's assertion that power corrupts with his (that is, Sherwood's) own belief that power ennobled Franklin Roosevelt.[9] But it was Sherwood's other subject, Harry Hopkins, who presumably uttered that epitome of corruption: "We will tax and tax, spend and spend, elect and elect." Lately, of course, even populists have been shaken by the imperial presidency of Johnson and Nixon, who, however popularly elected, persisted in a hated and oppressive war. In both cases the threat of the next election proved decisive for liberty because it made one not try for reelection and the other (ultimately) end the war. Even more impressive, the possibility of impeachment, a kind of negative election, made Nixon resign. Moreover, it was elections themselves, not just the threat of them, that as recently as 1977 disposed of two putatively tyrannical rulers in India and Sri Lanka.

The other part of Madison's concern was a fear of tyranny by the majority. This is a fear that officials acting for a majority created in the last election will persecute the minority of that election. Madison hoped that such oppression would be minimized by the fact of shifting majorities, so that a future majority might throw out of office the officials who oppressed in the name of the former majority. This is the reason he stressed diversity in the electorate. The way, he said, "to guard one part of society against the injustice of the other part" is to comprehend "in the society so many separate descriptions of citizens as will render an unjust combination of a majority of the whole very improbable, if not impracticable."[10]

Viewed statically, this sounds like just another version of the separation of powers.[11] Viewed dynamically, however, this is simply the claim that an unjust majority cannot last through several elections. Looking at the oppression of blacks, the most persistent issue in American politics and the clearest case of tyranny by the majority, it appears that the Madisonian hope has been justified. As long as blacks were excluded from the political system (from the beginning to 1867 and from the end of Reconstruction in 1877 to the emergence of a substantial number of black voters in the 1930s), they were persecuted. But including them in the system, especially as they became a marginal bloc between the political parties, led to political reform and even to reorientation of the judiciary, so that national political leaders (followed by the courts) have mitigated and are gradually eliminating that tyranny by the majority.

To consider the other danger to liberty (that officials be inefficient agents): The only possible remedy—and one recommended by both populists and liberals—is to elect new officials. So again the next election promotes liberty. Notice, however, that in the liberal view it is not assumed that the electorate is right. This assumption characterizes populism, as I will show. The liberal assumes not popular competence, but merely that the electorate can change officials if many people are dissatisfied or hope for better performance.

It may seem that in the liberal view officials, who are only negatively controlled by voting, cannot really act as agents of the electorate. By reason of regular elections, however, officials may be rejected. In their efforts to avoid rejection they usually act in some rough way as agents of the electorate, at least attempting to avoid giving offense to some future majority. Since this future majority cannot at any moment be clearly specified, officials seeking to placate it in advance must anticipate several kinds of potential majorities, the union of which is often most of the electorate. By reason of this anticipation of the next election, officials are, even in the liberal view, subject to electoral discipline as the agents of democratic self-control.

1.E. The Populist Interpretation of Voting

For the populist, liberty and hence self-control through participation are obtained by embodying the will of the people in the action of officials. The fundamental notion goes back at least to Rousseau. There is a social contract, which creates a "moral and collective body" that has "life" and "will," that is the famous "general will," the will of the incorporated people, the Sovereign. Individual liberty, for Rousseau and subsequent populists, is the participation of the citizen in this sovereignty. "Liberty," Rousseau says, "is obedience to a law we have prescribed for ourselves," understanding, of course, that the prescription is through the acts of the anthropomorphized Sovereign.[12] The way to discover the general will, which is the objectively correct common interest of the incorporated citizens, is to compute it by consulting the citizens. The computation will be accurate if each citizen, when giving an opinion or vote, considers and chooses only the common interest, not a personal or private interest. Thus, by summing the common interest regarding wills (votes) of real persons, one can arrive at the will of the great artificial person, the Sovereign.

In the Middle Ages it was sometimes (blasphemously) said that the voice of the people is the voice of God. Rosseau did not invest the people with quite such divine authority—indeed he believed they might be mistaken about the general will—but he did assert that the general will is always correct and embodies the objective good for society. Later populists have continued to attribute some special character to the voice of the people: What the sovereign people, when speaking for the public interest, want is justified because the sovereign people want it and because it is their liberty.

To summarize: According to the populist interpretation of voting, participation in rule-making is necessary for liberty. The rules thus made must be respected as right and proper because they embody that liberty. Were they not so respected, liberty itself might vanish.

1.F. Differences Between Liberal and Populist Interpretations of Voting

In the liberal view, since voting generates liberty simply by restraining officials (by popular election and limited tenure), there is no need to treat the output of government as the precious embodiment of liberty itself. Indeed, for the liberal, law is no more than the decree of legislators or judges, accepted and occasionally ratified by the citizens. But in the populist view, since voting generates liberty by participation, the output of government must be precious, for that very output *is* liberty.

We can understand the difference between the two views somewhat better, I believe, by recounting a controversy over Isaiah Berlin's distinction between positive and negative liberty.[13] Berlin defined *negative liberty* as the absence of interference by others (especially government) in one's activity. *Positive liberty,* on the other hand, is being one's own mentor. The burden of Berlin's argument is that these two apparently similar notions are at loggerheads. Berlin's explanation of this paradox is that ideas about self-mastery are turned into particular goals for society that people are then coerced into following: They are forced, that is, to be "free." His main example is the transformation of Kant's notions of individual ethical responsibility by, successively, Hegel and Marx into the justification for a monstrous dictatorship. Berlin's point is that positive liberty, which appears initially innocuous, is the root of tyranny.

C. B. MacPherson, in a clever effort to rescue positive liberty from Berlin's obloquy, redefined three kinds of positive liberty:

1. *Liberty as "self-direction" or "self-mastery":* "to live in accordance with one's own conscious purposes."

2. *Liberty as obedience to law:* "coercion, by the [supposedly] fully rational or those who have [supposedly] attained self-mastery [e.g., Lenin or Mao], of all the rest."

3. *Liberty as participation:* "the democratic concept of liberty as a share in the controlling authority." (Notice that this is the populist, not the liberal view of voting.)[14]

MacPherson's argument is that Berlin, lumping the three kinds of positive liberty together, used the obvious and admitted difference between negative liberty and populist voting to generate a contrast and (through liberty as obedience and coercion) an inconsistency between negative liberty and all kinds of positive liberty. MacPherson, as a populist and socialist, wants to save self-mastery as complementary to and not inconsistent with negative liberty, while banishing coercion, that Stalinist embarrassment to "democratic" socialists. MacPherson accomplishes his purpose by giving self-mastery a new name, "developmental liberty," so that it appears to be clearly separate from liberty as obedience and coercion.

The problem, however, is that populist voting is ineradicably different from negative liberty and yet is logically correlated with coercion. This association is precisely explained by Willmoore Kendall in his explication of Locke's version of majority rule.[15] Kendall sought to reconcile Locke's presumed belief in objective moral law with his conclusion that right is what the majority wills. The explanation Kendall proposes of this apparent paradox is that Locke assumed that most people are just and rational; consequently, "The individual can . . . covenant to obey the majority without subjecting himself to . . . arbitrary authority . . . since the judgments of the majority are those of reason and justice."[16]

Thus it is that MacPherson's populist voting unites self-mastery and coercion. All one has to do is to find that a majority (perhaps a putative or even a wholly imaginary and nonexistent majority like the "proletariat" conjured up by Marx) has willed some version of self-mastery. It then becomes both *reasonable* and *necessary* to impose that version of liberty by coercion. It is *reasonable* because the majority that produced the particular version of self-mastery is, in Kendall's words, "rational and just." And it is *necessary* because the particular self-mastery is the embodiment of that majority's liberty, and its liberty would vanish were it not translated into a coerced version.

If, however, one had not the populist view of voting, but merely the liberal view, then this totalitarian sleight-of-hand would not be possible. Indeed, if there were only the liberal view and if one banished the populist "share in the governing authority," then it would be easy for MacPherson to demonstrate the complementarity between negative liberty and self-mastery. But, as a socialist, MacPherson cannot give up populism, and so he is necessarily stuck with coercion. Clearly, Berlin's villain all along is really populism, not just self-mastery. He should have contrasted not negative and positive liberty, but rather negative liberty and the populist view of voting that is used to justify coercion in the name of temporary or spurious majorities.

I have emphasized the moral certainty implicit in the populist view of voting in order to correct the common misconception that populist democracy is simply majority rule. The customary distinction—often expressed in the cliché "majority rule versus minority rights"—is between (1) popular sovereignty or lodging power and decision in the hands of the majority and (2) limited government or reserving some rights for minorities (within an otherwise majoritarian framework). Dahl, for example, makes this distinction, in effect terming (1) Madisonian and (2) populist. This distinction cannot be maintained, however. All democracies involve popular government, equality, and the rule of decision according to the greater number—precisely the features Dahl attributes to populism. Conversely, all democracies (populist as well as liberal) actually limit government by the technique of shifting majorities. So the customary distinction is without a difference.

What is different between the liberal and the populist views is that, in the populist interpretation of voting, the opinions of the majority *must* be right and *must* be respected because the will of the people is the liberty of the people. In the liberal interpretation, there is no such magical identification. The outcome of voting is just a decision and has no special moral character.[17]

1.G. The Vitality of the Liberal and Populist Interpretations of Voting

To show that two interpretations of voting have existed does not prove that they continue today to influence thought. They may have been amalgamated, and if so there is not much point to discussing them, except as historical phenomena. Two writers I have quoted—Berlin (fatalistically) and MacPherson (hopefully)—have each tried to show that populism is absorbing liberalism. I believe, however, that the two traditions remain separate. My evidence is two recent books whose authors are deeply concerned in a practical way with changing American politics, who do not bother with abstract political philosophy, but who nevertheless reflect in more or less pure form the two interpretations I have described.

The books are William A. Rusher's *The Making of the New Majority Party,* which is the liberal offering, and Marcus Raskin's *Notes on the Old System,* which is the populist offering.[18]

Both writers were impelled to write by the Watergate crisis. Rusher observed the scandal weakening the Republican party at the very moment that a majority of citizens seemed to him to be abandoning the then-dominant statism for so-called conservatism (actually Madisonian liberalism). These citizens lacked, he feared, an appropriate vehicle through which to express their new values, not only because the Republican party was discredited, but also because it was infected with the statism of, for example, Nelson Rockefeller. Consequently, Rusher wrote to propose a new national party that would organize the now-leaderless putative majority.

Raskin, on the other hand, regarded Watergate as another compelling instance of the way that what he called "the System" (in which he included the imperial presidency, the CIA, rich people, the Joint Chiefs, the Democratic party, and capitalism) frustrated the supposed impulses of most people to take the positions he (Raskin) believed correct on public policy. Seizing the occasion, therefore, he wrote both to induce popular disgust and to propose a reform—namely, a nationwide system of grand juries to instruct members of Congress. This change, he believed, would amplify voices now supposedly muffled.

Both authors describe themselves as democrats, accurately, I believe, although Raskin displays tendencies toward MacPherson's preference for coercive liberty. Both Rusher and Raskin also denounce the huge bureaucratic apparatus of the contemporary state and seek to hook this Leviathan. But there the similarity ends, and each proceeds according to the tradition he represents.

Rusher thinks the Leviathan exists in large part because voters are often wrong, misled by demagogues who promise "benefits" that cannot be paid for and will, by inducing inflation, harm the ostensible beneficiaries. Clearly, he has no populist illusions that the people do what is right. On the other hand, he wants to make democracy work and rejects the possibility of limiting suffrage. Instead he proposes a new party to instruct and lead the people. "How," Rusher asks, "does an honest politician . . . run against some spellbinder who has invented a new 'benefit'?" The answer: "By telling the truth, of course, about the real cost and impact of the proposed 'benefit'" (p. 200). This answer is introduced by quoting Madison, who wrote that "knowledge will forever govern ignorance" and popular governments "must arm themselves with the power knowledge gives" (p. 198). Thus, Rusher's prescriptions are exactly liberal: Without supposing the people are especially wise, one should nevertheless try, at the polls at the next election, to hook the Leviathan, the king of the children of pride.

Raskin thinks that the Leviathan exists because an elite (politicians, bureaucrats, soldiers, corporate executives) uses the System to suppress the voice of the people and do all sorts of wrong things like building MIRVs and collecting withholding taxes. He is confident that the people, if they could speak, would do right. Like Rousseau, he wants to erase the special interests that stand between the people and the general will. His method is a huge number of grand juries to conduct inquiries and to instruct members of Congress. A Congress thus revitalized would, he believes, embody the true will of the people in law.

Raskin's scheme contains both features of the populist view. First, it stresses participation in local assemblies that will be "instruments of the people as people and as citizens" (p. 157). Second, what the people do will be good, for they will "express a quality of empathy, fairness, and inquiry" (p. 152). Raskin quotes approvingly these sentences from Martin Buber:

Though something of righteousness may become evident in the life of the individual, righteousness itself can only become wholly visible in the structure of the life of a people. . . . Only life can demonstrate an absolute, and it must be the life of the people as a whole.[19]

As applied by Raskin, this is the most extreme claim of populism I have ever seen. Apparently, Raskin believes that the works of the people embody not only their liberty and true justice, but also (and incredibly) *absolute* righteousness.

1.H. The Paradox of Voting

As a beginning of the discussion of the attainability of democratic justice, I have so far shown that the ideal as well as the method of democracy focuses on voting and that voting has been interpreted in two quite different ways. Now I want to show that the theory of social choice raises other disturbing questions about voting, questions that are as controversial as the issue between liberalism and populism and that may affect or even resolve that issue.

Historically, the theory of social choice arose out of the paradox of voting. Without here going into many subsequently developed niceties, one can explain the paradox with these primitive notions of preference and choice.

1. *Preference.* Assuming there are *alternatives, x, y, . . . ,* which may be objects, values, motions, candidates, and so on, a person, *i*, may prefer one alternative to another. This state of mind is represented as the relation of *preference, P,* between some pair of alternatives, *x* and *y*. Conventionally, one writes $x\ P_i\ y$, to mean "*i* prefers *x* to *y*." The relation, *P*, is *transitive,* which means that the following sentence is true:

If $x\ P_i\ y$ and $y\ P_i\ z$, then $x\ P_i\ z$.

Quantitative relations like equality ($=$) or greater than ($>$) are transitive. For example, if *a* equals *b* and *b* equals *c*, then *a* equals *c*. Other relations, such as parenthood, are not transitive. Clearly, if *a* is the father of *b* and *b* is the father of *c*, then it does *not* follow that *a* is the father of *c*. Preference is said to be transitive mainly because intransitive preferences usually seem bizarre. If a man says he likes Republicans better than Democrats and Democrats better than Communists, then we think he is indeed strange if he also says he likes Communists better than Republicans.

2. *Rules of Choice.* Given a society of *n* persons, where *i* is one individual, and given a set of alternatives, $X = (x, y, . . .)$, a rule of choice is a rule by which a choice, *C*, is made for all of the *n* persons (e.g., the selection of a winning alternative by voting or the selection of the alternative left after discussion has eliminated all expressions of dissent). Conventionally one writes $C(X) = y$ to mean "the social choice from *X* is *y*."

There are many rules of choice. A typical example is *simple majority voting between two alternatives.* By this rule, if more people prefer *x* to *y* than prefer *y* to *x*, then *x* wins. Conversely, if more people prefer *y* to *x* than *x* to *y*, then *y* wins. And if the same number prefer *x* to *y* as prefer *y* to *x*, then *x* and *y* tie.

With these primitive notions of preference and choice, the paradox of voting can now be stated: Suppose three people, 1, 2, 3, choose among three alternatives, *x, y, z,* by the method of simple majority rule applied successively to pairs. Suppose also that each person has the following transitive ordering of preference on *x, y,* and *z*:

Person 1: $x\,P_1\,y$, $y\,P_1\,z$, and $x\,P_1\,z$; or $x\,y\,z$

Person 2: $y\,P_2\,z$, $z\,P_2\,x$, and $y\,P_2\,x$; or $y\,z\,x$

Person 3: $z\,P_3\,x$, $x\,P_3\,y$, and $z\,P_3\,y$; or $z\,x\,y$

Then the social choices are:

$C(x, y) = x$ because $x\,P_1\,y$ and $x\,P_3\,y$, while $y\,P_2\,x$

$C(y, z) = y$ because $y\,P_1\,z$ and $y\,P_2\,z$, while $z\,P_3\,y$

$C(x, z) = z$ because $z\,P_2\,x$ and $z\,P_3\,x$, while $x\,P_1\,z$

Thus, although each individual in the society has a transitive ordering of preference, the outcome of voting is not transitive because x beats y, y beats z, and z beats x. If one tried to arrange the outcome of voting in a sequence of "social preference," one would not be able to do so because one could not say whether x or y or z stood first. Any one of these arrangements would be possible: $x\,y\,z\,x$, $y\,z\,x\,y$, $z\,x\,y\,z$.

If, on the other hand, one imposed transitivity by starting with $C(x, y) = x$ and $C(y, z) = y$ and concluding, by reason of transitivity, that $C(x, z) = x$, then person 1 would be a dictator, because only person 1 prefers x to z. Apparently, one is forced either to accept intransitivity for society or to achieve transitivity at the cost of creating a kind of dictator.

Many people are shocked by this result. One standard of consistency in sentences and coherence in thought is transitivity. We would consider a person claiming to like five dollars more than three dollars, three dollars more than one dollar, and one dollar more than five dollars to be quite confused. So we say that *preference* is a transitive relation. We can go further and say that social choice should also be transitive. If so, then, in the case of the voting paradox, we must affirm, paraphrasing Reinhold Niebuhr, "coherent man and incoherent society." Although individuals can arrive at a unique choice, in this case society cannot even choose. What makes all this so democratically unpalatable is that, apparently, the only way to make "society" choose coherently is to impose a dictator.

The possibility that social choice by voting produces inconsistent results raises deep questions about democracy. Can the democratic ideal be attained if the method used to attain it produces confusion? Given the possibility of inconsistency, does one interpretation of voting make more sense than another, or are both interpretations hopelessly flawed?

To raise the issues in the bluntest possible ways, I ask:

1. Can voting restrain officials if the outcome of voting is inconsistent? How can restraint occur if it is not clear what restraint is imposed?

2. Is someone, supposedly restrained at the polls, merely kept in or out of office accidentally? If the outcome of voting might be $x\,y\,z\,x$ or $y\,z\,x\,y$ or $z\,x\,y\,z$, does not an accident of institutions, rather than popular taste, select the winner? And if the antecedent constitution, rather than the people, chooses, how can any kind of democracy be said to operate?

3. If liberty is embodied in an inconsistent law, is not liberty itself defective? If alternative laws are in a cycle, $x\,y\,z\,x$, then which alternative ought to be regarded as the will of the people and their liberty?

4. When an absolute good produced by voting is inconsistent, can that absolute have any moral significance? To say that x is morally right because x beat y seems difficult to defend if z also beat x.

These are the kinds of questions raised when we allow the theory of social choice to confront the theory of democracy. In this book I will elaborate the theory of social choice in order ultimately to explore these questions.

2

Different Choices from
Identical Values

Democracy, however interpreted as a political ideal, uses, as a method of governing, social summaries of citizens' decisions in elections and legislators' decisions in representative bodies. The theory of social choice raises fundamental questions about the quality of these summaries: Are they coherent? Are they imposed by manipulation? This, then, is the problem: Are the doubts raised by social choice theory enough to necessitate a reinterpretation of democracy itself?

Before I begin the investigation, I want to point out that most citizens of democracies seem to be unaware of the problem. Although many people now complain about the adequacy of institutions like parties, they seem more or less satisfied with the fairness and integrity of the voting process (though not necessarily with the outcomes of voting). This satisfaction is easy to understand. We do not frequently have persuasive evidence of the defects in voting. When an election or a committee's decision procedure produces an outcome, evidence that another outcome *might* be socially preferred is usually never collected. One can seldom know, therefore, that the road not taken could have led to a better choice.

For example, when many candidates for an office are winnowed down to two by some nominating procedure (a primary election or a nominating convention), some candidate actually preferred to all others by a majority of voters may nevertheless be eliminated in the nominating process. Such a candidate, call him Golden Median, though very popular with independents as well as with many people in all parties, might lose by a narrow margin in his own party to another candidate, call her Bitter End, who is liked only by those who nominate her. In the election itself, Bitter End faces Blandly Mild, chosen by the other party. Blandly Mild easily beats Bitter End and is said, therefore, to be the voters' choice, even though Golden Median would defeat Blandly Mild if there were some way to conduct another election. But such information is seldom available, and in its absence we cannot know that the best choice was not made. So instead we take the victory of Blandly Mild as evidence that he was the choice of the majority against all others, when, strictly speaking, that victory is only evidence that he was the majority choice against Bitter End.

Lacking clear-cut evidence of the inadequacy of voting, we repress our doubts—if indeed we ever have any—and treat elected officials and enacted legislation as if they were the true embodiments of popular preference. Nevertheless, we ought not to be wholly satisfied with the integrity of voting summaries, for we do have some evidence that elections do not always select the "best" or "right" result.

This evidence is based on the fact that different methods of election and committee decision-making have produced different results from identical distributions of preference. If one method were clearly superior, we might be able to say that its choice was the right one. But, as I will show in detail in Chapter 4, it is not possible to prove or even to argue persuasively that any method of election or decision is clearly superior to all others. Thus the fact of different results from different methods is powerful and disturbing evidence that the social summaries on which democracy depends are of poor quality and possibly are inadequate for the function they are expected to perform. Chapter 2, therefore, is devoted to an examination of a few instances in which one has good reason to question the quality of social summaries of individual preferences.

2.A. Evidence from Elections

To present clear-cut evidence that different methods of voting produce different results, one must show that, with exactly the same structure of individual preferences, two methods each produce unique results. Although this is not easily proved, we can get a strong suggestion of it from the elections we know best—namely, elections of the president of the United States. Most people in the United States probably believe that the election of the president works out pretty well—except for the special problem of the electoral college. Many people fear that the electoral college will distort the outcome, but it has produced the "wrong" result at most twice—in 1888 and 1824. Much more serious is the fact that quite often candidates win with less than half of the votes cast; and, surprisingly, this does not seem to bother people. Doubtless many citizens recall the election of 1968, in which Nixon's plurality over Humphrey was only seven-tenths of 1 percent, while the third candidate (Wallace) received about 14 percent of the vote. If the supporters of Wallace had been forced to choose between Nixon and Humphrey, the election might have turned *probably not* out differently. Still, this possibility apparently disturbs very few people, although in the summer of 1980 it seemed likely that Anderson's candidacy would have an even more disturbing effect than Wallace's.

Perhaps most people believe this kind of election is an infrequent aberration. But, as Display 2-1 shows, such outcomes occurred in 14 of the 39 elections (36 percent) since 1824, when most states began popular voting for presidential electors. It might be said in defense of the "infrequent aberration" notion that some of these cases are not "serious" because the winner would have retained a substantial plurality under any reasonable reallocation of the ballots for third and fourth candidates. In 1948, for example, Truman's plurality was 4.4 percent and each minor party candidate had 2.4 percent of the total vote. In a reallocation, most of Wallace's votes would probably have gone to Truman and so might some of Thurmond's. If so, then Truman's failure to get a majority made no difference to the outcome. Nevertheless, before the 1948 election, most people correctly believed that Truman would get only a minority of the votes. Many voters, therefore, may have voted strategically (that is, not for their true preference) just because of this anticipation. Suppose most voters for Thurmond ordered the candidates thus: Thurmond, Dewey, Truman. Then, the assurance of Truman's loss led them to vote for Thurmond rather than for Dewey. Perhaps also potential voters for Dewey did not vote because they believed he was a sure winner. If these possibilities are realistic, then Dewey might have won, and at the very least the summary is flawed, no matter what the actual outcome.

If we discard the "infrequent aberration" notion on this basis, then we ought to add to the list in Display 2-1 the elections of 1832, 1852, 1924, and 1980. In those elections, despite the winner's simple majority over all other candidates, 5 percent or more of the ballots were cast for a third candidate, whose very presence thus casts doubt on the quality of the electoral summary—that is, his presence may have led people to vote contrary to their true tastes. If so, then 18 out of 39 elections (46 percent) might have turned out differently with a different method of summarizing. A different outcome would not, of course, be "right." It might simply reflect different strategic considerations. But the possibility of difference is itself disconcerting.

The problem is that, in the American system of choosing a single official in a single district of the whole country, choosing between two candidates by a simple majority and choosing among several candidates by a plurality are quite different procedures. There is no reason to suppose

Display 2-1

U.S. Presidents Who Won with a Minority of the Popular Vote, 1824–1976

Year	Winner	Percent for winner	Percent for runner-up	Percent for third place	Percent for fourth place	Percent for others
1824	Adams	31.0*	41.3	13.0	11.2	3.5
1844	Polk	49.6	48.1	2.3	—	—
1848	Taylor	47.3	42.5	10.1	—	0.1
1856	Buchanan	45.3	33.1	21.5	—	0.1
1860	Lincoln	39.8	29.5	18.1	12.6	—
1880	Garfield	48.27	48.25	3.3	—	0.2
1884	Cleveland	48.5	48.3	1.7	1.5	—
1888	Harrison	47.8	48.6	2.2	1.3	0.1
1892	Cleveland	46.0	43.0	8.5	2.3	0.2
1912	Wilson	41.8	27.4	23.6	6.0	1.6
1916	Wilson	49.2	46.1	3.2	1.2	0.3
1948	Truman	49.5	45.1	2.4	2.4	0.6
1960	Kennedy	49.7	49.5	0.2	0.1	0.5
1968	Nixon	43.4	42.7	13.5	0.1	0.3

*Elected by the House of Representatives.

Note. In 1876, Tilden apparently received over half of the votes cast; but the electoral commission recognized Hayes electors from three disputed states, and Hayes was elected in the electoral college.

they will turn out the same way. This is not, however, a defect unique to the single-member district system. Even under proportional representation, slightly different methods of summarizing can produce markedly different results. The French parliamentary election of 1951 provides a persuasive illustration of this fact.

In preparation for that election, the parties of the center, the so-called Third Force, which had jointly controlled the National Assembly from the election of 1946, *slightly* changed the electoral procedures in a way that *greatly* enhanced their opportunities to remain in control. It seems likely that the ordinary citizen did not observe much difference in the procedure. Indeed, in 1946 and 1951 he or she cast a ballot by exactly the same method. Furthermore, the ballots themselves appeared to be of exactly the same sort. Only the parties and the vote-counters did anything differently or perhaps even knew much about the difference. Nevertheless, the outcome in 1951 was grossly manipulated, enough to change the whole tone of French politics. Without this manipulation, both Gaullists and Communists would have had more seats, and that fact would very likely have changed the Cabinets between 1951 and 1955 from mostly Third Force coalitions to either right-leaning or left-leaning ones. Whether the contrived enhancement of the Third Force was fortunate or unfortunate I cannot say. But I can say for certain that the actual outcome and what might have been were very different reflections of voters' preferences.

The purpose of proportional representation is to reflect as accurately as possible in the legislature candidates' or parties' votes in the election: If a party has x percent of the total vote, then it ought to have exactly x percent of the seats in the legislature.[1] But it is seldom possible, especially with districts smaller than the whole nation, to achieve quite this objective in practice. And it was this fact that the French legislators exploited.

In both 1946 and 1951, elections were conducted in districts with from two to ten seats allocated roughly in proportion to district population. Each party, if it ran in a district, presented a list of as many candidates as the district had seats, and each voter cast a ballot for one list. In 1946 parties were assigned seats by districts using the formula of the highest average.

In 1951 two changes were made. In some districts, parties were permitted to form alliances and seats were assigned by the highest-average formula applied either to parties or to alliances. In other districts, alliances were not permitted, and seats were assigned by the largest-remainder formula.[2] The highest-average method favors large parties; the largest-remainder method does not systematically favor large or small parties.

In 1951, alliances among parties were permitted in all districts except Paris and its suburbs. The voters still voted for an individual party (not for a whole alliance). Since the ballots looked just like the ballots used in 1946 and did not indicate the existence of alliances, it is possible many voters did not know alliances existed. If, together, the parties in an alliance got more than half of the valid ballots, then *all* the seats in a district were divided among just the parties in the alliance by the highest-average formula. If an alliance did not get half of the votes, then seats were assigned, as in 1946, by the highest-average formula, to *all* parties that had enough votes. This procedure greatly helped the Third Force parties (the mildly conservative Radical Socialists, the barely socialistic Socialists, and the Catholic centrist Popular Republican Movement [MRP]). They were ideologically compatible, were already jointly running the government, and could get a bare majority in quite a large number of districts. In contrast, the largest parties, the Communists and the Gaullists, were at opposite ends of the ideological spectrum and had very few ideologically friendly parties to ally with (although the Gaullists made a few alliances with traditional rightist parties).

The total number of seats in districts permitting alliances was 508. Display 2-2 summarizes the gains and losses that actually occurred with alliances and the outcome that would have occurred under the 1946 law without alliances. The Display is based on two allocations of seats: (1) the actual allocation with alliances and (2) an imaginary allocation without alliances. Gains and losses are the differences between the two allocations. The calculation of the imaginary allocation is, for each legislative district, by the highest-average method, using the votes actually cast for the individual parties, but assuming that no alliances were made. The alliance procedure permitted parties of the governing coalitions to gain 85 of 508 seats or about 17 percent.

In Paris and its suburbs, Communists and Gaullists controlled probably two-thirds of the votes. The procedure of a majority alliance could not help the Third Force parties, and they did not permit it in the 75 seats there. Instead, they changed the formula of counting votes from the highest-average method to the largest-remainder method. Since the highest-average method sometimes penalizes small parties, while the largest-remainder method treats large and small parties indifferently, the relatively smaller parties of the Third Force could improve their chances by this change. The right and center parties gained 9 of 75 seats or about 12 percent of the Parisian seats. The actual gains and losses are summarized in Display 2-3.

As a consequence of these manipulations, the distribution of parties in the National Assembly in 1951 turned out to be quite different from

Display 2-2

Gains and Losses in 1951 from Using the 1951 Procedure of Alliances Rather Than the 1946 Procedure of Parties Standing Independently

Parties	Gains	Losses	Net change
Third Force			
Radicals	24	2	+22
Socialists	17	3	+14
MRP	26	—	+26
Rightist parties	25	2	+23
Communists	—	65	−65
Gaullists	2	22	−20
	94	94	0

Display 2-3

Gains and Losses in Paris in 1951 from Using the Largest-Remainder Method Instead of the Highest-Average Method

Parties	Gains	Losses	Net change
Third Force			
Radicals	3	1	+2
Socialists	1	—	+1
MRP	4	—	+4
Rightist parties	2	—	+2
Communists	—	4	−4
Gaullists	—	5	−5
	10	10	0

Display 2-4

Actual Outcome of the 1951 Election in Paris Compared to a Hypothetical Outcome from Using the 1946 Electoral Law to Calculate 1951 Results

Parties	Actual outcome		Hypothetical outcome	
Third Force				
Radicals	90		62	
Socialists	107		90	
MRP	97	294	65	217
Rightists				
Independent Republicans	52			
Center Republicans	42	94		82
Gaullists		120		146
Communists		101		170
Unassigned		18		12
Total*		627		627
Constitutional majority		314		314

*Includes 44 members from overseas.

what it would have been under the 1946 election law. This distribution, including 44 overseas members, is set forth in Display 2-4. As it illustrates, the Third Force could get a majority of 314 to form a Cabinet by attracting only 20 more supporters (314 − 294)—a few Rightists or Gaullists. In fact, the Gaullist party split up for just this reason within a few months. Consequently, most Cabinets from 1951 to 1955 were dominated by the Third Force along with a few Rightists and complaisant Gaullists. If the 1946 law had remained in effect, however, the Third Force would have needed 97 additional votes to form a Cabinet (314 − 217), and this would surely have forced the inclusion of either Gaullists or Communists. Since the latter option then appeared politically infeasible, the Third Force would probably have had to compromise with De Gaulle. One can always wonder whether such a compromise might have saved the Fourth Republic, which De Gaulle replaced in 1958. (One can also wonder whether the Fourth Republic was worth saving.)

2.B. Evidence from Experiment

The evidence cited so far of defects in the process of voting is inadequate because we do not have a full record of voters' preferences. Hence we cannot be absolutely certain whether the different possible results derive from different methods of summation or from quirks in voters' behavior such as strategic voting (that is, voting not in accord with one's true preferences). There is, however, at least one very well documented instance of voting for which we have an exhaustive record of preferences and to which we can apply different methods of summation in full confidence that only the methods vary, not the preferences themselves. The fact that in this case different methods produce different results seems to me to be definitive evidence of ambiguities in the process of aggregating preferences.

In preparation for a project to launch two Mariner (now Voyager) spacecraft in the summer of 1977 to fly by Jupiter in 1979 and Saturn in 1980 and then to escape from the solar system, the Jet Propulsion Laboratory of the California Institute of Technology (the manager of the project for the National Aeronautics and Space Administration) assembled about 80 outside scientists divided into ten teams concerned with various features of the observation of planets. Typical teams were Magnetic Fields (MAG), concerned with planetary and interplanetary magnetic fields, and Infrared Radiation (IRIS), concerned with energy-related topics such as the atmospheric composition and temperature of planets. One of the first tasks of the ten teams was the selection of specific trajectories for the two spacecraft, and it was in connection with the decision on this task that detailed data on preferences were collected.[3]

Initially, engineers at the Jet Propulsion Laboratory selected 105 trajectories satisfying certain fundamental navigational, scientific, and budget constraints. Pairs of trajectories—one trajectory for each of the two spacecraft—were then matched for the beginning and end of the feasible launching period in August and September 1977. After extensive analysis by the teams of outside scientists, 32 pairs of trajectories were selected for final consideration. In October 1973, each team ranked the 32 pairs according to their usefulness for the observations with which the team members were concerned. This ranking produced the ordinal utility of each team for the pairs. *Ordinal utility* is a measure of preferences in terms of rank orders—that is, first, second, etc. Once ordinal utility is determined, it is possible to transform it into cardinal utility. *Cardinal utility* is a measure of preferences on a scale of cardinal numbers, such as the scale from zero to one or the scale from one to ten. In this case, the experimenter used a standard method to elicit from each team its cardinal utility numbers from 0.0 for lowest to 1.0 for highest.[4] The ordinal and cardinal rankings by teams are the fundamental data on preferences to which various methods of summation can be applied.

There can be no doubt that the members of the teams took this task very seriously and calculated their preferences according to their own self-interest rather than according to any kind of general interest (as assumed in some populist theories). As two observers, Dyer and Miles, remarked, "The duration of the MJS77 Project is about ten years and may represent the only foreseeable opportunity for some of these scientists to be involved in a planetary mission."[5] Clearly a good part of the team members' professional lives and indeed of their scientific achievements was involved in the selection of good trajectories. Furthermore, the pairs of trajectories were of widely different value. Trajectory pair 24, for example, was ranked first by team UVS, third by team RSS, and thirty-second by teams LECP, MAG, and PRA.

The teams were given approximately one month to analyze the relative merits of the 32 pairs by mail and telephone, and then they were assembled physically for two days to carry through the actual ordinal rankings and to derive cardinal utilities. The result is, I believe, a thoughtful and careful ordering of preferences, more thoughtful and careful than is usually found in political decisions. Furthermore, the teams were isolated from each other when they measured their preferences, so it was not possible to report their preferences falsely in order to exploit intransitivities and other anomalies in the sum of other teams' preferences. Hence we can interpret the data as an honest, nonstrategic expression of the voters' (i.e., the teams') true tastes.

The data on preferences is set forth in Display 2-5. Using this data, Dyer and Miles applied four well-known and well-rationalized methods of summation:

1. *Sum of ordinal ranks comparison.* This method involves summing, for each pair of trajectories, the rank orders given that pair by each of the teams. This is an adaptation of the *Borda method* of rank order comparison, named after its eighteenth-century inventor.

2. *Sum of cardinal utilities comparison.* This method consists of summing, for each alternative, the cardinal utilities assigned to it by each team. The alternative with the highest sum is the winner. This can be called the *Bentham winner,* after Jeremy Bentham, the nineteenth-century philosopher who advocated "utilitarianism."

3. *Multiplicative cardinal utilities comparison.* This method consists of multiplying, for each alternative, the cardinal utilities assigned to it by each team. The winner is the alternative with the highest product and is called the *Nash winner* after the contemporary mathematician who proposed it.

4. *Ordinal pairwise comparison.* This method (see Display 2-6) involves setting each alternative (in this case, pairs of trajectories) against each other alternative in a head-to-head vote by simple majority rule. If any alternative can defeat each of the others by a simple majority, it is the *Condorcet winner,* so named after the eighteenth-century philosopher who first proposed this method.

By the Condorcet standard, pair 26 was the clear winner, for, as partially indicated in Display 2-6, it defeats all others in a head-to-head contest. Notice that team IRIS ranks pair 26 second and pair 31 third. Hence in pairwise voting between 26 and 31, IRIS should (and did) vote for pair 26.

By the Borda method of summing ranks, pair 31 won. By the Bentham method of adding utilities, pair 26 again won, while by the Nash method of multiplying utilities number 31 won a second time. Finally, although plurality voting probably ought not to be taken seriously in this case, pair 25 and pair 27 were tied, each with two first-place votes. Nevertheless, ignoring the plurality outcome, with four methods, each of which can be supported by strong and persuasive arguments, there are two distinct winners, each of which wins twice. Which one ought to be regarded as the "true" winner? I cannot say, and I think it is difficult to produce a convincing argument either for pair 26 or for pair 31. The best that one could possibly say is that probably one of these two pairs should have been chosen. Actually, the Jet Propulsion Laboratory, after some adjustment and improvement of pair 26, persuaded the teams to adopt it. But, as Dyer and Miles point out, if pair 31 had been similarly improved, it might just as easily have been chosen.

This example of real decision-making, the only one known to me in which full information on preferences was collected from real decision-makers, reveals the fundamental ambiguity in methods of summarizing preferences.[6] This example demonstrates that, even if an omniscient observer, call him Zeus, knew the true tastes of every voter, it would still be impossible for him to predict the social choice or the product of aggregating preferences unless he also knew the method of aggregation. This means that the social choice depends not simply on the wills of individuals, but also on the method used to summarize these wills.

Display 2-5

Ranking and Utilities of Ten Trajectory Pairs According to the Borda, Bentham, and Nash Methods

Trajectory pair	Borda method: Ordinal utility		Bentham method: Additive cardinal utility		Nash method: Multiplicative cardinal utility	
	Social ordering	Sum of team's rank numbers	Social ordering	Sum of team's cardinal utilities	Social ordering	Product of cardinal utilities
31	1	67.0	2	8.87	1	0.2703
29	2	75.0	3	8.75	3	0.2340
26	3	75.5	1	8.89	2	0.2701
27	4	100.0	4	8.56	4	0.1738
5	5	111.5	6	7.91	6	0.0796
25	6	113.0	5	8.22	5	0.1124
35	7	120.0	7	7.57	8	0.0524
17	8	131.0	10	7.38	10	0.0399
8	9	134.5	8	7.55	7	0.0537
10	10	136.5	12	7.28	12	0.0310

Adapted from James S. Dyer and Ralph E. Miles, Jr., "An Actual Application of Collective Choice Theory to the Selection of Trajectories for the Mariner Jupiter/Saturn 1977 Project," *Operations Research*, Vol. 24 (March 1976), pp. 220–244.

By the Borda method, each team ranks the 32 pairs first, second, etc., on to thirty-second. Then, for each alternative, the ranks are summed. The winner is the pair with the lowest sum, here pair 31, which has a sum of 67. (The minimum sum would be 10, if each team ranked the same alternative first. Display 2-9 contains an example of the Borda calculation in reverse ranking.)

To use the Bentham and Nash methods, the rank orders by each team are transformed to a cardinal scale, using 1 for the highest rank and zero for the lowest rank. Then, for the Bentham method, the cardinal numbers are summed for each alternative, while for the Nash method they are multiplied. The maximum values, which would occur if each of the ten teams put the same trajectory pair in first place, are 10 under the Bentham method (i.e., $1 + 1 + \ldots + 1 = 10$) and 1 under the Nash method (i.e., $1 \cdot 1 \cdot \ldots \cdot 1 = 1$). The minimum values, if each team put the same trajectory pair in last place, are zero in both cases.

Display 2-6

Ordinal Pairwise Comparison of Four Trajectory Pairs Ranked Highest by the Borda, Bentham, and Nash Methods

Teams' Ordinal Rank Numbers*

Trajectory pair	RSS	IRIS	ISS	PPS	UVS	CRS	LECP	MAG	PLS	PRA
31	20.5	3.0	5.0	8.5	6.0	8.0	4.0	3.0	4.0	5.0
29	20.5	5.0	19.0	6.5	9.0	3.0	2.0	2.0	4.0	4.0
26	20.5	2.0	10.0	11.0	7.0	17.5	3.0	1.0	1.5	2.0
27	20.5	1.0	30.0	16.0	3.0	17.5	1.0	4.0	4.0	3.0

Calculation of the Condorcet Winner: Pairwise Voting*

Contest		
Pair	vs.	Pair
26		31
IRIS		ISS
LECP		PPS
MAG		UVS
PLS		CRS
PRA		

Contest		
Pair	vs.	Pair
26		29
IRIS		PPS
ISS		CRS
UVS		LECP
MAG		
PLS		
PRA		

Contest		
Pair	vs.	Pair
26		27
ISS		IRIS
PPS		UVS
MAG		LECP
PLS		
PRA		

*Adapted from James S. Dyer and Ralph E. Miles, Jr., "An Actual Application of Collective Choice Theory to the Selection of Trajectories for the Mariner 1977 Jupiter/Saturn Project," *Operations Research*, Vol. 24 (March 1976), pp. 220–244.

I have been very much impressed with this deep ambiguity; and, as an additional exercise in demonstrating the defects of voting, I have concocted an imaginary voting situation with five alternatives. This imaginary, but nevertheless disconcerting, situation is set forth in Display 2-7. Each column shows the preference order of a single voter. The most-preferred alternative is at the top of the column, and the least-preferred alternative is at the bottom. The voter's cardinal utility for each alternative is in parentheses.

Notice that the plurality winner is alternative *b*, which is supported in first place by voters 4 and 5, or 40 percent of the voters. The Condorcet winner is alternative *a*. It wins in a head-to-head vote against each of the others, as shown in Display 2-8. By the Borda method, alternative *b* wins again as shown in Display 2-9. (Dyer and Miles inverted the Borda scale to simplify arithmetic for a large number of alternatives. Usually, however, the Borda count, for *n* alternatives, gives $n - 1$ points to a voter's first choice, $n - 2$ to his or her second choice, on down to zero points for the last choice. The winner is the alternative with the most points.) The Bentham winner (by additive cardinal utility) is alternative *d*, as shown in Display 2-10. And, finally, the Nash winner (the product of cardinal utilities) is alternative *e*. The Nash winner is calculated from the data in Display 2-9, except that the utilities in each row are multiplied together instead of summed. (For example, in the first row $1.00 \times .61 \times .70 \times .75 \times .60 = .192150$.) The products for each row are:

a. .19215

b. .19800

c. .07700

d. .20250

e. .20956

Of the five alternatives, *a, b, c, d,* and *e,* every one except *c* wins by some defensible method of aggregating preferences. Clearly, the outcome is just as much a function of the method as it is of the underlying tastes.

*   *   *

I have discussed a variety of methods of voting, methods in use in different cultures and in different kinds of social circumstances. In each example, alternative methods do not agree on the social choice, thereby suggesting doubts about the quality of the process of amalgamation. By reason of the variety, it is clear that something more general is involved

Display 2-7

Imaginary Ordinal and Cardinal Utilities for Five Alternatives and Five Persons

Rank order	Voter 1	Voter 2	Voter 3	Voter 4	Voter 5
Highest: 1	a (1.00)	d (1.00)	e (1.00)	b (1.00)	b (1.00)
2	d (0.90)	a (0.61)	c (0.80)	d (0.90)	e (0.96)
3	b (0.60)	b (0.60)	a (0.70)	a (0.75)	c (0.70)
4	c (0.55)	e (0.59)	b (0.55)	e (0.74)	a (0.60)
Lowest: 5	e (0.50)	c (0.50)	d (0.50)	c (0.50)	d (0.50)

Note. Cardinal utilities are in parentheses.

Display 2-8

Calculation of the Condorcet Winner for the Five-Person Society of Display 2-7

Number of Votes for the Alternative in the Row when Placed in Contest against the Alternative in the Column

	a	*b*	*c*	*d*	*e*
a	—	3	3	3	3 (Condorcet winner)
b	2	—	4	3	4
c	2	1	—	2	1
d	2	2	3	—	3
e	2	1	4	2	—

Since alternative *a* (top row) has a majority over each of the other alternatives, it is the Condorcet winner.

---

than a mere locally idiosyncratic feature of the process. I have not yet investigated the characteristics of the methods or attempted to judge their merits; yet each method has been recommended because it is believed to be appropriate and justifiable. We are thus driven to ask: Is there one method (and hence outcome) that *ought* to be chosen? In these examples I think that even Zeus, with, presumably, perfect knowledge of voters' tastes, could not predict the social choice. And if Zeus were required to impose some method of summation, which method would he say was morally right or even merely technically correct? I do not know, and, if Zeus existed, I doubt very much if he would know either. In the next two chapters, I will try to instruct him about how to choose.

Display 2-9

Calculation of the Borda Winner for the Five-Person Society of Display 2-7

Number of Points for Alternatives in Rows, Preference Orders in Columns

Alternatives	Points from Voter i					Total
	$i = 1$	$i = 2$	$i = 3$	$i = 4$	$i = 5$	
a	4	3	2	2	1	12
b	2	2	1	4	4	13 (Borda winner)
c	1	0	3	0	2	6
d	3	4	0	3	0	10
e	0	1	4	1	3	9

Borda calculation: Add the points for each alternative (in rows) across individuals (in columns). The winner is alternative b, with the most points in total.

Display 2-10

Calculation of the Bentham Winner for the Five-Person Society of Display 2-7

Utility for Alternatives in the Rows; Voters' Judgments in the Columns

Cardinal Utilities for Alternatives by Voter i

Alternatives	$i = 1$	$i = 2$	$i = 3$	$i = 4$	$i = 5$	Total
a	1.00	.61	.70	.75	.60	3.66
b	.60	.60	.55	1.00	1.00	3.75
c	.55	.50	.80	.50	.70	3.05
d	.90	1.00	.50	.90	.50	3.80 (Bentham winner)
e	.50	.59	1.00	.74	.96	3.75

Bentham calculation: Add the utilities for each alternative (in rows) across individuals (in columns). The winner is alternative d, with the largest sum.

3

Simple Majority Decision

The examples of Chapter 2 clearly indicate that different methods of summarizing the same underlying structure of preference produce different social choices. Still, this fact need not cause problems for democratic theory if one method of aggregation is clearly superior to all others. And, as it happens, there is one that is quite attractive and perhaps appears better than others—namely, simple majority decision when there are exactly two alternatives.

The procedure does have highly desirable properties, and one reason that most people are indifferent to the defects in voting may be that they believe that simple majority rule over two alternatives is in use most of the time. If this belief were correct, popular indifference would probably be justified. Unfortunately, simple majority rule displays its most desirable properties only when there are exactly two alternatives, and nature hardly ever offers us binary choices. We have, of course, many institutions, like primary elections, to reduce alternatives to exactly two. But simply because we force ourselves into a binary choice should not obscure the fact that we really start out with many alternatives and that we can never be certain that our institutions have narrowed the choice down to the right pair for us to choose between.

Rare as its natural occurrence is, however, simple majority decision is still very attractive, which is why some people want to realize it in institutions. In this chapter, therefore, I will explain in detail why it is attractive. Then, in conclusion, I will describe the tradition of democratic thought devoted to institutionalizing it. But I will also show that simple majority decision cannot be institutionalized without violating fundamental notions of fairness.

In this chapter and the next two, it will be necessary to define a number of technical terms in order to reveal some of the deep meaning of the issues raised. Definitions will always be stated in the text. Formal statements—if useful—will be placed in the Notes. Since this is an introductory discussion, no proofs of formal theorems will be given.

3.A. Introductory Definitions

In section 1.H several primitive notions were introduced. I will elaborate them here and introduce a few more.[1]

1. A set, $X = (x, y, \ldots)$, of alternatives, which can be motions, candidates, platforms, bundles of goods, and so on. Since in this chapter the concern is with simple majority choice between pairs, the set X will here be limited to exactly two members, $X = (x, y)$; later it may be indefinitely or even infinitely large. Here, x and y may be thought of as two candidates (x is, say, candidate A, and y is then candidate B) or as yea or nay votes on a motion (x is for yea, and y is for nay).

2. A set, $N = (1, 2, \ldots, n)$, of people, which is a society of n members or eligible participants, where i is any one of the n members, that is, $i = 1$ or 2 or $\ldots$ or n.

3. For each i, a relation, P_i, of preference over X. Each P_i is asymmetric: If a judgment is made between x and y, then either $x\,P_i\,y$ or $y\,P_i\,x$ but not both. Notice that P_i need not be complete so that, for some x and y in X, neither $x\,P_i\,y$ nor $y\,P_i\,x$.

4. For each i, a relation, I_i, of indifference, which, given a judgment between x and y, is defined as: not $(x\,P_i\,y)$ and not $(y\,P_i\,x)$. Hence I is symmetric: if $x\,I_i\,y$, then $y\,I_i\,x$.

5. For each i, a relation, R_i, of P_i and I_i combined, which is defined as: $x\,R_i\,y$ is equivalent to not $(y\,P_i\,x)$.[2] Notice that R_i is complete so that either $x\,R_i\,y$ or $y\,R_i\,x$.

6. The concept of a social choice, $C(X)$, where $C(X) = z$ means "When the society follows a given rule for choosing, the choice from X is z." If the context does not make clear the rule being followed, say, simple majority (SM) or plurality (P), then the rule in use will be indicated as a subscript to C, thus: $C_{SM}(X)$ or $C_P(X)$.

It is a delicate matter to determine just what P_i, I_i, and R_i involve. One possible interpretation is that they refer to private individual judgments. We learn of such judgments, however, only through their public expression, as when a person says, "I like y better than x," or when a person votes for x. Unfortunately, public expressions may or may not truly reflect private judgments. A person may dissemble opinions, for strategic reasons, and perhaps vote contrary to true tastes (either because of being manipulated or because of trying to manipulate). It is not quite clear, therefore, just what the statement $x\,P_i\,y$ means. For convenience I will adopt this convention: Except when I expressly note that private judgment and public action may differ, I shall equate the two. Hence $x\,P_i\,y$ will mean both private preference for x over y and the public (though possibly secret) act of voting for x, and $x\,I_i\,y$ will mean both private indifference and abstention from voting.

For each i in N, there is a structure, D_i, of individual judgment over the members of X. In the two-alternative case, D_i is just one of $x\,P_i\,y$, $x\,I_i\,y$, or $y\,P_i\,x$. These forms can be represented conveniently by the integers $(1, 0, -1)$:

$$
\begin{array}{lll}
D_i = 1 & \text{means} & x\,P_i\,y \\[4pt]
D_i = 0 & \text{means} & x\,I_i\,y \\[4pt]
D_i = -1 & \text{means} & y\,P_i\,x
\end{array}
\tag{3-1}
$$

For the whole set N, there is a vector, D, of all the individual judgments, where $D = (D_1, D_2, \ldots, D_n)$. Using (3-1), some profile, D, of a society may be thought of as a string of integers chosen from $(1, 0, -1)$, where each integer stands for an individual judgment. For example, on a five-person committee, where the first, fourth, and fifth members favor and vote for a motion, the second is undecided and abstains, and the third opposes and votes against, $D = (1, 0, -1, 1, 1)$. Finally, the vector D is a member of a set $\mathbf{D}$, which is the set of all possible social profiles. For example, if N consists of two people (that is, $n = 2$), then $\mathbf{D}$ is as set forth in Display 3-1.

Thus, D_i is some particular person's preference or values, D is the profile on a particular occasion of the preference or value structure of all members of the society, N, and $\mathbf{D}$ is the set of all possible social profiles that N might display.

Inasmuch as our concern is with some kind of *social* choice, based ultimately on individual judgment, there must be a rule by which the D_i in each D are amalgamated. This rule is a function, F, which is stated in complete form so that it can operate on any D in $\mathbf{D}$. The social choice from X, given D and F, is referred to as $F(X, D)$. I will abbreviate this to $F(D)$. Note that $F(D)$ is thus a special case of $C(X)$, special in the sense that a profile, D, and a rule, F, are stipulated. For the case where X has

Display 3-1

Members of *D* for Two Persons

$$D = \begin{cases} (1, 1), (0, 1), (-1, 1) \\ (1, 0), (0, 0), (-1, 0) \\ (1, -1), (0, -1), (-1, -1) \end{cases}$$

Each pair of D_i in parentheses indicates a possible choice by the two voters. Thus $(0, 1)$ means that $D_1 = 0$ (for $x\, I_1\, y$) and $D_2 = 1$ (for $x\, P_2\, y$). The set of nine possibilities in large brackets is all possibilities of **D**.

---

just two members, I define $F(D)$ parallel to the interpretation of D_i:

$F(D) = 1$ means x is the social choice from X by F, given D.

$F(D) = 0$ means x and y tie and are together the social choice by F from X, given D. (Many rules of amalgamation do not exclude ties. Practically, however, there are usually ad hoc rules to break ties—tossing coins, extra votes for presiding officers, etc.—which have nothing to do with the amalgamation itself.)

$F(D) = -1$ means y is the social choice by F from X, given D.

$$(3\text{-}2)$$

Obviously, there are a large number of possible rules or functions. To convey a sense of the wide variety, I will list a few to be discussed:

1. *Constant functions*
    a. *Indecisive.* x and y always tie, regardless of the individuals' preferences in D; that is, $F(D) = 0$, for all D in **D**.
    b. *Imposed.* x (or y) always wins, regardless of the individuals' preferences in D; that is, $F(D) = 1$ (or -1), for all D in **D**.

2. *Simple majority functions.* That alternative wins which has more votes than the other (or, if the number of voters is even, alternatives may tie), where members of N may vote or abstain. Many variations can be obtained by weighting votes and declaring the winner to be that alternative with the greater sum of weights.

3. *Absolute majority functions.* That alternative wins which has more votes (or weights) than half of the total votes or weights in N, with abstention permitted or not permitted as the case may be.

4. *Special majority functions.* That alternative wins which has more than some specified proportion of the votes or weights (e.g., ratios like 2/3 or 3/4), when the proportion is calculated from those voting or from all members of N.

3.B. Properties of Simple Majority Decision: Monotonicity

The method of simple majority decision, in which voters are weighted equally and in which they can either vote or abstain, is defined thus: If more people vote for x than for y, x wins; if the same number vote for x and y, they tie; and if more vote for y than for x, y wins. Using the terminology of D_i, if the sum of the D_i in D is greater than zero, x wins; if equal to zero, x and y tie; and if less than zero, y wins.[3] The method has three independent properties—monotonicity, undifferentiatedness, and neutrality. An examination of each of them will permit a full appreciation of this rule.[4]

By *monotonicity* is meant that an increase in the value of some D_i implies an increase, or at least not a decrease, in the value of $F(D)$. That is, if one or more voters change preference in a direction favorable to x (i.e., change from favoring y either to being indifferent between x and y or to favoring x, or change from being indifferent to favoring x), then the resulting change, if any, in the fate of x should be an improvement for x.

Monotonicity is an especially important feature of any decision rule that amalgamates individual tastes into a social outcome. It would be perverse in the extreme if increased votes for an alternative contributed to its defeat. Consequently, it seems an elementary requirement of sensible and fair choice that the decision rule respond positively, or at least nonnegatively, to increases in individual valuation of an alternative. This is precisely what monotonicity (or, as it is sometimes called, *responsiveness* or *nonperversity*) provides for. Desirable as monotonicity may seem, however, there are, quite surprisingly, a number of widely used social choice functions that fail to satisfy it.

To define monotonicity, consider some D and D' both in $\mathbf{D}$. They may be identical; but for every i in N, $D_i \geq D_i'$. Specifically, any change from D' to D involves a change, for one or more i, in the direction of favoring x over y. Thus, for any person, i, whose values change, if $D'_i = -1$ (i.e., $y\,P_i\,x$), then $D_i = 0$ or 1; or if $D'_i = 0$ (i.e., $x\,I_i\,y$), then $D_i = 1$. This means that, for the whole society, the sum of D_i is equal to or greater than the sum of D'_i, because, if any change occurs from D'_i to D_i, it must increase the sum of D_i relative to D'_i. Hence monotonicity for a rule, F, means that if some D_i increases over D'_i, then $F(D)$ is not less than $F(D')$.[5]

To state this definition in another way, suppose an alternative is rendered more preferred in private judgment and individual voting. Then, if any change in outcome results, that change *must* not hurt the alternative that has come to be more attractive. But, of course, no change in outcome need result. Indeed, this condition on F does allow for a wide range of ties and hence for a wide range of situations in which, despite shifts in preference or valuation, no change in outcome results. Specifically it might happen, for an F satisfying equation (N3.2) (see note 5),* that some person changes $D'_i = 0$ to $D_i = 1$, yet nevertheless $F(D') = F(D) = 0$. This means that an individual valuation of x rises, but the tie between x and y is not broken.

A commonly used method of social choice that displays such a wide range of ties is the rule used on juries. For a jury, where x means conviction and y means acquittal, the jury function is the rule that x or y wins only if the jury is unanimous and that otherwise x and y tie in a hung jury.[6] For this F in situation D' the jury might be split nine to three for conviction (i.e., $\sum_{i=1}^{n} D'_i = 6$). Then to create situation D some juror, i, might switch from acquittal to conviction so that $D'_i = -1$ and $D_i = 1$. (Consequently, $\sum_{i=1}^{n} D_i = 8$.) But the jury would still be hung, so $F(D') = F(D) = 0$.

In simple majority decision, ties are not so persistent, which is one of the merits, I believe, of this rule for large electorates. To describe simple majority decision, therefore, one needs the notion of *strong monotonicity:* If a tie exists and just one voter shifts his or her position, the tie is broken.[7] Thus, if just one person shifts from abstaining ($D'_i = 0$) to voting ($D_i = 1$ or -1), strong monotonicity requires that the tie be broken, provided no one else changes a vote. On, for example, a seven-member committee with six members present and split three to three on election of a chairman, the absent member will, when brought in to vote, break the tie.

As this example indicates, simple majority voting is strongly monotonic because a single person can always break a tie if no one else changes. The jury rule, while monotonic, is not strongly monotonic, because changes by several persons may be required to break a tie.

---

*The prefix "N" indicates that the equation appears in the Notes at the back of the book.

3.C. Violations of Monotonicity

Given the fundamental importance of monotonicity for constructing a consistent relation between individual valuations and social outcomes, it is truly astonishing that several widely used social choice functions violate this condition. Although violators are probably rare when restricted to binary choice—I shall, however, offer one example—they are quite common among functions that operate on more than two alternatives, and I shall describe several.

Social Choices Operating on Two Alternatives

One widely used method of choosing a winner in contests of musical performance violates a condition of unanimity. Since unanimity is closely related to and implied by monotonicity, a violation of unanimity also constitutes a violation of monotonicity. There are two forms of the unanimity condition: (1) *unanimity,* which means that, if everyone favors x, then x wins (and vice versa for y); and (2) *weak unanimity,* which means that, if everyone favors x, at least y does not win (and vice versa for y).[8] For F nonconstant and admitting values of 1, 0, and -1, strong monotonicity implies unanimity and monotonicity implies weak unanimity, so forms of unanimity are special cases of forms of monotonicity. This is as it should be, for there is a congruence of sense between the two conditions. Certainly, if we believe that improving the private valuation of an alternative *ought* not to make it worse off (monotonicity), then a unanimous preference for that alternative *ought* to guarantee that it not lose (weak unanimity).

In judging performances in musical contests, the following rule is often used: For n judges and m performers (here I present an example with $m = 2$ to preserve binary choice and $n = 3$ to save arithmetic, though typically m and n are both much larger), each judge awards each performer from 1 to 25 points.[9] For each performer, the judges' awards are ordered from highest to lowest, the median award is determined, any awards in excess of 8 points difference from the median are discarded, and the remaining points are summed. The performer with the highest sum wins. Under this rule it is possible for a performer who is unanimously preferred to lose.

Let three judges award two performers points as shown in Display 3-2. Each judge prefers A to B, yet B wins in clear violation of weak unanimity and monotonicity. To see these violations, suppose judge 3 had given performer A only 7 points, with all other points the same. Since judge 3's points for A would not count, B would win. If judge 3 increased

Display 3-2

Voting in a Musical Contest

	Performer A	Performer B
Judge 1	15	10
Judge 2	16	10
Judge 3	25*	15
Total	31	35

*Excluded from the total because it exceeds the median, 16, by more than 8 points.

the points for A to 8 on up to 24, A would win. But as judge 3 increases A's points to 25, A turns into a loser in spite of the increased support and unanimous preference.

Doubtless this rule was devised to minimize favoritism in judging (often judges in such contests find their own students among the contenders). Ignoring outliers appears, therefore, to be an appropriate remedy. Nevertheless, it allows perverse results.

Social Choices Operating on More Than Two Alternatives

It has been shown that any social choice function providing for the elimination of alternatives violates monotonicity.[10] Of course, when X has more than two alternatives, we must think of monotonicity in a slightly different way. Let $F(D)$ now mean the choices by F from X, given a profile of preference structures, D. If an alternative x is in $F(D')$ and D differs from D' only in that x has risen in some individual preference order(s) in D from D', then monotonicity requires that x be in $F(D)$. That is, a higher individual valuation and more votes cannot hurt an alternative.

Two voting rules, by providing for dropping alternatives, violate this condition: (1) the single transferable vote method of proportional representation,[11] used for national legislatures in Ireland and Malta and in local governments and private societies in most of the English-speaking world; and (2) the two-stage majority system, currently used in France for national elections and in many local primaries and elections in the United States.

The rule for the *single transferable vote method* is: For districts with S seats and m candidates ($m \geq S$), the voters, V in number, mark ballots for first choice, second choice, ..., and m^{th} choice. A quota, q, is calculated thus:

$$q = (V/S + 1) + 1$$

and q is rounded down to the largest integer contained in it.

If a candidate receives at least q first-place votes, he or she wins, and any surplus votes (i.e., the number of first-place votes in excess of q) are transferred to nonwinning candidates in proportion to the appearance of these candidates in next place on all ballots for the initial winner. Another candidate who then has q first-place and reassigned votes wins, and his or her surplus is transferred to the next nonwinning candidate on his or her supporters' ballots (again in proportion to their appearance in next place) and so on until all seats are filled. If at any point in the process (including the beginning) no candidate has q first-place and reassigned votes, the candidate with the fewest first-place and reassigned votes is eliminated and all the ballots for her or him are transferred to candidates in the second (or next) place on those ballots; and this is repeated until some candidate has q votes.

Doron and Kronick have devised an example in which monotonicity is violated by this rule.[12] In Display 3-3 two seats are to be filled from four candidates by 26 voters, where q rounds down to 9. The two situations, D' and D, are identical except that, for the two voters, i, in the third row, $D'_i = y\,x\,z\,w$ and $D_i = x\,y\,z\,w$. That is, these two voters increase their valuation of x in D as against D'. In both situations, w has nine first-place votes and is initially elected. No surplus exists and no other candidate has enough first-place votes to win. So in both situations, the candidate with the fewest first-place votes must be eliminated, and his or her votes are transferred to the candidate in second place on these ballots. In situation D', z is eliminated and his or her five votes go to x, who is elected with eleven votes. In situation D, y is eliminated and his or her four votes go to z, who is elected with nine votes. In going from D' to D, x has risen in two preference orders and nothing else has changed. Since D differs from D' only by two voters increasing their valuation of x in D, it is a violation of monotonicity that x, which won in D', loses in D.

The same kind of situation can arise in *two-stage majority voting*, in which, if no candidate receives an absolute majority of votes cast in a first stage (where more than two candidates are offered), then a runoff election is held between the two highest candidates. If voters retain the same preference structures between the two elections, then the situation is like

Display 3-3

A Profile of Preference Orderings in Situations D' and D Using Single Transferable Vote

Situation D'

Number of voters	First choice	Second choice	Third choice	Fourth choice
9	w	z	x	y
6	x	y	z	w
2	y	x	z	w
4	y	z	x	w
5	z	x	y	w

Situation D

Number of voters	First choice	Second choice	Third choice	Fourth choice
9	w	z	x	y
6	x	y	z	w
2	x	y	z	w
4	y	z	x	w
5	z	x	y	w

Note. $q = (V/S + 1) + 1 = (26/3) + 1 = 9.67 \approx 9$ (using the customary procedure of rounding down).

Adapted from Gideon Doron and Richard Kronick, "Single Transferable Vote: An Example of a Perverse Social Choice Function," *American Journal of Political Science,* Vol. 21 (May 1977), pp. 303–311.

the single transferable vote in the sense that voters initially supporting an eliminated candidate vote for the remaining candidate who stands higher in their preference orders. Exactly the same kind of perversities can arise as in the single transferable vote method, although, of course, the elections themselves never reveal enough data about preferences to make the perverse outcomes visible to the voters.

Monotonicity is primarily a technical requirement that one would want to impose on *any* voting system. If we assume that the purpose of voting is to amalgamate individual tastes into a social decision, then monotonicity requires that voting actually do so by counting all individual judgments in generating an outcome. Moral (as distinct from technical) considerations may arise in choosing between forms of monotonicity. For example, one might prefer a two-thirds majority (monotonic) to a simple majority (strongly monotonic) on ethical grounds. But that some kind of monotonicity be required is hardly a moral question. It is simply a straightforward matter of making the voting system do what it is supposed to do.

Theoretically, therefore, one should, on technical grounds, reject all nonmonotonic systems, although practically compromise may be appropriate. Two-stage majority rule, though nonmonotonic, may be better than the plurality system it replaces. It is hard to believe there is any good justification for the single transferable vote, however, when there exist proportional representation systems (such as list systems) that are at least weakly monotonic. In rejecting the single transferable vote, technical considerations ought to dominate.

3.D. Properties of Simple Majority Decision: Undifferentiatedness (Anonymity)

As we turn now to other properties of simple majority decision, moral rather than technical considerations dominate. The property of undifferentiatedness (or anonymity, as it is usually called) is imposed primarily because of preferences about political values, although the condition itself is technical.

Undifferentiatedness is often said to be the same as equality and to embody the principle of "one man, one vote." Actually, however, it is the technical condition underlying equality and is quite distinct from equality. The best name for the condition is *undifferentiatedness* because this is primarily what it provides—namely, that one vote cannot be distinguished from another. This feature allows for anonymity, and anonymity in turn allows for equality. In the next few paragraphs, I will explain the sequence from technical antecedent to moral consequent.

Sometimes voters are clearly distinguished by the differentiated votes they cast. They may, for example, be assigned unequal numbers of votes. These may be thought of as weights, w_i, where $i = 1, 2, \ldots, n$. On the New York City Board of Estimate, the mayor, comptroller, and president of the City Council each have four votes, while the five borough presidents have two votes each. In effect, each official's judgment on a motion is multiplied by the number of assigned votes. This fact can be described by writing $D = (w_1 D_1, w_2 D_2, \ldots, w_n D_n)$, where $w_i \geq 0$. Calculating the sum of the weights, W, the rule for weighted voting is: That alternative wins which receives more than half of the sum of the weighted votes; and, if both alternatives get the same weighted votes, they tie.[13]

Naturally, votes must be differentiated from each other so that vote-counting will be accurate. One possible formulation of the condition of undifferentiatedness is, therefore, that weights be equal: $(w_1, w_2, \ldots, w_n) = (1, 1, \ldots, 1)$. This formulation is inadequate, however, because votes are also differentiated by the roles the voters play in the system. For example, in the United Nations Security Council, for a (substantive) motion to pass, all five permanent members (US, USSR, China, Britain, France) must vote yea and so must four of the ten temporary members. The permanent members' rights of veto clearly require that their votes be differentiated. Several scholars have translated rules for this sort of differentiation into weights in a weighted voting system.[14] Unfortunately, the methods of translation vary in assumptions and therefore disagree in results, sometimes wildly.[15] It seems to me wise, therefore, not to try to reduce all differentation to a matter of unequal weights. Since roles as well as weights require that votes be differentiated, it is essential that the definition of undifferentiatedness capture the fact that neither makes a difference.

To do so, I introduce the notion of a *permutation*. Let $(1, 2, \ldots, n)$ be a sequential arrangement of n objects. One can rearrange them by replacing the first object in the sequence with another object (including possibly itself), the second object with another, and so forth through the nth object. If we signify the replacement itself with $\sigma_{(i)}$ where σ indicates the replacement and the subscript indicates the object replaced, a permutation of $(1, 2, \ldots, n)$ is then a new arrangement: $(\sigma_{(1)}, \sigma_{(2)}, \ldots, \sigma_{(n)})$. For example, if the initial arrangement is $(1, 2, 3)$ and $\sigma_{(1)} = 2$, $\sigma_{(2)} = 1$, and $\sigma_{(3)} = 3$, then the permutation is $(2, 1, 3)$.

Undifferentiatedness is the condition that any permutation of a set of individual judgments leads to the same social choice.[16] This means that the votes cannot be differentiated either in weight or in the roles played by the voters because if judgments are rearranged among voters *in any way* the same outcome is produced. Thus, for example, on a five-member committee, undifferentiatedness requires $F(1, 0, -1, 1, 1) = F(-1, 1, 1, 0, 1)$. If we use simple majority rule, $F(D) = 1$ for both these sequences.

Undifferentiatedness provides the technical base for anonymity but is not the same thing. Votes are undifferentiated, while voters are anonymous. Suppose in some society undifferentiated votes are bought and sold. Buyers do not care which votes they buy because votes are undifferentiated. Hence the purchase of k individual judgments in one permutation produces the same outcome as the purchase of k votes in another permutation. Thus the definition of undifferentiatedness (which is also the usual definition of anonymity) is satisfied. Nevertheless, in that society voters cannot be anonymous because their names are necessary for enforcement of contracts.

Once votes are undifferentiated, however, it is possible to detach names, and historically this is precisely what happened. In the Anglo-American tradition, the content of legally undifferentiated votes was, in the eighteenth and early nineteenth centuries, recorded by the name of the voters in poll books. Since this practice was believed to admit both corruption and coercion of voters, it gradually gave way to printed ballots. Since the ballots were produced and distributed by party workers, they knew how voters voted, and corruption and coercion were still possible—and indeed widespread. Finally, the secret ballot, a late-nineteenth-century invention, effectively provided anonymity. Notice, however, that it was historically a necessary condition of anonymity that votes be undifferentiated.

The same development from undifferentiatedness to anonymity occurred in a curious way in ancient Athens. As the selection of officials by heredity gave way to election by legally undifferentiated voters, political leaders developed groups of clients whose votes they coerced. Two devices were then developed to provide anonymity: Most officials were selected by a lottery, and the size of juries, which decided many political questions, was increased in some cases to sixteen hundred jurors whose votes were, presumably, hard to supervise.

The motive for providing anonymity for persons who cast otherwise undifferentiated votes is a belief in the ethical principle of equality, which is especially attractive to leaders who have relatively few clients. Those who cast undifferentiated votes may not be equal, for the operative principle can be "one important man, many (clients') votes; one client, no personally decided vote." Anonymity permits this rule to change to "one man, one vote," because all voters can then have an equal personal impact on the outcome (assuming monotonicity). Hence it is the ideal of equality that (morally) justifies anonymity, and it is the fact of anonymity that admits the practice of equality.

Whether it is desirable to impose undifferentiatedness and, further, anonymity on a method of social choice depends on whether one wants to achieve equality of influence on outcomes. In business corporations, where, presumably, influence on outcomes is roughly proportional to ownership, neither anonymity nor differentiation is desired. In representative bodies, legislators are expected to be legally undifferentiated but not anonymous. Citizens need to know how their representatives vote. Furthermore, in the operation of party government, legal undifferentiation is replaced by de facto extra weighting of party leaders by giving them the weights of disciplined backbenchers. Thus, party government requires that nonanonymous legislators have identifiable (nonanonymous) votes; but in order to guarantee equality of representation, these identifiable votes must be undifferentiated. On the other hand, for popular elections of government officials it is usually desired that voters be treated equally, and for this, undifferentiated votes must also be cast by anonymous persons.

To illustrate the significance of undifferentiatedness for equality, I will conclude with a comparison and contrast of a system intended to promote inequality—the so-called demand-revealing process that Tideman and Tullock have recently proposed to extend to ordinary elections.[17] This process was invented as a device to motivate truthful statements of the demand for public goods such as schools and armies. It operates like this when applied for more than two voters on a binary choice: Each voter, i, offers to pay money, m_i, to obtain a preferred alternative, x or y. The amounts for x are summed over all who offer to pay for x into an S_x, and similarly for y into an S_y. The alternative with the largest sum wins. To motivate truthfulness, each person, i, on the winning side, say x, who offers to pay more than the margin of winning—that is, when $m_i > (S_x - S_y)$—must pay a tax of the amount of his or her contribution to the victory of x, which is $[S_y - (S_x - m_i)]$, when that number is positive. This tax is then destroyed. For example, suppose there are voters who offer the amounts shown in Display 3-4.

Since $S_x > S_y$, x wins. Person 2 must pay $[S_y - (S_x - m_2)] =$ $10 - (15 - 12) = \$7$, which is destroyed. (Were the \$7 given to person 1 and person 4 or used to run government, the losers would have a motive to bid up to \$14.99, which would increase taxes on persons 2 and 3 to \$14.98.) On the other hand, since $[S_y - (S_x - m_3)]$ is negative (i.e., $10 - (15 - 3) = -2$), person 3 pays no tax since x would win without his or her vote.

A voter in this process who offers more than his or her true valuation on an alternative may have to pay a tax higher than his or her true valuation. For example, if persons 1 and 4 each offered \$8 to make y win, they would each have to pay a \$7 tax, which is more than y is really worth to them. A voter who offers less than his or her true valuation risks losing.

Display 3-4

The Demand-Revealing Process
for Two Alternatives

Money Offers, m_i, for Alternatives x and y

	x	y
Person 1	—	$ 5
Person 2	$12	—
Person 3	$ 3	—
Person 4	—	$ 5
Total	$S_x = \$15$	$S_y = \$10$

In either case, he or she is somewhat motivated to tell the exact truth, if it is known.[18]

As Tideman and Tullock point out, this process is like simple majority rule with secret ballots in that an abstainer gets what the higher bidders want, except when the abstainer decides to vote and can change the outcome and thus get what he or she wants. There the similarity of procedures ends, although they share the goal of truthful revelation. By treating voters anonymously, simple majority decision by secret ballot is intended to minimize coercion and corruption and thus allow voters to express their true preferences, although they may misrepresent their preferences if they find doing so to their advantage. Demand-revelation is also aimed at revealing true preferences, but it operates by treating voters unequally and requiring public revelation. The two systems are thus at loggerheads, and the difference between them is the moral value placed on equality.

It seems to me that the demand-revealing process promotes inequality in two ways:

1. Since utilities for money differ and since therefore more prosperous people (other than misers) are more likely to offer large amounts than are less prosperous people, demand-revelation clearly gives an advantage to the better-off. Indeed it might be described as a method to make wealth count for more.

2. Demand-revelation admits and encourages coercion because the winners' tax depends on the size of the losers' bids, which are necessarily revealed. (As pointed out in note 18, the tax is zero when $S_x > S_y$ and, for all i who have $x P_i y$, $m_i > S_y$. Surely this is an invitation to intimidation and coercion of exactly the sort that the secret ballot was intended to minimize.)

The strength of these forces toward inequality emphasizes by contrast just how deeply undifferentiated and anonymous voting provides for and is justified in terms of the notion of equality. Observe that item 1 violates the criterion of undifferentiated votes and that item 2 violates the criterion of anonymous voters. This joint violation renders equality impossible and thus reveals how equality is built on the sequential layers of undifferentiatedness and anonymity.

3.E. Properties of Simple Majority Decision: Neutrality

The third condition of simple majority decision is *neutrality* (or, as it is also known, *duality*), which means that the method does not favor either alternative. Many decision rules give an advantage to the status quo or to expediting motions in a committee (and there are often good reasons to do so). By contrast, the condition of neutrality, which seems especially appropriate for contests between candidates, provides that neither has an advantage.

One way of characterizing this idea is to note that, if neither alternative has an advantage, reversed preferences will lead to a reversed result. This statement is not generally true of rules that favor one alternative. For example, under the two-thirds rule, where x stands for the yea side, y is advantaged because it can win with no more than one-third plus 1 of the vote. Suppose y does win minimally and then the individual judgments are reversed so that x has one-third plus 1 of the vote. Still y wins. Under simple majority rule, however, if x wins minimally with just over half of the vote and preferences are reversed, y will have just over half and win.[19]

One important feature of neutrality is that decision rules embodying this condition typically allow for ties. Consequently this condition is inappropriate when decisions must be made. *Decisive* rules, which do not admit ties and are not neutral, have therefore a role in social choice. Here are some examples of decisive rules:

1. *Simple majority decision with a rule for breaking ties.* Ordinarily, under simple majority rule, neither side wins if the sum of D_i is zero. But if there is a rule to pick a winner, then that alternative has an advantage and the procedure is not neutral. Here are two examples of commonly used winner-picking rules (with their rationales, some of which appear dubious):
   a. In a legislature, when yeas and nays tie, nays win. (Rationale: In the absence of a clear majority, the status quo ought not be changed.)
   b. On an appellate court, on a motion to reverse a lower court decision, a tie sustains the lower court decision. This rule favors the alternative chosen by the lower court. (Rationale: In the absence of a majority to reverse, a lower court decision ought to stand.)

2. *Minority decision rules.* By these rules, if any number larger than a minority of specified size approves, a motion passes; otherwise not. Typically these rules are intended to expedite procedure or to protect minorities. Two examples:
   a. The constitutional requirement that in Congress one-fifth of a house may order the recording of the yeas and nays.
   b. The rule that four judges of the Supreme Court can grant *certiorari* (i.e., they can force the Court to hear a case).

3. *Special majority decision rules.* Under these rules, if a motion receives a specified special majority, say two-thirds, of the votes cast (or possible), it wins; otherwise not. An example of a *relative* special majority is the rule for constitutional amendments in Congress, where the motion to submit an amendment to the states passes with the assent of two-thirds of the votes cast. An example of an *absolute* special majority is the rule that three-fourths of all the states is necessary to ratify an amendment. The motive for such rules is not so much to force decision as it is to protect minorities by supporting the status quo. An extreme form is unanimity, the famous *librum veto* of the Polish Diet, where if $D = (1, 1, \ldots, 1)$, then $F(D) = 1$; otherwise $F(D) = -1$. This rule protects a minority of one.

On the other hand, where a decision is not absolutely necessary and where there is no minority to protect, it is often desirable to use rules that satisfy neutrality. Some of these are:

1. *The jury rule.* As described in section 3.B, unanimity results either in conviction or in acquittal; a tie is a mistrial. The wide range of ties

protects the defendant, and owing to the existence of ties the rule is neutral.

2. *Simple absolute majority decision with no tie-breaking rule.* This method requires that the winner get more than half of the possible votes. If neither alternative does, they tie. This rule is often used on committees such as city councils, to elect a chairperson, and, as is well known, there is often a deadlock when some member abstains.

3. *Rules for more than two alternatives.* This situation is not relevant to the main theme of this chapter, but it does pertain to the condition of neutrality, which must be redefined for the cases of three or more alternatives. Instead of requiring a complete reversal of preference orders, D_i, it is enough to require consistent permutations of the alternatives in them. Then, if the choice from a profile of permuted preference orders is the same as the permutation of the choice from the initial profile, the rule is neutral.[20] The rules discussed in Chapter 2—plurality, Condorcet, Borda, and Bentham rules—all satisfy this neutrality. Although none of them prevents ties, they do guarantee that no alternative has an advantage.

As can be seen from these examples, neutrality is inappropriate when either decisiveness or delay is desired. It is appropriate, however, when one wants to treat alternatives as impartially as possible. In this sense, neutrality is to alternatives what undifferentiatedness is to votes: a technical base for equality. Undifferentiatedness requires that votes be treated equally; neutrality requires that alternatives be treated equally. Hence neutrality is especially appropriate for choice between two candidates, where, in fact, simple majority decision is mainly used, except when tie-breaking is necessary.

3.F. Simple Majority Decision and Fairness

In Chapter 2, I emphasized that different methods of voting could result in different social choices when applied to the same profile of individual preferences. I concluded that, since all the methods appeared, superficially, to be fair, no social choice could be justified on the ground that it was fairly chosen but others were not. If, for any choice that is supposedly fair because it comes out of a fair procedure, there is another choice from another procedure that is fair in a different and conflicting way, then it is difficult to justify the fairness of any choice. Two methods based on mutually exclusive assumptions cannot both be fair. Simple majority voting, which is said to be fair because it is undifferentiated, and demand-revealing voting, which is said to be fair because it is not undifferentiated, cannot both be fair. Yet if there is no obvious way to choose between them, it is hard to say that either one is fair. The only escape from this relativistic, even nihilistic, conclusion is to find that some method is uniquely the fairest and thus clearly superior on moral grounds to all others.

Simple majority decision between two alternatives is said to be just that. As revealed in Kenneth May's theorem (see note 4), this method of decision is the *only* method that simultaneously satisfies the criteria of monotonicity, undifferentiatedness, and neutrality. And since these three criteria are sometimes thought to be necessary (both individually and together) for fairness, the unique method of decision that satisfies them all must be fairer than other methods. Such are the grounds for believing that simple majority voting on binary alternatives is indeed so superior a method that the relativistic conclusion of Chapter 2 is unjustified.

It is indeed true that simple majority voting is, on the grounds just set forth, an attractive method of social decision. But it is limited in application. If it could be used universally, then we might be justified in conceding its general superiority. Unfortunately, it is probably extremely rare for binary alternatives to occur naturally without any human intervention. Instead, society acquires binary alternatives, which allow for a fair procedure, only by reducing the size of the set of alternatives—a reduction that is often (possibly always) in itself unfair.

I will conclude this chapter by examining this contradiction in the concrete case of democratic voting. In this case, however fair simple majority decision on binary alternatives is in the abstract, it is unfair in practice because the institutions to generate binary alternatives are unfair, mainly because they are not neutral. The institutions give some alternatives advantages over others.

3.G. Democratic Thought About Simple Majority Decision

Simple majority decision on binary alternatives is consistent with the democratic purposes of voting (by reason of strong monotonicity); it is fair to all voters (by reason of undifferentiatedness); and it is fair to all candidates (by reason of neutrality). Consequently, it satisfies most of what is expected from democratic voting. Naturally, therefore, it has entranced many theorists of democracy, who have tried to find ways to force the world to use it.

Unfortunately, there is no fair way to ensure that there will be exactly two alternatives. Usually the political world offers many options, which, for simple majority decision, must be reduced to two. But usually also the *way* the reduction occurs determines *which* two will be decided between. There are many methods to reduce the many to two; but, as has long been obvious to politicians, *none* of these methods is particularly fair because their different ethical principles cannot be effectively ordered and, worse still, because *all* methods can be rigged.

Consequently, although the notion of achieving democracy by simple majority decision on binary alternatives is a will-o'-the-wisp, there has been (or, better, was) a long academic tradition in the United States about the notion of a "responsible" two-party system. The scholars in that tradition did not use the language of social choice, but they were, I believe, trying to realize simple majority decision as the regular, indeed only, method of choice. I think they saw in it, perhaps dimly, exactly the features of consistency and fairness that I have described. In this tradition, which started with Woodrow Wilson and reached its zenith with the report in 1950 of the Committee on Political Parties of the American Political Science Association, the writers were perturbed by compromise and incoherence in American politics.[21] They believed that responsible parties to generate clear binary choices would result in national public policy in a national interest. I am not sure which they thought was the engine of coherence—either binary choice itself or the system of two responsible parties associated with binary choice. Whichever way they saw it, they really were proponents of simple majority decision.

Unfortunately, these writers were profoundly wrong, largely because they did not know the theory of voting summarized in this book. If there were exactly two alternatives (i.e., party platforms), then the notion of responsible parties might make sense because such parties might clarify each alternative. (There is good reason to believe, however, that they would do the exact opposite.) Since there are always more than two alternatives, the most that responsible parties can do is select two of them—usually in an unfair way. So the democratic advantage of simple majority decision is nonexistent.

Many early exponents of the tradition of responsible parties were Anglophiles who, like Woodrow Wilson and A. Lawrence Lowell, admired the parliamentary discipline in British parties, where backbenchers usually supported the leaders' programs. They believed—doubtless mistakenly—that these programs were internally consistent and sharply different from each other (for they also thought it was a two-party system, despite the very obvious Irish). Consequently, they believed that British voters were always given a clear, programmatic choice in elections. The theme of Wilson's *Congressional Government* is that American parties in Congress lack a national program and that local and trivial interests, voiced through congressional committees, dominate policy outcomes. "It is ever the little foxes," Wilson quoted, "that spoil the grapes."[22] Lowell, in one of the first important accumulations of political statistics, demonstrated that American parties were quite undisciplined in comparison to the British.[23]

These themes persist. The report of the Committee on Political Parties was motivated in good part by an animosity toward special interests: "By themselves, the interest groups cannot . . . define . . . policy democratically. Coherent public policies do not emerge as the mathematical result of the claims of all the pressure groups" (p. 19). Its authors' remedy was a party system that would be "democratic, responsible, and effective," by which they meant parties that "are able to bring forth programs to which they commit themselves, . . . that . . . possess sufficient internal cohesion to carry out these programs" (pp. 17–18). This was their ideal and their argument:

When there are two parties identifiable by the kinds of action they propose, the voters have an actual choice. On the other hand, the sort of opposition presented by a coalition that cuts across party lines, as a regular thing, tends to deprive the public of a meaningful alternative. When such coalitions are formed after the elections are over, the public usually finds it difficult to understand the new situation and to reconcile it with the purpose of the ballot. Moreover, on that basis it is next to impossible to hold either party responsible for its political record. This is a serious source of public discontent [pp. 18–19].

It is difficult to imagine more populistic enthusiasm for discovering the people's will in simple majority decision. But enthusiasm for this particular nostrum has waned. Just at the time of the report, Pendleton Herring and David Truman were reviving Arthur Bentley's picture of public policy as a vector of group interests.[24] And, soon after, Robert Dahl replied in a sense to the report with his influential description of American "polyarchy":

The making of governmental decisions [Dahl argued] is not a majestic march of great majorities united upon certain matters of basic policy. It is the steady appeasement of relatively small groups. Even when these groups add up to a numerical majority at election time it is usually not

*useful to construct that majority as more than an arithmetic expression
. . . . It is the various components of the numerical majority that have the
means for action.*[25]

As Dahl cast doubt on the doctrine of responsible parties using a
more or less inductively arrived-at description of American politics,
Anthony Downs presented a wholly deductive argument that parties
would not offer those "meaningful alternatives" for which the committee
had asked.[26] Suppose there is a single issue dimension, x, which might, for
example, concern the degree of government regulation of the economy,
where the left end represents a high degree and the right end a low degree.
Citizens can be arranged along that dimension according to their individual choices. The horizontal axis in Figure 3-1 is such a dimension, with
point x_1 indicating the value judgment of a particular citizen on that issue.
The position of all citizens is indicated by the curve in Figure 3-1, which
shows the number, $f(x)$—on the vertical axis—of citizens at each point
on the horizontal axis. Downs showed that, if the distribution $f(x)$ was
unimodal, both political parties would adopt platforms near the median,
x_m, which is the point on the horizontal axis from which a perpendicular
line, p, erected parallel to the vertical axis divides the distribution $f(x)$
exactly in half.

Downs' argument is distressingly simple: Suppose one party goes to
the median while the other goes to x_1. The party at x_1 gets the votes to the
left of x_1 and the votes to the right of x_1 but to the left of the midpoint
between x_1 and x_m. Clearly, therefore, the party at x_1 loses and has every
incentive to get as close to x_m as it can. The same kind of analysis applies
to parties to the right of x_m. If both parties move to x_m, they tie.

Downs presented his argument for the unimodal case, but it applies
to any distribution in one dimension. Consequently, far from providing
"meaningful alternatives," parties should be expected to be as much alike
as possible. Peter Ordeshook extended this observation by allowing for
nonvoters and more than one dimension with, however, several fairly
severe restrictions.[27] Richard McKelvey, imposing fewer restrictions
than Ordeshook, nevertheless showed that "uncommitted citizens" near
the median of a multidimensional distribution have the most influence
on party platforms and that "there is a tendency for candidates to move
away from their strongest supporters" at the extremes, a quite counter-
intuitive result.[28]

We will later observe that, in the wholly unrestricted case of n
dimensions, the tendency toward equilibrium at the median does not
survive—a fact discovered by McKelvey himself. Still, the drag of institutions guarantees that, in the short run, party positions will converge

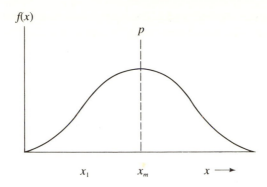

Figure 3-1   Distribution of citizens in one dimension.

to a median, even though in the long run there may be considerable divergence. In any event there is no theoretical comfort here for the doctrine of responsible parties. If Downs, Ordeshook, and McKelvey are right, the theory that two parties, however "responsible," would give voters a clear choice between distinct alternatives is simply wrong. Furthermore, American experience in the 1960s and 1970s has tarnished somewhat the ideal of presidential leadership to create coherent parties. Perhaps for this reason, political parties themselves have rapidly lost identifiers and loyalty. So the experiential justification for responsible parties has now also failed.

In a sense, political science and political events have passed the adherents of "responsible parties" by. It may seem foolish to waste time now on their mistake of expecting a clear binary choice. Still, we can understand their mistake a little better today. It is not simply an empirical matter—as Dahl, for example, argued—that the American (or any other) system does not work in the neat way the Wilsonians wanted. More important is the fact that what they wanted was itself morally wrong from a liberal democratic view, because to get binary choice one must *enforce* some method of reducing options. This is precisely the coercion involved in populist liberty. The populist expectation of a coherent program is not attainable by weaving together individual judgments, either for a small group or for a large nation. To attribute human coherence to any group is an anthropomorphic delusion. Worse, however, the populists expected to calcify politics on *their* own issues, progressivism or the New Deal. That is fundamentally unfair. Winning politicians are, of course, happy to stick with the issues on which they are winning. Losing politicians are not so entranced with that future. The losers of the last election become the winners of the next by changing issues, revealing new dimensions of choice, and uncovering covert values in the electorate. To create and enforce coherent parties with stable programs is to foreclose this artistry. It is the nature of politics that issues are in continuous creation. No institutional device to force binary choice can stop that creation and, furthermore, no device should stop it. Fairness to losers and an interest in what losers create forbid the imposition of binary choice.

*   *   *

So I conclude: Simple majority decision on binary alternatives satisfies three fundamental criteria of fairness and in that sense seems superior to other methods. But it cannot be fair in a democratic sense because the imposition of binary alternatives is itself unfair. Hence the relativistic conclusion of Chapter 2 still stands.

4

Voting Methods with Three
or More Alternatives

Simple majority decision on binary alternatives requires some social embodiment of Procrustes, who chopped off the legs of his guests to fit them into the bed in his inn. The number of alternatives *must* be reduced to exactly two, and this means that some alternatives worthy of consideration must be excised. Furthermore, there must be some Procrustean leader or elite to excise them. Even the apparently unbiased method of reducing alternatives by a series of binary elections requires that someone decide on the *order* of elections—and control of the order is often enough to control the outcome, as we shall see. Thus, however democratic simple majority decision initially appears to be, it cannot in fact be so. Indeed, it is democratic only in the very narrow sense of satisfying certain formal conditions. In any larger sense, it is not democratic because its surrounding institutions must be unfair.

If a voting system is to be really fair, more than two alternatives must be allowed to enter the decision process; a decision method must be able to operate on three or more alternatives. But here is a snag. Many decision methods can deal with several alternatives, but no one method satisfies all the conditions of fairness that have been proposed as reasonable and just. Every method satisfies some and violates others. Unfortunately, there are, so far as I know, no deeper ethical systems nor any deeper axioms for decision that would allow us to judge and choose among these conditions of fairness. Hence there is no generally convincing way to show that one decision method is truly better than another.

So we are faced with a dilemma. Simple majority decision between two alternatives, while narrowly fair, is unattractive because it requires unfair institutions to operate it. On the other hand, no particular decision methods for three or more alternatives can be unequivocally demonstrated to be fair or reasonable. The problem is that we cannot prove that any method truly and fairly amalgamates the judgments of citizens simply because we do not know what "truly and fairly amalgamates" means.

Chapter 4 is devoted to a demonstration of that proposition. I have no deep preference for any method of decision, and I am not trying to prove that one is better or worse than another. I want merely to show that the notion of true and fair amalgamation is neither obvious nor simple, which is why we cannot easily choose among the voting methods discussed in Chapter 2.

4.A. Some Preliminaries

Because no method for decision among three or more alternatives is entirely satisfactory, many methods have been invented. Despite the variety, they can be classified into three families, the members of which are enough alike that their merits and deficiencies can be discussed together. I call the three families (1) majoritarian methods, (2) positional methods, and (3) utilitarian methods. To begin the discussion I will define the categories and offer some examples.

As a preliminary, however, the vocabulary must be revised and expanded. The set, X, of alternatives now must have $m > 2$ members, $X = (1, 2, \ldots, m)$, which will be referred to with lower-case italic letters, x, y, a, b, and so on. The relations, P, I, and R, remain binary in that they represent individual judgments and votes between a pair of alternatives. But now it must be decided whether they are also transitive—namely, that, if $x R_i y$ and $y R_i z$, then $x R_i z$. (For simplicity, I will write $x y z$ to mean "$x R_i y, y R_i z,$ and $x R_i z$," and $x(yz)$ to mean "$x P_i y, y I_i z,$ and $x P_i z$.") Many arguments are offered for and against individual transitivity.[1] I will, however, conventionally assume that $P, R,$ and I are transitive, except when it is stated otherwise for I and R.

Furthermore, I will also assume that, for all i in the set, N, of decision-makers, some one of these relations connects every pair, x and y, in X. This means that D_i, which is the individual judgment on members of X, is an *ordering*—that is, a transitive and complete arrangement of X. By ordering is meant that the position of each alternative in a particular arrangement is unambiguous. Since X is connected, this means that, for each x and y in X, either $xy, yx,$ or (xy) must be true for each i in N; that is, D_i is one of $\{xy, yx, (xy)\}$. This establishes an unambiguous order in every pair of alternatives. Since D_i is transitive, if it contains $x y$ and $y z$, then it must contain $x z$ (rather than $z x$ or $(x z)$), which establishes an unambiguous order in every triad of alternatives. And since triads can overlap (e.g., $w\,x\,y$ and $x\,y\,z$), transitivity establishes an order over an X of any finite size.

The profile, D, will be a set of (not necessarily different) orderings, D_i, of X, for each of n participants; and $\mathbf{D}$ will be the set of all possible profiles. Finally, the social choice, F, will now be the result of a decision rule, g, operating on a specified set, X, and a particular profile, D, of judgments to produce a choice: $F_g(X, D)$. Notice that now the set, X, from which the choice is taken will customarily be specified because sometimes the discussion will concern choices from two different sets, X and X'. Typically, if the decision rule, g, is clear from the context, it will not be indicated in the identification of F.

For the time being, except when expressly stated otherwise, I will also assume that all voting is in accordance with preferences. Hence, if $x\,P_i\,y$, person i votes for x over y; and, if $x\,I_i\,y$, person i does not vote for either x or y.

4.B. Majoritarian Methods of Voting

Majoritarian systems are those in which the principles of simple majority voting are extended to three or more alternatives. The rationale is that majority decision is fair and reasonable in its logical structure, and it is assumed that the defect of limiting alternatives can be offset by admitting all desired alternatives. This assumption, however, is profoundly dubious, as we shall see in the discussion of positional voting in section 4.E.

The way of extending the method of majority decision from two to more alternatives is the so-called Condorcet method, in which a winner is defined as that alternative which can beat *all* others in X in a simple majority vote. When X has two members, this is merely simple majority decision. But when X has more than two, this is the requirement that the winner beat $m - 1$ others in $m - 1$ pairwise decisions.

Unfortunately, there are many situations in which the Condorcet winner is undefined simply because no alternative can beat $m - 1$ others. One extreme example, in Display 4-1, is the so-called paradox of voting (see section 1.H). In Display 4-1 each alternative beats one other and loses to another. Which, if any, ought to win?

A more confusing example is set forth in Display 4-2. There, since w ties or beats x, y, and z, presumably w ought to be among the winners. But what of x and y? They tie and so might reasonably win along with w; but although x ties w, y does not, so just as reasonably only w and x

Display 4-1

The Paradox of Voting

D_1: $x\ y\ z$
D_2: $y\ z\ x$
D_3: $z\ x\ y$

Number of Votes for the Alternative in the Row When Placed in Contest Against the Alternative in the Column

	x	y	z
x	—	2	1
y	1	—	2
z	2	1	—

A Condorcet winner would have a majority (here at least 2) in every cell (except the blank one) in a row, signifying that the alternative in the row beats all others. In the paradox, no alternative can beat all others, and so each row has at least one cell with less than a majority (here, at most, 1).

---

might win. In the absence of a Condorcet winner, problems like these inevitably arise.

Different resolutions of such problems result in different decision methods. Those called *majoritarian* or *Condorcet extensions* have the common property that they select the Condorcet winner, if one exists; if one does not exist, they provide for some further resolution. All such rules depend on knowing whether one alternative beats another in a simple majority vote. Thus I define a *social* relation of majority, M, so that $x\ My$ means "more people prefer x to y than prefer y to x."[2] In any event, to use the Condorcet criterion and its extended rules, it is necessary, as a practical matter, either for each voter to report his or her entire preference structure, D_i, or for the group to hold a number of ballotings, perhaps as many as a round robin, $m(m-1)/2$.

Display 4-2

A Profile for Which the Choice of a Winner Is Not Clear

D_1: $w \; y \; x \; z$
D_2: $x \; w \; z \; y$
D_3: $y \; z \; w \; x$
D_4: $x \; w \; y \; z$

Number of Votes for the Alternative in the Row When Placed in Contest Against the Alternative in the Column

	w	x	y	z
w	—	2	3	3
x	2	—	2	3
y	1	2	—	3
z	1	1	1	—

While w beats or ties all others, x and y tie. Ought x to win? It is true that x ties with w, the alternative that otherwise beats all others. But x ties y, which otherwise loses. Should y win? Its only claim is a tie with x, which in turn ties w, which beats y.

4.C. Examples of Majoritarian Methods

There are many rules that utilize paired comparisons of alternatives to discover a Condorcet winner. If a Condorcet winner exists, then all these methods come out the same way. If a Condorcet winner does not exist, however, these rules typically produce different results, no one of which, in my opinion, seems more defensible than another.

The Amendment Procedure

The only widely used Condorcet extension, the goal of the amendment procedure is to select the Condorcet winner, if there is one, or, if there is not, to select the status quo. (Hence the procedure is not neutral, since the status quo is favored.) It works as intended on three alternatives—(1) motion, (2) amendment, (3) neither; but it does not ensure its objective for more than three.

The actual rule is: Alternatives (motions) are put forward to form X, which always includes the implicit motion to sustain the status quo. The winner of an identified pair is chosen by simple majority decision. That winner is placed against another identified motion and a second winner is chosen, and so forth until a just-previous winner is placed against the status quo, and a final winner is chosen by simple majority. In the typical American procedure, X can actually have six members:

t. Original motion

w. Amendment

x. Amendment to the amendment

y. Substitute amendment

z. Amendment to substitute

s. Status quo

The six are voted on by this rule:

Step 1: z vs. y

Step 2: x vs. w

Step 3: Survivor of step 1 vs. survivor of step 2

Step 4: Survivor of step 3 vs. t

Step 5: Survivor of step 4 vs. s^3

With just three alternatives—motion (t), amendment (w), and status quo (s)—this procedure actually works as intended, for it discovers the Condorcet winner, if one exists, or, if none exists, it chooses the status quo. With three alternatives, this procedure reduces to two steps:

Step 1: w vs. t

Step 2: Survivor of step 1 vs. s

If a substantive motion (w or t) wins, it must beat both other alternatives and is thus the Condorcet winner (see Figure 4-1). Thus outcome 1 means

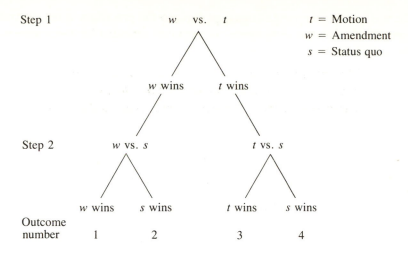

Figure 4-1 Parliamentary voting on three alternatives.

w has beaten both t and s, and outcome 3 means t has beaten w and s. When outcomes 2 or 4 occur, it is not clear whether s is the Condorcet winner or simply the tie-breaker. Outcome 4, for example, could be reached from either profile D or profile D' of Display 4-3.

In profile D, s beats both substantive alternatives and is the Condorcet winner. In profile D', no alternative can beat both others; so, by the non-neutral rule, s is chosen. The failure in this case to reveal whether D or D' exists is irrelevant because, by the procedure, s is intended to win in either case. It might be argued that s ought not win in D' because, if w had not been eliminated by t, then w would have beaten s and *should* in fact do so. Still, the assumption in the procedure is that, since w loses to t, it is better to do nothing than to adopt w. For that reason, the procedure is designed to make s win.

The fact that the amendment procedure embodies a reasonable extension of the Condorcet criterion to three alternatives is what, in my opinion, has made it generally acceptable. Nevertheless, when X has four or more members, this procedure is quite arbitrary and may select a *substantive* motion that fails the Condorcet test, even one that is unanimously believed inferior to a rejected motion. Thus, for motion (t), amendment (w), amendment to the amendment (x), substitute amendment (y), and status quo (s), a profile like that in Display 4-4 might occur.[4]

In this profile, x (the initially rejected amendment) is *unanimously* preferred to t (the original and winning motion). Clearly here the proce-

Display 4-3

Alternate Profiles Leading to a Victory for the Status Quo Under the Amendment Procedure with Only One Amendment

$$D$$
(with a Condorcet winner)

D_1, D_2:	$s\ t\ w$
D_3, D_4:	$t\ s\ w$
D_5:	$w\ s\ t$

Number of Votes for the Alternative in the Row When Placed in Contest Against the Alternative in the Column

	s	t	w
s	—	3	4 (Condorcet winner)
t	2	—	4
w	1	1	—

Alternative s is the Condorcet winner in profile D.

$$D'$$
(without a Condorcet winner)

D'_1, D'_2:	$t\ w\ s$
D'_3:	$s\ t\ w$
D'_4:	$s\ w\ t$
D'_5:	$w\ s\ t$

**Number of Votes for the Alternative
in the Row When Placed in Contest
Against the Alternative in the Column**

	s	t	w
s	—	3	2
t	2	—	3
w	3	2	—

There is no Condorcet winner, and s wins by default in profile D'.

---

dure fails to achieve the intended goal of identifying and selecting a clear-cut winner.

The Successive Procedure

The successive procedure is the analogue for electing candidates of the amendment procedure for selecting motions, but it is neutral since all candidates may lose. It guarantees the choice of the candidate with an absolute majority, if one exists; but it does not choose at all when there is no Condorcet winner, and it may even reject a Condorcet winner.

The set X is composed of nominated candidates, who are voted upon individually in some specified order until one wins or the list is exhausted. If at the end no winner has been selected, the procedure is abandoned or repeated. At each stage the procedure in effect divides the alternative candidates into two sets, the singleton $\{x\}$ and the remainder $(X - \{x\})$, and places them against each other. Each voter then decides how to vote by this rule: If i prefers x to all other members of X, then i votes yes on $\{x\}$; but if i prefers some y in X, where $y \neq x$, then i votes no on $\{x\}$—in effect choosing $(X - \{x\})$ over $\{x\}$. If $\{x\}$ wins, x must, by definition, be able to beat *all* of the others simultaneously. Even a Condorcet winner can lose, as in the example in Display 4-5, where the alternative x is the Condorcet winner but the singleton set $\{x\}$ will lose to $(X - \{x\})$. If there is no winner, this rule has no method of resolution among nominees, although in practice it probably often influences voters to reorder their preferences to obtain a winner.

Display 4-4

A Profile in Which a Losing Alternative Is Unanimously Preferred to the Winning Alternative

	D
D_1:	$w \; x \; t \; y \; s$
D_2:	$y \; w \; x \; t \; s$
D_3:	$s \; x \; t \; y \; w$

Number of Votes for the Alternative in the Row When Placed in Contest Against the Alternative in the Column

	s	t	w	x	y
s	—	1	1	1	1
t	2	—	2	0	2
w	2	1	—	2	1
x	2	3	1	—	2
y	2	1	2	1	—

Amendment Procedure by Which t Wins Although All Voters Prefer x to t

Step 1: x vs. w; w wins

Step 2: w vs. y; y wins

Step 3: y vs. t; t wins

Step 4: t vs. s; t wins

Runoff Elections

Runoff elections combine plurality decision (a positional method to be discussed in section 4.E) with simple majority decision in a two-stage process. Although the intent is probably to ensure a Condorcet winner,

Display 4-5

A Profile in Which the Condorcet Winner Loses Under the Successive Procedure

D_1:	$w\ x\ y\ z$
D_2:	$y\ x\ w\ z$
D_3:	$z\ x\ y\ w$

Number of Votes for the Alternative in the Row When Placed in Contest Against the Alternative in the Column

	w	x	y	z	
w	—	1	1	2	
x	2	—	2	2	(Condorcet winner)
y	2	1	—	2	
z	1	1	1	—	

Although x is the Condorcet winner, in a contest between the singleton set $\{x\}$ and the set $(X - \{x\})$, $\{x\}$ loses, which means, of course, that x loses.

	Contest		
	$\{x\} = x$	vs.	$(X - \{x\}) = w, y, z$
Voters	None		1, 2, 3

runoff elections may fail to do so. Typically, positional methods do not satisfy the Condorcet criterion, and in this combination the plurality feature introduces violations of it. The rule is: When X contains three or more members, choose that alternative which receives more than half of the total vote. If none do, then hold a runoff election between the two alternatives with the largest numbers of votes, deciding between them by simple majority.

That this method can fail to satisfy the Condorcet criterion is easily seen in Display 4-6. Although x wins, z has a simple majority over x and y, and z is the Condorcet winner. Furthermore, as Smith has proved (see section 3.C and Chapter 3, note 10), this method is not necessarily monotonic because alternatives are eliminated. An example of the failure of runoff elections to satisfy monotonicity is seen in Display 4-7, where an increase from D' to D in support for alternative x results in its defeat in D even though it had won in D'. The reason is that the weakening of w changes the runoff from "x vs. w" in D' to "x vs. y" in D and, in both D' and D, x loses to y.

There are other Condorcet extensions, a few of which I will discuss in the following paragraphs. They have not been widely used, if at all, and are of interest because they show the difficulty of defining winners when no Condorcet winner exists. There is no good reason, in my opinion, for preferring one to another, yet they can lead to different outcomes (see note 8).

The Copeland Rule

The Copeland rule is based on the notion that those alternatives ought to be selected that win relatively most frequently in simple majority contests with all other alternatives. The rule is: Select that alternative, x, with the largest Copeland index, $c(x)$, which is the number of times x beats other alternatives less the number of times x loses to other alternatives.[5] Of course, if there is a Condorcet winner, $c(x) = m - 1$; if not, there may be ties.[6]

The Schwartz Rule

If no alternative beats all others, then some alternatives are in a cycle: $x \, M \, y \, M \, z \, M \, x$. The "top" cycle is one that either extends over the whole set X, or, if not, each alternative in the top cycle beats all alternatives not in it. The goal of the Schwartz rule is to select the top cycle, which is a unique alternative if a Condorcet winner exists, but may be most or all of the alternatives otherwise.[7]

The Kemeny Rule

The goal of the Kemeny rule is to find a permutation, P, of the members of X that is "closest" to all the D_i in D. A permutation of X is a transitive ordering of X and consists of ordered pairs, so that if xy is in P, then yx cannot be. Thus, for $X = (x, y, z)$, one permutation is zxy or the

Display 4-6

A Profile in Which the Condorcet Winner Loses Under the Runoff Procedure

D_1, D_2:	x z y
D_3, D_4:	y z x
D_5:	z x y

Plurality Stage

First-place votes:

x: 2

y: 2

z: 1

The alternative with the fewest first-place votes, z, is eliminated.

Majority Stage

Contest		
	x vs.	y
Votes	3	2

Alternative x, supported by voters 1, 2, and 5, wins. Nevertheless, z is the Condorcet winner.

Number of Votes for the Alternative in the Row When Placed in Contest Against the Alternative in the Column

	x	y	z	
x	—	3	2	
y	2	—	2	
z	3	3	—	(Condorcet winner)

Display 4-7

Why Runoff Elections Do Not Satisfy the Criterion of Monotonicity

D'		D	
D'_1, D'_2:	$w\ x\ y\ z$	D_1, D_2:	$x\ w\ y\ z$
D'_3, D'_4:	$w\ y\ x\ z$	D_3, D_4:	$w\ y\ x\ z$
D'_5, D'_6, D'_7, D'_8:	$x\ w\ y\ z$	D_5, D_6, D_7, D_8:	$x\ w\ y\ z$
D'_9, D'_{10}, D'_{11}:	$y\ z\ x\ w$	D_9, D_{10}, D_{11}:	$y\ z\ x\ w$
D'_{12}, D'_{13}:	$z\ w\ y\ x$	D_{12}, D_{13}:	$z\ w\ y\ x$

Profile D'

Plurality stage, first-place votes:

w: 4

x: 4

y: 3

z: 2

The alternatives with the fewest first-place votes, y and z, are eliminated.

Majority stage:

Contest	
w vs. x	
Votes 6	7

Alternative x, supported by voters 5, 6, 7, 8, 9, 10, and 11, wins.

Profile D

Profile D differs from Profile D' only in that voters 1 and 2 have raised x from second place to first place and lowered w to second place.

Plurality stage, first-place votes:

w: 2

x: 6

y: 3

z: 2

The alternatives with the fewest first-place votes, *w* and *z*, are eliminated.

Majority stage:

	Contest		
	x	vs.	*y*
Votes	6		7

Alternative *y*, supported by voters 3, 4, 9, 10, 11, 12, and 13, wins. Thus an increase in support of *x* in *D* as against *D′* brought about the defeat of *x* in *D* even though *x* had won in *D′*.

---

pairs *zx*, *zy*, *xy*. To find the "closest" permutation to *D*, the rule is: For each *P*, sum the number of ordered pairs in all the D_i of *D* that are the same as pairs in *P*. There is a set *P** of those *P* with the largest sum of ordered pairs in *D* and the winner(s) are those alternative(s) standing first in the permutations in *P**.

Although the detail of this extremely complicated calculation is not in itself important, an example (illustrating, perhaps, the desperation of theorists to discover an adequate Condorcet extension) is set forth in Display 4-8, where the ordered pairs in the six possible permutations of the members of *X* are checked against the ordered pairs in the D_i of *D*. The pairs in P_6 are found more frequently in *D* than are the pairs of any other permutation. Hence, $P* = P_6$; and *z*, which is first in P_6, is the Kemeny winner. Notice that, if a Concorcet winner exists, it will be chosen; but if one does not exist, there is still likely to be a unique winner. Although the Kemeny rule is based on a clever and defensible idea, the

Calculation of the Kemeny Winner

D		P		
D_1:	$z\ y\ x$	P_1:	$x\ y\ z$	P_4:	$y\ z\ x$
D_2:	$y\ z\ x$	P_2:	$x\ z\ y$	P_5:	$z\ x\ y$
D_3:	$x\ z\ y$	P_3:	$y\ x\ z$	P_6:	$z\ y\ x$

Comparison of Ordered Pairs in D_i and P_1 to P_6

P_1: $x\ y\ z$

Pairs in P_1	Pairs in D		
	D_1	D_2	D_3
xy	0	0	1
xz	0	0	1
yz	0	1	0
Total	$0 + 1 + 2 = 3$		

P_2: $x\ z\ y$

Pairs in P_2	Pairs in D		
	D_1	D_2	D_3
xz	0	0	1
xy	0	0	1
zy	1	0	1
Total	$1 + 0 + 3 = 4$		

P_3: $y\ x\ z$

Pairs in P_3	Pairs in D		
	D_1	D_2	D_3
yx	1	1	0
yz	0	1	0
xz	0	0	1
Total	$1 + 2 + 1 = 4$		

P_4: $y\ z\ x$

Pairs in P_4	Pairs in D		
	D_1	D_2	D_3
yz	0	1	0
yx	1	1	0
zx	1	1	0
Total	$2 + 3 + 0 = 5$		

P_5: $z\ x\ y$

Pairs in P_5	Pairs in D		
	D_1	D_2	D_3
zx	1	1	0
zy	1	0	1
xy	0	0	1
Total	$2 + 1 + 2 = 5$		

P_6: $z\ y\ x$

Pairs in P_6	Pairs in D		
	D_1	D_2	D_3
zy	1	0	1
zx	1	1	0
yx	1	1	0
Total	$3 + 2 + 1 = 6$		

Since the pairs in P_6 are found more frequently in D than the pairs of any other permutation, the Kemeny winner is z, which is the alternative ordered first in P_6.

Kemeny winner may not be the same one chosen by Copeland's rule or by Schwartz's rule, which are also based on clever and defensible ideas.[8]

Conclusions

Two features stand out in this survey of majoritarian rules. First, majority choice over three or more alternatives, though not easy to operate, usually has a clear meaning when a Condorcet winner exists. Second, when a Condorcet winner does not exist, the rules actually used to pick a winner may in fact pick what many would regard as a loser, and there is no consensus on what ought to be regarded as the winner.

One can therefore say that, if the Condorcet criterion is not satisfied, majoritarian decision is only partially adequate from a practical point of view. It can pick winners, but they need not be unique. From a theoretical point of view, majoritarian decision is even worse because it is hard to define and, furthermore, the several definitions do not necessarily lead to the same winner from the same profile.

4.D. Positional Methods of Voting

The fact that majoritarian methods are clearly defined when a Condorcet winner exists does not win universal approval for them. As I mentioned at the beginning of section 4.B, majoritarian methods assume that the defect in simple majority decision of limiting alternatives can be cured by the easy solution of admitting more of them. But the remedy creates a new disease. One is the difficulty, just discussed, of stating an adequate rule when a Condorcet winner is undefined. This is, however, only the first and simplest difficulty. A more profound one is that majoritarian methods use only information about binary relations in the social profile, D, even though, once X is expanded to more than two members, much more information exists—namely, the position of each alternative in the individual orderings, D_i, of D.

Positional methods are intended to resolve this more profound difficulty by taking some or all of the information about whole individual orderings into account. These methods include (1) plurality voting (which uses only information about first places), (2) approval voting (which uses information about a variable number of places), and (3) scoring functions such as the Borda count, which uses information about all places. The Borda count—the most systematic of the three positional methods—has each individual assign $m - 1$ points to her or his first-place alternative, $m - 2$ points to the second-place alternative, and so on, to zero points to the mth-place (that is, last) alternative. The Borda score for an alternative is the sum of points given it by the n voters. The Borda winner, then, is the alternative with the highest Borda score.[9]

The main argument for the positional approach is that it uses some or all of the information added by expanding X and thus expanding the D_i from paired comparisons to orderings of three or more alternatives. This added information makes a great difference. In an especially interesting example, Peter Fishburn points to the following pair of situations for $X = (x, y, a, b, c)$ and five voters:[10]

D: By binary majority decision: $x \, M \, y \, M \, a \, M \, b \, M \, c$

D': x has: 2 first-place votes y has 2 first-place votes
            1 second-place vote   2 second-place votes
            1 fourth-place vote   1 third-place vote
            1 fifth-place vote

As Fishburn remarks, although one might reasonably choose x to win in D and y to win in D' (since, in D', y has the same number of first-place votes and more second- and third-place votes), the interesting fact is that it is possible that $D = D'$, as shown in Display 4-9.

Clearly the kind of information used makes a difference. Paired comparisons lead to the choice of x, and positional comparisons lead to the choice of y. Furthermore, as Condorcet himself pointed out, the conflict is profound and does not depend at all on the particular method of numbering positions.[11] One can generalize the Borda method into a scoring system to count relative positions without using points at all—thereby implicitly revealing the justification for positional methods: For each alternative, x, determine a score $s(x)$, by counting the number of times x precedes $y, z, \ldots$ in all of the D_i of D and then subtracting the number of times x succeeds $y, z, \ldots$. The alternative with the highest score wins, which means the winner most frequently stands ahead of others in the whole profile.[12] For the example just given, $s(y) = 12$, $s(x) = 4$, $s(a) = -4$, $s(b) = -6$, $s(c) = -6$.[13] Since this is a count of positions (not points), it follows that y will beat x for *any* system that uses data on the entire profile.

Dodgson invented an excellent example, set forth in Display 4-10, to point up the ethical conflict between majoritarian and positional methods.[14] There are 11 voters. Although b is clearly the Condorcet winner, in some sense a has an excellent claim because

Display 4-9

A Profile in Which the Borda Winner Seems Appropriate Even Though a Different Condorcet Winner Exists

$D = D'$	
D_1:	$x\ y\ a\ b\ c$
D_2:	$y\ a\ c\ b\ x$
D_3:	$c\ x\ y\ a\ b$
D_4:	$x\ y\ b\ c\ a$
D_5:	$y\ b\ a\ x\ c$

Majoritarian Decision: Number of Votes for the Alternative in the Row When Placed in Contest Against the Alternative in the Column

	x	y	a	b	c	
x	—	3	3	3	3	(Condorcet winner)
y	2	—	5	4	4	
a	2	0	—	3	3	
b	2	1	2	—	3	
c	2	1	2	2	—	

Borda Count: Number of Points for Alternatives in Rows, Preference Orders in Columns

	D_1	D_2	D_3	D_4	D_5	Total	
x	4	0	3	4	1	12	
y	3	4	2	3	4	16	(Borda winner)
a	2	3	1	0	2	8	
b	1	1	0	2	3	7	
c	0	2	4	1	0	7	

Display 4-10

A Profile in Which the Condorcet Winner Has a Majority of First-Place Votes While a Different Borda Winner Has a Much Higher Score Than the Condorcet Winner

D	
D_1, D_2, D_3:	b a c d
D_4, D_5, D_6:	b a d c
D_7, D_8, D_9:	a c d b
D_{10}, D_{11}:	a d c b

Majoritarian Decision: Number of Votes for the Alternative in the Row When Placed in Contest Against the Alternative in the Column

	a	b	c	d	
a	—	5	11	11	
b	6	—	6	6	(Condorcet winner)
c	0	5	—	6	
d	0	5	5	—	

Borda Count: Number of Points for Alternatives in Rows, Preference Orders in Columns

	D_1	D_2	D_3	D_4	D_5	D_6	D_7	D_8	D_9	D_{10}	D_{11}	Total	
a	2	2	2	2	2	2	3	3	3	3	3	27	(Borda winner)
b	3	3	3	3	3	3	0	0	0	0	0	18	
c	1	1	1	0	0	0	2	2	2	1	1	11	
d	0	0	0	1	1	1	1	1	1	2	2	10	

a has 5 first-place votes b has 6 first-place votes
            6 second-place votes   5 fourth- (last-) place votes

Everybody who likes b better than a nevertheless likes a second-best, while everybody who likes a better than b puts b at the bottom of the list. Accordingly, a wins by a dramatic margin under the Borda count.

4.E. Examples of Positional Methods

I do not intend at this point to render a moral judgment on the relative merits of majoritarian and positional methods. I wish now merely to observe that the use of one rather than the other makes a great difference in outcomes. Furthermore, because the kind of positional voting one uses also makes a great difference, I will describe three kinds briefly.

Plurality Voting

In constitutional structure, the plurality method is close to simple majority decision. Both require single-member districts or unique outcomes, and which one occurs is determined by the number of candidates or alternatives put forward. If there are only two, then simple majority decision occurs; if more than two, plurality occurs. *Plurality* means selecting the alternative with the most votes (which may or may not be a majority of the votes cast). This method of voting thus in effect selects the alternative most frequently placed first in voters' preference orders. Naturally, this need not be a Condorcet winner and probably often is not. For example, in Display 4-11, x is the plurality winner, y is the Condorcet winner, and x loses to *all* other candidates in a majority decision. Elections in which something like this may have occurred are the presidential election of 1912 and the New York senatorial election of 1970, for which I have guessed at voters' orderings, as depicted in Displays 4-12 and 4-13.

This feature of plurality voting appears illogical and inadequate to many social choice theorists. In terms of a particular election, it may lead to an undesirable choice. In terms of a series of elections, however, it has the effect of encouraging politicians to offer exactly two candidates, thus achieving simple majority decision without the unfairness involved in the notion of monolithic "responsible" parties. The motive is, as in the foregoing cases, that supporters of the losers (y and z in Display 4-11, Taft and

Display 4-11

A Profile in Which the Plurality Winner Loses to All Other Alternatives Under Majority Decision

D	
D_1, D_2, D_3, D_4:	$x\,y\,z$
D_5, D_6, D_7:	$y\,z\,x$
D_8, D_9:	$z\,y\,x$

Plurality Winner

Number of First-Place Votes	
x	4 (Plurality winner)
y	3
z	2

Majoritarian Decision: Number of Votes for the Alternative in the Row When Placed in Contest Against the Alternative in the Column

	x	y	z	
x	—	4	4	
y	5	—	7	(Condorcet winner)
z	5	2	—	

Notice that x loses to both y and z.

Display 4-12

Possible Profiles
of the 1912 Presidential Election

First-place votes	Possible orderings by voters with given first-place votes
42% Wilson	Wilson, Roosevelt, Taft
27% Roosevelt	Roosevelt, Taft, Wilson
24% Taft	Taft, Roosevelt, Wilson
7% Others	

The plurality winner is Wilson.

Majoritarian Decision: Percent of Votes
for the Alternative in the Row
When Placed in Contest Against
the Alternative in the Column

	Wilson	Roosevelt	Taft
Wilson	—	42%	42%
Roosevelt	51%	—	69% (Condorcet winner)
Taft	51%	24%	—

Display 4-13

Possible Profiles of the
1970 New York Senatorial Election

First-place votes	Possible ordering by voters with given first-place votes
39% Buckley (Con.)	Buckley, Ottinger, Goodell
37% Ottinger (Dem.)	Ottinger, Goodell, Buckley
24% Goodell (Rep.)	Goodell, Ottinger, Buckley

The plurality winner is Buckley.

Display 4-13 (Continued)

**Majoritarian Decision: Percent of Votes
for the Alternative in the Row
When Placed in Contest Against
the Alternative in the Column**

	Buckley	Ottinger	Goodell	
Buckley	—	39%	39%	
Ottinger	61%	—	76%	(Condorcet winner)
Goodell	61%	24%	—	

Roosevelt in Display 4-12, and Ottinger and Goodell in Display 4-13) like
the winner least of all, *and* they know that their failure to compromise is
the proximate cause of the winner's success. In the next election, therefore, they *want* to compromise, and this is what produces a two-candidate
election.

In the instances cited, this is precisely what happened. After 1912,
Progressives returned to the Republican fold. After the 1970 election,
where many Republicans could not vote for their second choice, Ottinger,
because they believed him quite incompetent, the Democrats compromised by offering an obviously intelligent candidate, Moynihan, and obtained thereby much moderate Republican support against Buckley, who
ran in 1976 as a Republican. Thus plurality voting, while often defective
in single elections, is probably the main force maintaining over time the
simple majority decision that most people regard as desirable.[15]

Approval Voting

Approval voting permits the voter to cast one vote for as many
candidates as she or he chooses, and the candidate with the most votes
wins. This method is used, so far as I know, only for honorary societies,
but it has recently been proposed for national primaries and elections.[16]

It is an essentially positional or point-count system, where one point
is given for each of the j places, $j < m$, in the preference ordering, D_i, for
which i chooses to vote. So approval voting is somewhere between plural-

ity voting and the Borda count. As a positional system, approval voting can lead to the defeat of the Condorcet winner. Indeed, it can lead to the defeat of a candidate with a large absolute majority. If all voters decide to cast two approval votes—one for each of the first two positions, as in Display 4-14—then y wins, though x is the Condorcet winner.

Display 4-14

A Comparison of Approval Voting and Majoritarian Voting

D	
D_1–D_{61}:	$x\ y\ z$
D_{62}–D_{81}:	$y\ x\ z$
D_{82}–D_{101}:	$z\ y\ x$

Approval Voting, Assuming Each Voter Votes for Two Alternatives

	First-place votes	Second-place votes	Total
x	61	20	81
y	20	81	101 (Approval winner)
z	20	0	20

Majoritarian Decision: Number of Votes for the Alternative in the Row When Placed in Contest Against the Alternative in the Column

	x	y	z
x	—	61	81 (Condorcet winner)
y	40	—	81
z	20	20	—

The reason approval voting is urged as a replacement for the plurality method is that it would probably select the Condorcet winner in cases like those of 1912 and 1970, where supporters of the losers rate the winners last. Furthermore, in presidential primaries it would probably encourage the selection of moderates, because party members of all beliefs would be likely to vote for the moderates. Still, its dynamic effect would probably be to increase the number of candidates offered (especially in primaries), so that simple majority decision would almost never occur.

The motive would be that supporters of a minority candidate might believe that they could collect enough second-, third-, . . . , j^{th} place votes to win. In primaries, this dynamic fractionalization would simply split up the parties. But in elections the effect would probably be worse: The force in the plurality system toward simple majority decision might be dissipated. It does seem myopic to abandon a system dynamically moving toward two-candidate choice and to accept one kind of failure to choose a Condorcet winner (namely, permanent multipartyism or multifactionalism), simply to avoid another kind of failure (occasional plurality winners).

The Borda Count

The Borda count is, as noted in section 4.D, a simple version of scoring methods—that is, of ascertaining the order of alternatives based on the net number of positions of precedence. It is important not to think of the Borda score as some kind of utility function.[17] Just because a voter places x first among five (4 points) does not mean he or she likes x twice as much as y in third place (2 points). The points are simply a device to count "aheadness." This definition of winning in terms of aheadness is what renders the Borda count especially attractive for many people. It is also, however, what renders it especially vulnerable to strange and paradoxical results when the number of alternatives (and hence of positions) is varied. In such circumstances, there are problems with all voting systems, but the Borda count seems particularly prone to such distortions. For example, Fishburn has shown the possibility of these bizarre results:[18]

1. If the ordering induced on X by the Borda count is $y\,a\,b\,c$, and if y is then removed from X, the ordering on $(X - \{y\})$ can then be reversed to $c\,b\,a$, as in Display 4-15.

2. The inverse of this paradox is: If the ordering on X is $a\,b\,c\,y$, then the ordering on $(X - \{y\})$ can be $c\,b\,a$.

3. Suppose y is the Borda winner in X. It may be that, for all the possible proper subsets of X containing y and at least one other alternative, y is

the Borda winner in only *one* subset. (A proper subset is a subset that does not include all members of the set.) So, if X has, say, $m = 6$ alternatives, there are $(2^{m-1} - 2) = 30$ proper subsets containing y and at least one other alternative, and it is possible that y loses in 29 of them and still wins in X.

The implicit justification of the Borda count is that positional information should be considered. These perversities, however, suggest that the method is quite sensitive to the number of positions, and that fact casts some doubt on the justification.

Finally, there is a practical difficulty with the Borda method, one it shares with Condorcet extensions such as Kemeny's. That difficulty is the onerous task of collecting complete preference orders, D_i, from all i in N. For more than three alternatives, many voters find ordering difficult.

Conclusions

Positional methods are sensitive to the positions used. Indeed, it is possible that with exactly the same profile, D, plurality voting will produce one winner, approval voting another, and the Borda count yet another. This is perhaps as it should be, because each involves adding some positional information; but it also suggests that the outcome is as much dependent on the method of counting votes as it is on the voters' judgments. In Display 4-16 is an example where D is constant, $X = (a, b, c, d)$, and $n = 13$; the winners are

Plurality: a

Approval: b, where each voter votes for two candidates

Approval: c, where each voter votes for three candidates

Borda: d

Incidentally, there is no Condorcet winner; but the Copeland winners are a and d; the Schwartz winners are a, b, c, d; and the Kemeny winners are b and d.

In Display 4-16, with just one profile of preferences, there are four different social choices from four methods of aggregation. Furthermore, these methods are not wildly different. They are all based on the notion of aheadness, which is implicit in positional methods. The inescapable inference is that social choice depends as much on methods of aggregation (that is, on social institutions) as it does on individual values and tastes.

Display 4-15

A Paradox with the Borda Count

Let $X = (y, a, b, c)$.

D on X	
D_1, D_2:	$y\ c\ b\ a$
D_3, D_4:	$a\ y\ c\ b$
D_5, D_6:	$b\ a\ y\ c$
D_7:	$y\ c\ b\ a$

Borda Count for D on X: Number of Points for Alternatives in Rows, Preference Orders in Columns

	D_1	D_2	D_3	D_4	D_5	D_6	D_7	Total
y	3	3	2	2	1	1	3	15
a	0	0	3	3	2	2	0	10
b	1	1	0	0	3	3	1	9
c	2	2	1	1	0	0	2	8

The ordering induced on X by the Borda count is $y\ a\ b\ c$.

Let $(X - \{y\}) = \{a, b, c\}$.

D on $(X - \{y\})$	
D_1, D_2:	$c\ b\ a$
D_3, D_4:	$a\ c\ b$
D_5, D_6:	$b\ a\ c$
D_7:	$c\ b\ a$

Borda Count for D on (X − {y}):
Number of Points for
Alternatives in Rows,
Preference Orders in Columns

	D_1	D_2	D_3	D_4	D_5	D_6	D_7	Total
a	0	0	2	2	1	1	0	6
b	1	1	0	0	2	2	1	7
c	2	2	1	1	0	0	2	8

The ordering induced on $(X − \{y\})$ by the Borda count is $c\,b\,a$.

Display 4-16

A Profile of Four Alternatives
in Which Four Positional Methods
Each Lead to a Different Winner

	D
D_1, D_2, D_3, D_4:	$a\,d\,c\,b$
D_5:	$b\,a\,d\,c$
D_6, D_7:	$b\,a\,c\,d$
D_8, D_9, D_{10}:	$c\,b\,d\,a$
D_{11}, D_{12}:	$d\,b\,c\,a$
D_{13}:	$d\,c\,b\,a$

Plurality Method

Number of First-Place Votes

a	4 (Plurality winner)
b	3
c	3
d	3

Display 4-16 (Continued)

Approval Voting
Assuming Each Voter Casts Two Votes

	First-place votes	Second-place votes	Total votes
a	4	3	7
b	3	5	8 (Winner)
c	3	1	4
d	3	4	7

Approval Voting Assuming
Each Voter Casts Three Votes

	First-place votes	Second-place votes	Third-place votes	Total votes
a	4	3	0	7
b	3	5	1	9
c	3	1	8	12 (Winner)
d	3	4	4	11

Borda Count: Number of Points
for Alternatives in Rows,
Preference Orders in Columns

	D_1	D_2	D_3	D_4	D_5	D_6	D_7	D_8	D_9	D_{10}	D_{11}	D_{12}	D_{13}	Total	
a	3	3	3	3	2	2	2	0	0	0	0	0	0	18	
b	0	0	0	0	3	3	3	2	2	2	2	2	1	20	
c	1	1	1	1	0	1	1	3	3	3	1	1	2	19	
d	2	2	2	2	1	0	0	1	1	1	3	3	3	21	(Borda winner)

4.F. Utilitarian Methods of Voting

Majoritarian methods base decision on how many times x is ahead of one other alternative. Positional methods base decision on how many times x is ahead of all other alternatives. Neither bases decision on voters' direct valuation of alternatives, although positional methods are sometimes mistakenly so interpreted. Many writers, however, have argued that the intensity of judgment or direct valuation *ought* to be incorporated into the decision.[19] The voting method should reveal not only that x is ahead of y, but by *how much*. Methods that attempt this are here called *utilitarian* because they involve the construction and summation of utility numbers.

Utility is a measure on preference. Given two objects, x and y (such as yea and nay votes), and an individual choice of x over y (which is a judgment of preference), the act of choice reveals to an observer that the chooser likes x better than y. But nothing in the act itself reveals *how much* better. The task of measurement is to state "how much" on some scale or another. Distances on the scale are utilities and as such are a measure on preference.

Until recently, most social scientists were reluctant to use notions of cardinal utility because all methods of measurement seemed arbitrary. In the last generation, however, the Von Neumann–Morgenstern method has come to be accepted, and proposals for utilitarian voting depend, at least theoretically and conceptually, on the *existence* of this method.[20]

The theme of the Von Neumann–Morgenstern method is that the outside observer can, by conducting an experiment, arrive at an exact, external, cardinal measure of the chooser's ordinal preference. The protocol of the experiment is:

1. Offer the subject three or more alternatives and obtain a transitive and complete ordering (e.g., $x \, R_i \, w \, R_i \ldots R_i \, z$).

2. For three alternatives, the most and least preferred and the one in between (say, x, y, and z), give the most preferred, x, a utility, $u(x)$ of some maximum, u_{max} (e.g., let $u(x) = 1$); and similarly for the least preferred, z, give some minimum, u_{min} (e.g., let $u(z) = 0$). This generates a scale from zero to 1 on which y must be located.

3. Offer the subject a choice between two alternatives.
   a. The lottery alternative: Using some chance mechanism, the subject receives x with probability p and z with probability $(1 - p)$. Here p is an ordinary probability number, $0 \leq p \leq 1$ and $p + (1 - p) = 1$. The expected utility of this gamble is: $p \, u(x) + (1 - p) \, u(z)$.

b. The certain alternative: The subject receives y for certain.

Of course, the subject's choice will be affected by the value of p. If p is large (i.e., close to 1), then the expected value of the lottery is large, which means that, when the chance mechanism is operated, the subject is likely to receive the most-preferred alternative. Hence he or she is likely to choose alternative a (the lottery alternative). If, however, p is small (i.e., close to zero), then the expected value of the lottery is low, which means that the subject is likely to receive the least-preferred alternative. Hence he or she is likely to choose b, (the certain alternative), which assures the receipt of the medium alternative.

4. Offer the subject these choices repeatedly, beginning with p sufficiently high that he or she chooses the lottery. Repeat, lowering p systematically, until the subject cannot decide between alternatives a and b. This indecision is interpreted as meaning that the expected utility of the lottery is exactly equal to the utility of the certain alternative, which thus generates a value for $u(y)$. That is

$$p\,u(x) + (1 - p)\,u(z) = u(y)$$

Recall that $u(z) = 0$, so the equation reduces to

$$p\,u(x) = u(y)$$

And since $u(x) = 1$,

$$u(y) = p$$

5. For other alternatives besides y, repeat using $u(x) = 1$ and $u(z) = 0$.

This experimental procedure is an externalized analogue of what people probably go through—in a casual, private, unformalized way— when they decide whether to take a risk, for example, whether to buy insurance at a particular price. Hence it assumes just about what is assumed in the notion of risks. Specifically, to produce cardinal utilities by this experiment, the following axioms must be assumed to be true:

1. *Transitivity and completeness.* The relations of preference and indifference are transitive and complete over the set of alternatives, X, and $x\,P_i\,y$ for at least one pair, x and y.

2. *Axiom of Archimedes.* There is a probability number, p, and a lottery, $L(p)$, based on p, such that the chooser is indifferent between the

utility of the lottery and the utility of an alternative y that is neither best nor worst.

Let the chooser order the alternatives from best to worst, say, $x, \ldots, z$, so that the maximum utility, u_{max}, is the utility of x, $u(x)$, and the minimum utility, u_{min}, is the utility of z, $u(z)$. Then

$$u\,L\,(p) = p\,u_{max} + (1 - p)\,u_{min}$$

Then the axiom is that

$$u\,(y)\,I_i\,u\,L\,(p)$$

3. *Continuity*. As p varies from zero to 1, $u\,L\,(p)$ varies from u_{min} to u_{max}.

4. *Substitutability*. An alternative y can be replaced by its equivalent lottery, $L\,(p)$, as identified by the axiom of Archimedes (axiom 2).

It is apparent that axioms 1, 3, and 4 are simply technical conveniences for the experiment, though axiom 1 does impose the substantive limitation that X consist of comparable things. Axiom 1 is necessary to justify the subject's initial ordering in the experiment. Axiom 3 is a conventional continuity axiom to justify the use of p. Axiom 4 is necessary to justify the lottery procedure. The main substantive assumption is, therefore, axiom 2, which is often expressed bluntly as "Everything has a price."

Does everything, or rather every risk, have a price? People do indeed price trading risks, and the experiment externalizes the internal risk-pricing mechanism. Consequently, cardinal utility is quite usable in economic theory. But what about political theory? It seems to me that many alternatives outside the economic sphere are unpriceable or, more accurately, incommensurate in value with other alternatives. Doubtless it is easy to measure some political values such as how much someone would prefer more police officers to more trash collectors or how much one would prefer lower taxes to either or both. But it is probably impossible to measure how much one prefers more national sovereignty to less national wealth, or vice versa. Many persons might find such tradeoffs incalculable simply because in their judgments independence (or wealth) must first be achieved before the other can be considered at all. If so, the goals are incommensurate, and there is no tradeoff and no price. So one can make ordinal, but not cardinal, comparisons.

Nevertheless, several kinds of voting with cardinal utilities have been proposed.

4.G. Examples of Utilitarian Methods

The common theme of the following methods is that the supposed intensity of each voter's preference is included in the social summation. The differences among them are mainly to remedy technical defects, no one of which is as serious as the misguided attempt to measure incommensurables.

Summation of Cardinal Utility

Apparently, Bentham considered the summation of cardinal utility as a decision process, even evidently using money as a measure.[21] It is now well understood, as it was not in Bentham's day, that the relation between money and the utility of money is not linear (that is, one may want a second dollar over a first far more than one wants a millionth over a 999,999th). Hence, today Bentham might opt for Von Neumann–Morgenstern utility rather than for money; but the notion of summation of some kind of cardinal utility is fundamental to his idea of maximizing social happiness by choosing the alternative with the largest sum.[22]

Demand-Revealing Methods

These methods of decision, described in section 3.D, can be extended easily to three or more alternatives.[23] They are a summation method with the added feature of (partially) encouraging a true revelation of judgment.

Multiplication of Utilities

This method consists of measuring all persons' utilities, using as the origin some status quo point, and, for each alternative, multiplying voters' utilities for it, selecting the alternative with the largest product.[24] The rationale for using the maximum product rather than the maximum sum is that the former satisfies an axiom of consistency in choosing from a set and its subsets. (See section 5.F.)

Conclusions

Utilitarian methods are neither majoritarian nor positional. Because they base decision on intensity, not on numbers, they can easily select alternatives not favored by a majority, even when a Condorcet winner exists. Simultaneously, they can fail any one of the positional tests by selecting alternatives not more frequently standing ahead of others in *D*. One reason some people reject utilitarian methods is that the emphasis on intensity might lead people to exaggerate their desires simply to make them count for more. Demand-revealing methods tend to squelch that maneuver, but they do not otherwise change the nonmajoritarian, non-positional character of the utilitarian decision process.

4.H. Criteria for Judging Voting Methods

It is clear from the foregoing survey that majoritarian, positional, and utilitarian methods of voting lead to different social results, often strikingly different, from the same underlying individual judgments. It seems natural to wonder, therefore, if there is any way to discriminate among this plethora of devices and to discover a way to amalgamate judgments fairly and truly. There are many criteria for discrimination, and I will discuss some here. Whether they lead to the discovery of a fair and true method I leave to the reader's judgment—though my own belief is that they do not.

I will begin by showing how the properties of simple majority decision discussed in Chapter 3—undifferentiatedness (anonymity), neutrality, and monotonicity—can be generalized to accommodate three or more alternatives. Those three criteria are, in some sense, elementary requirements of fairness and consistency, and most of the voting methods discussed in this chapter satisfy most of them. I will then introduce three deeper requirements of fairness, which embody some of the moral requirements raised in this chapter.

Undifferentiatedness

If the choice from *D* is *x*, and if the individual orderings are reassigned among voters to form *D'*, the social choice in *D'* remains *x*. Since permuting the preference orders does not change the outcome, it follows that the identity of voters has no effect on the social choice, which is exactly what undifferentiatedness should mean.[25]

Neutrality

If a social profile yields a choice *x*, and if the elements of *X* are permuted, thereby creating a new profile, then the choice from the new profile is the permutation of x. Since a rearrangement of alternatives leads to a corresponding rearrangement of outcomes, it follows that no alternative has a favored position in the voting system, which is exactly what neutrality should mean.[26]

Monotonicity

If a profile changes because some person raises the valuation of x relative to other alternatives, then, if x was originally the social choice, it remains so. Conversely, if a person lowers the valuation of an x that was not originally the social choice, it does not become so. This means that a higher judgment on a winning alternative cannot make it lose; nor can a lower judgment on a loser make it win.[27]

A similar generalization applies to unanimity, as an implication from monotonicity. For unanimity, corresponding to the weak unanimity of equation (N3.6), if, for some alternative, y, all persons prefer some other alternative(s) to it, then y cannot be the social choice. This means that an alternative unanimously beaten by one or more others cannot win.[28]

The Condorcet Criterion

According to the first "deeper" requirement of fairness and consistency, the Condorcet criterion, if an alternative beats (or ties) all others in pairwise contests, then it ought to win.[29] This notion is closely related to the notion of equality and "one man, one vote," in the sense that, when an alternative opposed by a majority wins, quite clearly the votes of some people are not being counted the same as other people's votes.

Consistency

The consistency requirement concerns the way votes are taken from the electorate. If the electorate is divided into two parts for election purposes and if one alternative is chosen in both parts, then it ought to be chosen in the whole.[30]

That this requirement contains a fundamental kind of fairness seems obvious. If a winner is a true winner, subdividing the electorate ought not to make it a loser. If consistency fails to hold, therefore, manipulation is rendered easy. Suppose x wins in the whole electorate and the voting method fails to satisfy consistency. Then opponents of x have merely to set up two appropriately chosen subelectorates, define the winner as that alternative which wins in both, and thereby make y win.

Independence from Irrelevant Alternatives

The independence criterion requires that a method of decision give the same result every time from the same profile of ordinal preferences.[31] This too seems a fundamental requirement of consistency and fairness to prevent the rigging of elections and the unequal treatment of voters; but it has nevertheless been seriously disputed.[32]

4.I. Judgments on Voting Methods

Do the methods described in this chapter satisfy the criteria just listed? The answer is unequivocally negative. I will dispose first of what seem obvious (and, in some cases, minor) violations, so that I can then discuss the main (and mostly serious) violations by each method of voting.

Minor Violations of Fairness

Monotonicity is satisfied by all the voting methods except runoff elections. (*All* elimination procedures can violate monotonicity and are thus highly suspect.) All methods here discussed except the Schwartz rule satisfy unanimity. The Schwartz rule fails simply because, when there is an all-inclusive cycle, it includes all alternatives, even those unanimously dominated.[33]

The neutrality criterion is satisfied by all but the amendment procedure, and it is precisely this violation that allows the procedure to work reasonably well on three alternatives—although the violation does not help on more alternatives.

Except for the violation of neutrality, the foregoing are indeed serious; but there are even more significant violations, to which I now turn.

No one of the three categories of voting methods satisfies all criteria:

Majoritarian methods violate the consistency criterion.

Positional methods violate the Condorcet criterion; moreover, the Borda count violates independence, and approval voting violates undifferentiatedness (anonymity).

Utilitarian methods violate the independence criterion and, as pointed out in section 3.D, demand-revealing methods violate undifferentiatedness.

Violation of Consistency
by Majoritarian Methods

That majoritarian methods violate the consistency criterion has been shown by H. P. Young, who also proved in general that "scoring functions" (which are positional methods) are the only ordinal methods that satisfy consistency.[34] Utilitarian methods, involving summations of cardinal numbers, also satisfy this criterion. The reason majoritarian methods fail is that, since they count only simple majorities on pairs, an alternative that wins or comes close in N^1 but fails in N^2 may pick up enough votes in N^2 to win in N. Positional methods, which keep track of the pairwise relations, do not admit this anomaly.

For example, in Display 4-17, using some majoritarian methods (say, the Copeland rule or the Schwartz rule), if 75 voters are divided into district 1 ($N^1 = 30$ voters) and district 2 ($N^2 = 45$ voters), with D^1 and D^2 on three alternatives, then x wins in N^1 and ties in N^2 but loses to y in $N^1 + N^2$—in clear violation of consistency, which requires that a winner in both N^1 and N^2 also win in $N^1 + N^2$. As Gideon Doron remarks, the failure of consistency is an invitation to gerrymander.[35]

The failure of majoritarian methods to satisfy consistency is, practically, a very serious defect. This is illustrated in the history of senatorial elections in the United States. Initially, state legislatures used several voting methods. From 1866 to 1913, however, the uniform majoritarian rule was: If a candidate obtains a simple majority in both houses sitting separately, he wins; otherwise, the houses sitting together elect by simple majority. This is exactly the situation of the consistency criterion. As might be expected, there were many deadlocks—45 out of about 130 from 1891 to 1905, of which 14 resulted in no election at all.[36] Almost certainly some of these deadlocks resulted from the failure to satisfy the consistency criterion.

To see how deadlock might occur, assume some candidate, y, can win on the joint ballot, as in Display 4-18, while some other candidate, w, can win or tie in both houses separately. Some of the supporters of w—namely, the six members of group IV in the Display—are crucial for y to beat x on the joint ballot. Since the members of group IV have a strong motive not to allow y to win, one can expect deadlock in the houses sitting together, thus:

41 votes for x

43 votes for y

6 votes for w

Display 4-17

Violation of Consistency
by Majoritarian Methods

D^1 (for N^1)	
D_1–D_{17}:	$x\,y\,z$
D_{18}–D_{25}:	$y\,z\,x$
D_{26}–D_{30}:	$z\,x\,y$

D^2 (for N^2)	
D_{31}–D_{44}:	$x\,z\,y$
D_{45}–D_{60}:	$y\,x\,z$
D_{61}–D_{75}:	$z\,y\,x$

Number of Votes for the Alternative
in the Row When Placed in Contest
Against the Alternative in the Column

D^1	x	y	z
x	—	22	17
y	8	—	25
z	13	5	—

D^2	x	y	z
x	—	14	30
y	31	—	16
z	15	29	—

In N^1, x is the Condorcet winner. In N^2, x, y, and z tie in the cycle $x\,z\,y\,x$.

Using the Copeland or Schwartz methods, x is chosen in N^1, and x, y, and z are chosen in N^2.

$D^1 + D^2$ (for $N^1 + N^2$)	
D_1–D_{17}:	$x\,y\,z$ (17 voters)
D_{31}–D_{44}:	$x\,z\,y$ (14 voters)
D_{18}–D_{25}:	$y\,z\,x$ (8 voters)
D_{45}–D_{60}:	$y\,x\,z$ (16 voters)
D_{26}–D_{30}:	$z\,x\,y$ (5 voters)
D_{61}–D_{75}:	$z\,y\,x$ (15 voters)

Display 4-17 *(Continued)*

Number of Votes for the Alternative in the Row When Placed in Contest Against the Alternative in the Column

$$D^1 + D^2$$

	x	y	z
x	—	36	47
y	39	—	41 (Condorcet winner)
z	28	34	—

Notice that, while x is chosen in both N^1 and N^2 (that is, x is the Condorcet winner in N^1 and is in the cycle of tied alternatives in N^2), still y wins under any majoritarian method in $N^1 + N^2$. Since consistency requires that, if an alternative wins in N^1 and in N^2, then it must win in $N^1 + N^2$, and since x wins in N^1 and in N^2 but loses in $N^1 + N^2$, the majoritarian methods fail to satisfy consistency. If, however, the Borda count, as a typical positional method, is used, then consistency is satisfied.

Number of Points for Alternatives in Rows, Preference Orders in Columns

$$D^1 \text{ (for } N^1)$$

	$D_1–D_{17}$	$D_{18}–D_{25}$	$D_{26}–D_{30}$	Total
x	34	0	5	39 (Borda winner)
y	17	16	0	33
z	0	8	10	18

$$D^2 \text{ (for } N^2)$$

	$D_{31}–D_{44}$	$D_{45}–D_{60}$	$D_{61}–D_{75}$	Total
x	28	16	0	44
y	0	32	15	47 (Borda winner)
z	14	0	30	44

$$D^1 + D^2 \text{ (for } N^1 + N^2)$$

	D_1–D_{17}	D_{18}–D_{25}	D_{26}–D_{30}	D_{31}–D_{44}	D_{45}–D_{60}	D_{61}–D_{75}	Total
x	34	0	5	28	16	0	83 (Borda
y	17	16	0	0	32	15	80 winner)
z	0	8	10	14	0	30	62

Notice that, since no alternative wins by the Borda method in both N^1 and N^2, consistency imposes no requirement on the winner of $N^1 + N^2$.

Failing consistency, then, majoritarian methods are at least impractical as well, perhaps, as unfair.

Violation of Independence by the Borda Count

The failure of the Borda count to satisfy independence can be seen in Display 4-19. Suppose a committee (members 1, 2, 3) is to award a scholarship to one of three applicants (a, b, c), using the Borda count. Initially, in profile D', the vote results in a tie between a and c. Suppose member 2 revises his ordering to $c\ b\ a$, producing a new profile, D. Then c wins. The independence criterion requires that identical profiles on a subset, S, of a set, X, produce identical outcomes. Letting $S = (a, c)$ and $X = (a, b, c)$, then D' and D are identical on S because member 2 changed only the relation of a and b in D, not of a and c. In D' applicants a and c tie, but in D applicant c wins in direct violation of the independence criterion. It is true that in both D and D' the Condorcet winner is c and member 2 can be said to have produced a "fairer" outcome by his switch; but the switch nevertheless reveals a violation of independence. The criterion of independence from irrelevant alternatives, by requiring that the same order on S in profiles D' and D produce the same result, reveals a serious defect in the Borda rules themselves.

Violation of Undifferentiatedness by Approval Voting

Undifferentiatedness requires that the choice remain the same when preference orders are permuted among voters.[37] Since, however, different

Display 4-18

Deadlock in a Senatorial Election

D^1 (for N^1 with 30 voters)

Group	Alternatives
I. D_1-D_{16}:	$w\ x\ y\ z$ (16 voters)
II. $D_{17}-D_{26}$:	$y\ w\ x\ z$ (10 voters)
III. $D_{27}-D_{30}$:	$z\ y\ x\ w$ (4 voters)

Number of Votes for the Alternative in the Row When Placed in Contest Against the Alternative in the Column

D^1

	w	x	y	z	
w	—	26	16	26	(Condorcet winner)
x	4	—	16	26	
y	14	14	—	26	
z	4	4	4	—	

D^2 (for N^2 with 60 voters)

Group	Alternatives
IV. $D_{31}-D_{36}$:	$w\ y\ x\ z$ (6 voters)
V. $D_{37}-D_{61}$:	$x\ z\ y\ w$ (25 voters)
VI. $D_{62}-D_{84}$:	$y\ z\ w\ x$ (23 voters)
VII. $D_{85}-D_{90}$:	$z\ y\ w\ x$ (6 voters)

D^2

	w	x	y	z
w	—	35	6	6
x	25	—	25	31
y	54	35	—	29
z	54	29	31	—

Thus D^2 results in a cycle: $w\ x\ z\ y\ w$.

$D^1 + D^2$ (for $N^1 + N^2$ with 90 voters)

Group	Alternatives
I. D_1–D_{16}:	$w\,x\,y\,z$ (16 voters)
IV. D_{31}–D_{36}:	$w\,y\,x\,z$ (6 voters)
V. D_{37}–D_{61}:	$x\,z\,y\,w$ (25 voters)
II. D_{17}–D_{26}:	$y\,w\,x\,z$ (10 voters)
VI. D_{62}–D_{84}:	$y\,z\,w\,x$ (23 voters)
III. D_{27}–D_{30}:	$z\,y\,x\,w$ (4 voters)
VII. D_{85}–D_{90}:	$z\,y\,w\,x$ (6 voters)

**Number of Votes for the Alternative
in the Row When Placed in Contest
Against the Alternative in the Column**

	w	x	y	z
w	—	61	22	32
x	29	—	41	57
y	68	49	—	55 (Condorcet winner)
z	58	33	35	—

Notice that the six voters in group IV prefer w, who is the absolute winner in N^1 and is tied in N^2, and that they are crucial for the success of y in $N^1 + N^2$—all of which gives them a strong motive to promote deadlock in the joint ballot.

voters can have different intentions about how many votes to cast, and since a permutation of D_i does not necessarily permute i's intentions about the number of votes to be cast, the choice from D will not necessarily remain constant under permutations of D_i. For example, in Display 4-20, for $X = (a, b, c, d)$ and $n = 4$, voter 1 casts three votes in both D and D^σ and voters 2, 3, and 4 cast two votes in both profiles. Then candidate c wins in D and candidate d wins in D^σ in direct violation of the condition of undifferentiatedness.

Display 4-19

The Failure of the Borda Count to Satisfy Independence from Irrelevant Alternatives

$$D'$$

D'_1:	$a\ b\ c$
D'_2:	$c\ a\ b$
D'_3:	$c\ a\ b$

Number of Points for Alternatives in Rows, Preference Orders in Columns

	D'_1	D'_2	D'_3	Total
a	2	1	1	4 (Tied with c)
b	1	0	0	1
c	0	2	2	4 (Tied with a)

$$D$$

D_1:	$a\ b\ c$
D_2:	$c\ b\ a$
D_3:	$c\ a\ b$

Number of Points for Alternatives in Rows, Preference Orders in Columns

	D_1	D_2	D_3	Total
a	2	0	1	3
b	1	1	0	2
c	0	2	2	4 (Borda winner)

In D as against D' member 2 has revised the relation of a and b but has not changed the relation of a and c; yet the social choice between a and c has changed in D from D'.

Display 4-20

The Failure of Approval Voting to Satisfy Undifferentiatedness

	D
D_1:	$a\ b\ c\ d$
D_2:	$b\ c\ d\ a$
D_3:	$c\ d\ a\ b$
D_4:	$d\ a\ b\ c$

Assume voter 1 casts three votes and voters 2, 3, and 4 each cast two votes:

Number of Votes for Candidates

Candidates	First place	Second place	Third place	Total
a	1	1	0	2
b	1	1	0	2
c	1	1	1	3 (Approval winner)
d	1	1	0	2

Assume now that persons 1 and 2 trade preference orders in the following permutation, where $D_{\sigma(i)}$ means "the preference order that replaces D_i":

$$D_{\sigma(1)} = D_2$$
$$D_{\sigma(2)} = D_1$$
$$D_{\sigma(3)} = D_3$$
$$D_{\sigma(4)} = D_4$$

This permutation produces a new profile, D^σ.

Display 4-20 (Continued)

D^σ	
$D_{\sigma(1)}$:	b c d a
$D_{\sigma(2)}$:	a b c d
$D_{\sigma(3)}$:	c d a b
$D_{\sigma(4)}$:	d a b c

Assume, as in D, that voter 1 casts three votes and voters 2, 3, and 4 each cast two votes:

Number of Votes for Candidates

Candidates	First place	Second place	Third place	Total
a	1	1	0	2
b	1	1	0	2
c	1	1	0	2
d	1	1	1	3 (Approval winner)

Hence $F_{approval}(X, D) = c$; and $F_{approval}(X, D^\sigma) = d$.

The practical effect of this violation is that the indifferent voters or the voters with a broad tolerance for positions dominate in the choice. As is well known, simple majority decision—and even plurality voting insofar as it contributes to simple majority—places a premium on the median voter in a distribution. One can be at or near the median either (1) because of reasoned judgment or (2) because one does not care. Whether one wants to exaggerate the influence of type 2 voters in social decision seems to me doubtful.

Violation of Independence by Utilitarian Methods

That utilitarian voting violates the independence criterion is immediately apparent from the example in Display 4-21 of two voters and three alternatives. Although D and D' are ordinally identical, still by a utilitarian F x wins in D and y in D'. The moral question derived from this fact is whether a change in cardinal numbers without a change in ordinal relations should make a difference in choice. The utilitarian argument is that the change between D and D' involves a true change in the intensity of valuation. From D to D', voter 1 upgraded y and voter 2 downgraded x. Surely, the argument runs, y should now replace x as the winner.

The counterargument is that, since the cardinal sums are not soundly based and ought not therefore to affect the outcome, x and y should tie in both D and D'. The doubt about the soundness of the cardinal sums arises from the way they were initially constructed. A scale was created for an individual person, and alternatives were located on it by individual comparison. Hence, the numbers created are uniquely personal. They are useful to study behavior by the subject and even useful, perhaps, for the subject to guide his or her own behavior. But these personal numbers cannot be compared between people because they do not mean the same thing to each person. The sums are therefore meaningless. If one adds oranges and apples to get oranapps, one knows nothing more because one doesn't know what an oranapp is. Neither does one know what the sum of utilities is.

Of course, one may insist that the cardinal relations be fixed so long as the ordinal relations are, but then one loses the main advantage of cardinal utility—namely, the reflection of intensity of preference. If, however, one allows cardinal relations to reflect intensity, then the independence criterion may be violated, whenever, as in Display 4-21, ordinal relations remain constant.[38]

4.J. The Absence of True and Fair Amalgamations

In the beginning of this chapter I promised to show that we cannot prove that any method of voting truly and fairly amalgamates the judgments of voters. I think I have done so. I have shown that all members of each of the three main categories of methods violate at least one reasonable criterion of fairness or consistency. Furthermore, I have shown that many methods violate several criteria. Had space permitted, I would have introduced many additional criteria, some of which are violated by every category of voting methods. To assert, therefore, that one method truly and fairly amalgamates, one must show that the criterion or criteria it violates is or are unreasonable or trivial. But there is a good rationale in terms of fairness or consistency or both for every one of the criteria I have discussed as well as for many I have omitted. So it seems unlikely that

Display 4-21

The Failure of Utilitarian Methods to Satisfy Independence from Irrelevant Alternatives

	D
D_1:	$x\ y\ z$
D_2:	$y\ x\ z$

For Profile D:
Utility of the Alternative in the Row;
Utility to the Voter in the Column

	U_1	U_2	Total
x	1.0	0.6	1.6 (Utilitarian winner)
y	0.5	1.0	1.5
z	0	0	0

	D'
D'_1:	$x\ y\ z$
D'_2:	$y\ x\ z$

For Profile D':
Utility of the Alternative in the Row;
Utility to the Voter in the Column

	U_1	U_2	Total
x	1.0	0.5	1.5
y	0.6	1.0	1.6 (Utilitarian winner)
z	0	0	0

Although $D = D'$, the winner in D is x, and the winner in D' is y.

these criteria can be rejected as morally or logically irrelevant. If not, then we are inexorably forced to the conclusion that every method of voting is in some applications unfair or inadequate.

For my own taste, I would use different methods in different circumstances. In legislatures, I would use the amendment procedure on three alternatives and, somewhat hesitantly, the Borda count or Kemeny's method for more than three alternatives. In elections of executives or legislators, I would use the plurality method, more for its dynamic effects of maintaining the two-party system than for its effectiveness of choice in particular elections. In primary elections, I would use approval voting— though I would avoid it absolutely in general elections, where its effect would be to destroy the two-party system. In planning an economy, if that activity were forced upon me, I would use a kind of utilitarianism— namely, demand-revealing procedures—recognizing, of course, that however "honest" they are supposed to be, it is easy enough to manipulate them.

There is some niche, it seems to me, for majoritarian, positional, and utilitarian methods of voting. Nevertheless, we have now learned, I think, that we should never take the results of any method always to be a fair and true amalgamation of voters' judgments. Doubtless the results often are fair and true; but, unfortunately, we almost never know whether they are or are not. Consequently, we should not generally assume that the methods produce fair and true amalgamations. We should think of the methods, I believe, simply as convenient ways of doing business, useful but flawed. This gives them all a place in the world, but it makes none of them sacrosanct.

5

The Meaning of Social Choices

In Chapter 4 I showed that no method of voting could be said to amalgamate individual judgments truly and fairly because every method violates some reasonable canon of fairness and accuracy. All voting methods are therefore in some sense morally imperfect. Furthermore, these imperfect methods can produce different outcomes from the same profile of individual judgments. Hence it follows that sometimes—and usually we never know for sure just when—the social choice is as much an artifact of morally imperfect methods as it is of what people truly want. It is hard to have unbounded confidence in the *justice* of such results.

It is equally hard, as I will show in this chapter, to have unbounded confidence in the *meaning* of such results. Individual persons presumably can, if they think about it deeply enough, order their personal judgments transitively. Hence their valuations mean something, for they clearly indicate a hierarchy of preference that can guide action and choice in a sensible way. But the results of voting do not necessarily have this quality. It is instead the case that *no* method of voting can simultaneously satisfy several elementary conditions of fairness and also produce results that always satisfy elementary conditions of logical arrangement. Hence, not only may the results of voting fail to be fair, they may also fail to make sense. It is the latter possibility that will be analyzed in this chapter.

5.A. Arrow's Theorem

Kenneth Arrow published *Social Choice and Individual Values* in 1951. Although his theorem initially provoked some controversy among economists, its profound political significance was not immediately recognized by political scientists.[1] In the late 1960s, however, a wide variety of philosophers, economists, and political scientists began to appreciate how profoundly unsettling the theorem was and how deeply it called into question some conventionally accepted notions—not only about voting, the subject of this work, but also about the ontological validity of the concept of social welfare, a subject that, fortunately, we can leave to metaphysicians.

The essence of Arrow's theorem is that no method of amalgamating individual judgments can simultaneously satisfy some reasonable conditions of fairness on the method and a condition of logicality on the result. In a sense this theorem is a generalization of the paradox of voting (see section 1.H), for the theorem is the proposition that something like the paradox is possible in *any* fair system of amalgamating values. Thus the theorem is called the *General Possibility Theorem*.

To make the full meaning of Arrow's theorem clear, I will outline the situation and the conditions of fairness and of logicality that cannot simultaneously be satisfied.[2] The situation for amalgamation is:

1. There are n persons, $n \geq 2$, and n is finite. Difficulties comparable to the paradox of voting can arise in individuals who use several standards of judgment for choice. Our concern is, however, *social* choice, so we can ignore the Robinson Crusoe case.

2. There are three or more alternatives—that is, for the set $X = (x_1, \ldots, x_m)$, $m \geq 3$. Since transitivity or other conditions for logical choice are meaningless for fewer than three alternatives and since, indeed, simple majority decision produces a logical result on two alternatives, the conflict between fairness and logicality can only arise when $m \geq 3$.

3. Individuals are able to order the alternatives transitively: If $x\,R_i\,y$ and $y\,R_i\,z$, then $x\,R_i\,z$. If it is not assumed that individuals are able to be logical, then surely it is pointless to expect a group to produce logical results.

The conditions of fairness are:

1. *Universal admissibility of individual orderings (Condition U)*. This is the requirement that the set, **D**, includes all possible profiles, D, of individual orders, D_i. If each D_i is some permutation of possible orderings of X by preference and indifference, then this requirement is that individuals can choose any of the possible permutations. For ex-

ample, if $X = (x, y, z)$, the individual may choose any of the following 13 orderings:

1. $x\,y\,z$	7. $x\,(y\,z)$	10. $(x\,y)\,z$	13. $(x\,y\,z)$
2. $y\,z\,x$	8. $y\,(z\,x)$	11. $(y\,z)\,x$	
3. $z\,x\,y$	9. $z\,(x\,y)$	12. $(z\,x)\,y$	
4. $x\,z\,y$			
5. $z\,y\,x$			
6. $y\,x\,z$			(5-1)

The justification for this requirement is straightforward. If social outcomes are to be based exclusively on individual judgments—as seems implicit in any interpretation of democratic methods—then to restrict individual persons' judgments in any way means that the social outcome is based as much on the restriction as it is on individual judgments. Any rule or command that prohibits a person from choosing some preference order is morally unacceptable (or at least unfair) from the point of view of democracy.

2. *Monotonicity.* According to this condition, if a person raises the valuation of a winning alternative, it cannot become a loser; or, if a person lowers the valuation of a losing alternative, it cannot become a winner. The justification for monotonicity was discussed in section 3.B. Given the democratic intention that outcomes be based in some way on participation, it would be the utmost in perversity if the method of choice were to count individual judgments *negatively,* although, as I have shown, some real-world methods actually do so.

3. *Citizens' sovereignty or nonimposition.* Define a social choice as imposed if some alternative, x, is a winner for any set, D, of individual preferences. If x is always chosen, then what individuals want does not have anything to do with social choice. It might, for example, happen that x was everyone's least-liked alternative, yet an imposed choice of x would still select x. In such a situation, voters' judgments have nothing to do with the outcome and democratic participation is meaningless.

4. *Unanimity or Pareto optimality (Condition P).* This is the requirement that, if everyone prefers x to y, then the social choice function, F, does not choose y. (See Chapter 3, note 8, and Chapter 4, note 28.) This is the form in which monotonicity and citizens' sovereignty enter all proofs of Arrow's theorem. There are only two ways that a result contrary to unanimity could occur. One is that the system of amalgamation is not monotonic. Suppose in D' everybody but i prefers x to y

and $y\ P'_i\ x$. Then in D, i changes to $x\ P_i\ y$ so everybody has x preferred to y; but, if F is not monotonic, it may be that x does not belong to $F(\{x, y\}, D)$. The other way a violation of unanimity could occur is for F to impose y even though everybody prefers x to y. Thus the juncture of monotonicity and citizens' sovereignty implies Pareto optimality.

Many writers have interpreted the unanimity condition as purely technical—as, for example, in the discussion of the Schwartz method of completing the Condorcet rule (see section 4.C). But Pareto optimality takes on more force when it is recognized as the carrier of monotonicity and nonimposition, both of which have deep and obvious qualities of fairness.

5. *Independence from irrelevant alternatives (Condition I)*. According to this requirement (defined in section 4.H), a method of amalgamation, F, picks the same alternative as the social choice every time F is applied to the same profile, D. Although some writers have regarded this condition simply as a requirement of technical efficiency, it actually has as much moral content as the other fairness conditions (see section 4.H). From the democratic point of view, one wants to base the outcome on the voters' judgments, but doing so is clearly impossible if the method of amalgamation gives different results from identical profiles. This might occur, for example, if choices among alternatives were made by some chance device. Then it is the device, not voters' judgments in D, that determines outcomes. Even if one constructs the device so that the chance of selecting an alternative is proportional in some way to the number of people desiring it (if, for example, two-thirds of the voters prefer x to y, then the device selects x with $p = \frac{2}{3}$), still the expectation is that, of several chance selections, the device will choose x on p selections and y on $1 - p$ selections from the same profile, in clear violation of Condition I. In ancient Greece, election by lot was a useful method for anonymity; today it would be simply a way to by-pass voters' preferences. Another kind of arbitrariness prohibited by the independence condition is utilitarian voting. Based on interpersonal comparisons of distances on scales of unknown length, utilitarian voting gives advantages to persons with finer perception and broader horizons. Furthermore, independence prohibits the arbitrariness of the Borda count (see section 5.F).

6. *Nondictatorship (Condition D)*. This is the requirement that there be no person, i, such that, whenever $x\ P_i\ y$, the social choice is x, regardless of the opinions of other persons. Since the whole idea of democracy is to avoid such situations, the moral significance of this condition is obvious.

Finally, the condition of logicality is that the social choice is a weak order, by which is meant that the set, X, is connected and its members can be *socially* ordered by the relation, R, which is the transitive social analogue of preference and indifference combined. (This relation, as in $x R y$, means that x is chosen over or at least tied with y.) In contrast to the previous discussion, in which the method of amalgamation or choice, F, simply selected an element from X, it is now assumed that F selects repeatedly from pairs in X to produce, by means of successive selections, a social order analogous to the individual orders, D_i. And it is the failure to produce such an order that constitutes a violation of the condition of logicality.[2]

Since an individual weak order or the relation R_i is often spoken of as individual rationality, social transitivity, or R, is sometimes spoken of as collective rationality—Arrow himself so described it. And failure to produce social transitivity can also be regarded as a kind of social irrationality.

Arrow's theorem, then, is that every possible method of amalgamation or choice that satisfies the fairness conditions fails to ensure a social ordering. And if society cannot, with fair methods, be certain to order its outcome, then it is not clear that we can know what the outcomes of a fair method mean. This conclusion appears to be devastating, for it consigns democratic outcomes—and hence the democratic method—to the world of arbitrary nonsense, at least some of the time.

Naturally there has been a variety of attempts to interpret and sidestep this conclusion. One line of inquiry is to raise doubts about its practical importance; another is to look for some theoretical adjustment that deprives the theorem of its force. The rest of this chapter is devoted to a survey of both branches of this huge and important literature, so that in Chapter 6 it will be possible to assess fully the political significance of Arrow's theorem.

I will begin with inquiries about the practical importance of the theorem. One such inquiry is an estimate of the expected frequency of profiles, D, that do not lead to a transitive order.

5.B. The Practical Relevance of Arrow's Theorem: The Frequency of Cycles

One meaning of Arrow's theorem is that, under any system of voting or amalgamation, instances of intransitive or cyclical outcomes can occur.

Since, by definition, no one of the alternatives in a cycle can beat all the others, there is no Condorcet winner among cycled alternatives. All cycled alternatives tie with respect to their position in a social arrangement in the sense that $x\,y\,z\,x$, $y\,z\,x\,y$, and $z\,x\,y\,z$ have equal claims to being the social arrangement. Borda voting similarly produces a direct tie among cycled alternatives. Hence a social arrangement is indeterminate when a cycle exists. When the arrangement is indeterminate, the actual choice is arbitrarily made. The selection is not determined by the preference of the voters. Rather it is determined by the power of some chooser to dominate the choice or to manipulate the process to his or her advantage. Every cycle thus represents the failure of the voting process. One way to inquire into the practical significance of Arrow's theorem is, therefore, to estimate how often cycles can occur.

For this estimate, a number of simplifying assumptions are necessary. For one thing, majority voting (rather than positional voting or any other kind of amalgamation) is always assumed. This assumption of course limits the interpretation severely. For another thing, only cycles that preclude a Condorcet winner are of interest. Voting may fail to produce a weak order in several ways:

1. With all three alternatives, there may be a cycle: $x\,R\,y\,R\,z\,R\,x$ or simply $x\,y\,z\,x$.
2. With four or more alternatives, there may be
   a. A Condorcet winner followed by a cycle: $w\,x\,y\,z\,x$
   b. A cycle among all alternatives: $w\,x\,y\,z\,w$; or intersecting cycles: $s\,t\,w\,x\,y\,z\,w\,v\,s$
   c. A cycle in which all members beat some other alternative: $x\,y\,z\,x\,w$

If one is interested in social welfare judgments involving an ordering of all alternatives, then all cycles are significant no matter where they occur. But if one is interested in picking out a social choice, as in the voting mechanisms discussed here, then the significant cases are only 1, 2(b), and 2(c), where there is no unique social choice. (These are often called *top cycles*.) Attempts to estimate the significance of Arrow's theorem by some sort of calculation have all been made from the point of view of social choice rather than welfare judgments and have therefore concerned the frequency of top cycles.

For Arrow's theorem, Condition U allows individuals to have any weak ordering, R_i, of preference and indifference, as in (5.1). Calculation is simpler, however, based on strong orders—that is, individual preference orders, P_i, with indifference not allowed.

With m alternatives, there are $m!$ (i.e., $1 \cdot 2 \cdot \ldots \cdot m$) such linear orders possible; and, when $m = 3$, these are:

$$x\,y\,z, \qquad x\,z\,y, \qquad y\,x\,z, \qquad y\,z\,x, \qquad z\,x\,y, \qquad z\,y\,x$$

Each such order is a potential D_i. When each of n voters picks some (not necessarily different) D_i, a profile, D, is created. Since the first voter picks from $m!$ orders, the second from $m!$, . . . , and the last from $m!$, the number of possible different profiles, D, is $(m!)^n$, which is the number of members of the set, D, of all profiles, when voters have only strong orders.

A calculation that yields some estimate of the significance of cycles is the fraction, $p(n, m)$, of D in D without a Condorcet winner:

$$p(n, m) = \frac{\text{Number of } D \text{ without a Condorcet winner}}{(m!)^n}$$

If one assumes that each D is equally likely to occur (which implies also that, for each voter, the chance of picking some order is $1/m!$), then $p(n, m)$ is an a priori estimate of the probability of the occurrence of a top cycle. Several calculations have been made, as set forth in Display 5-1.[3] As is apparent from the Display, as the number of voters and alternatives increases, so do the number of profiles without a Condorcet winner. The calculation thereby implies that instances of the paradox of voting are very common. Most social choices are made from many alternatives (though often we do not realize this fact because the number has been winnowed down by various devices such as primary elections and committees that select alternatives for agendas) and by many people, so the calculations imply that Condorcet winners do not exist in almost all decisions.

But, of course, there are a number of reasons to believe that such calculations are meaningless. People do not choose an ordering with probability $1/m!$. Rather, at any particular moment, some orders are more likely to be chosen than others. The six strong orders over triples generate two cycles:

"Forward Cycle"	"Backward Cycle"	
1. $x\,y\,z$	4. $x\,z\,y$	
2. $y\,z\,x$	5. $z\,y\,x$	
3. $z\,x\,y$	6. $y\,x\,z$	(5-2)

Display 5-1

Values of $p(n, m)$: Proportion of Possible Profiles Without a Condorcet Winner

| | $n = $ Number of Voters | | | | | | |
m = Number of Alternatives	3	5	7	9	11	. . .	Limit
3	.056	.069	.075	.078	.080		.088
4	.111	.139	.150	.156	.160		.176
5	.160	.200	.215				.251
6	.202						.315
Limit	1.000	1.000	1.000	1.000	1.000		1.000

The entry in the row for four alternatives and in the column for seven voters—namely, .150—is the ratio of the number of profiles without a Condorcet winner to the number of profiles possible when seven voters order four alternatives.

Cycles occur when voters concentrate on one or the other of these sets of three orders. But suppose voters are induced by, for example, political parties, to concentrate heavily on, say, (1), (2), and (5). Then there is no cycle. Furthermore, there is good reason to believe that debate and discussion do lead to such fundamental similarities of judgment. Calculations based on equiprobable choices very likely seriously overestimate the frequency of cycles in the natural world.

On the other hand, it is clear that one way to manipulate outcomes is to generate a cycle. Suppose that in Display 5-2 profile D exists and that person 2 realizes that his or her first choice, y, will lose to the Condorcet winner, x. Person 2 can at least prevent that outcome by generating a cycle (or a tie) by voting as if his or her preference were $y z x$ as in D'.

The tendency toward similarity may thus reduce the number $p(n, m)$, while the possibility of manipulation may increase the number. It seems to me that similarity probably reduces the number of profiles without Condorcet winners on issues that are not very important and that no one has a motive to manipulate, while the possibility of manipulation

Display 5-2

The Generation of a Cycle

D			D'		
D_1:	x y z		D'_1:	x y z	
D_2:	y x z		D'_2:	y z x	
D_3:	z x y		D'_3:	z x y	

Note. Majoritarian ordering of *D*: $x\,P\,y\,P\,z$.

Note. Cycle in *D'* under majoritarian voting: $x\,P\,y\,P\,z\,P\,x$.

In *D'* person 2 has reversed *z* and *x* from *D*, thereby generating a cycle.

increases the number of such profiles on important issues, where the outcome is worth the time and effort of prospective losers to generate a top cycle. Neither of these influences appears in the calculations and thus renders them suspect from two opposite points of view.

5.C. The Practical Relevance of Arrow's Theorem: Conditions for Condorcet Winners

Another approach to estimating the practical significance of Arrow's theorem is to inquire into what kinds of profiles are certain to produce a Condorcet winner. As in the previous approach, only majoritarian voting is considered, which limits the relevance of the inquiry to the theorem but does say something about its practical effect on this kind of decision process. For example, as can be seen in Display 5-1, for $m = n = 3$, the number of elements of $D = (m!)^n = 216$ and $p(n, m) = 12/216 = .056$. It is natural to look for the features that guarantee a Condorcet winner for 204 of the profiles in *D*. If one can generalize about the sets of preference orders that produce these results, then it may be possible to estimate the practical significance of the theorem for majoritarian voting.

To give a simple example: If each voter chooses the same preference order, D_i, then under majoritarian rules the social order for the profile D will be identical with the chosen D_i, and the unique social choice will be the first alternative in that social order.

The goal of this approach is to identify kinds of preference orders, D_i, such that when the whole profile, D, is composed of such orders, then D will lead by majoritarian methods to a weak order and a Condorcet winner as a social outcome.

Even before Arrow's theorem was uttered, Duncan Black observed one such pattern of orders in D—namely, that the profile can be expressible as a set of single-peaked curves.[4] A preference order can be graphed as in Figure 5-1. On the vertical axis is measured the degree of preference from lowest at the origin to highest at the top. On the horizontal axis is placed some ordering of the alternatives in X, an ordering appropriately chosen to depict one particular D_i as a single-peaked curve. This is always possible if D_i is a strong order (with indifference not allowed). The general definition of single-peaked curves (with indifference permitted at the top) is, as displayed in Figure 5-2, reading from left to right: (1) always downward sloping, (2) always upward sloping, (3) sloping upward to a particular point and then sloping downward, (4) sloping upward to a plateau and then sloping downward, (5) horizontal and then downward sloping, (6) upward sloping and then horizontal. Curves that are *not* single-peaked are shown in Figure 5-3.

A profile, D, is single-peaked if some ordering of alternatives on the horizontal axis allows every D_i in D to be drawn as a single-peaked curve. As already observed, for a single D_i, it is always possible to find such an ordering. But with three or more D_i, an ordering that renders D_j single-peaked may preclude that D_k be single-peaked. Indeed, it is exactly when cycles exist that single-peakedness cannot be attained for D. In Figure 5-4 assume there are three persons who have chosen different preference orders in the forward cycle (5-2). Then *all* possible orderings of $X = (x, y, z)$ on the horizontal axis result in a set of curves that fail to be single-peaked, as in Figure 5-4a–4f, where the axes are *all* the $m!$ permutations of $\{x, y, z\}$. The same is true of the backward cycle. So to say a profile, D, is single-peaked is to say it does not admit of cycles. In general, if D is single-peaked, then:

1. If all D_i are strong orders and n is odd, the social ordering is strong.

2. If all D_i are weak orders, n is odd, and no D_i involves complete indifference over a triple, the social ordering is a weak order.[5]

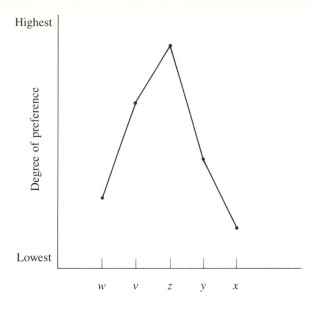

Figure 5-1   A single-peaked curve with the linear order *z v y w x*.

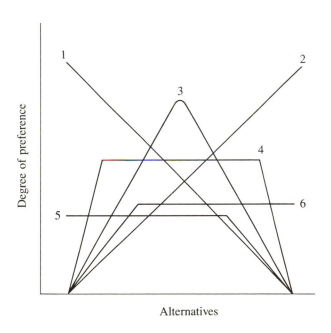

Figure 5-2   Single-peaked curves.

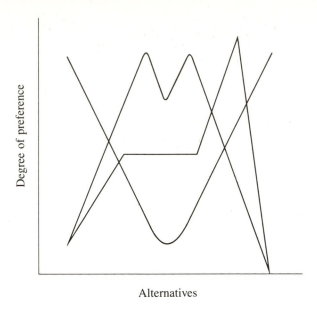

Figure 5-3   Non-single-peaked curves.

So single-peakedness implies transitivity and hence ensures the existence of a Condorcet winner.

It is furthermore a remarkable fact that, if D is single-peaked and n is odd, the Condorcet winner is immediately identifiable as the alternative on the horizontal axis beneath the median peak.[6] (If n is even, the winner is some alternative between the $n/2^{\text{th}}$ peak and the $(n/2) + 1^{\text{th}}$ peak, if such an alternative exists. And, if none exists, the alternatives at these peaks tie.) In Figure 5-5, with five peaks, the alternative beneath the median peak (3) is identified as x_{med}. If x_{med} is put against some alternative to its left, say x_1, then x_{med} wins because a majority consisting of voters 3, 4, and 5 prefer x_{med} to x_1 (that is, their curves are upward sloping from x_1 to x_{med}). Similarly, x_{med} can beat any alternative to its right, say x_4, with a majority consisting of voters 1, 2, and 3, whose curves are downward sloping from x_{med} to x_4, which means they prefer x_{med} to x_4. Hence x_{med} can beat anything to its right or left and is a Condorcet winner.

Single-peakedness is important because it has an obvious political interpretation. Assuming a single political dimension, the fact that a profile, D, is single-peaked means the voters have a common view of the political situation, although they may differ widely on their judgments. Person i may choose $D_i = x\, y\, z$, and person j may choose $D_j = z\, y\, x$; yet

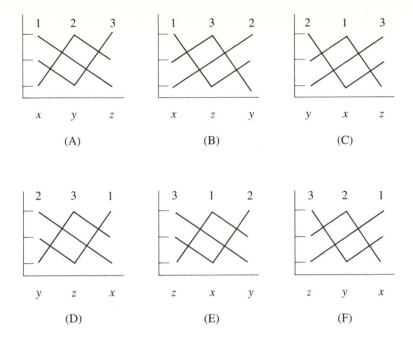

Figure 5-4   Non-single-peakedness for the forward cycle.

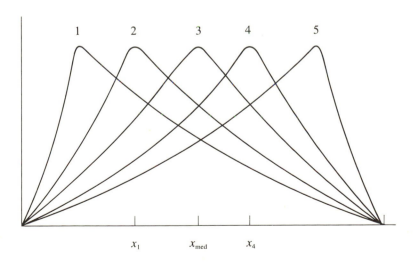

Figure 5-5   Single-peaked curves with Condorcet winner.

they agree that x is at one end of the scale, z at the other, and y in the middle, which means they agree entirely on how the political spectrum is arranged. This kind of agreement is precisely what is lacking in a cycle, where voters disagree not only about the merits of alternatives but even about where alternatives are on the political dimension.

If, by reason of discussion, debate, civic education, and political socialization, voters have a common view of the political dimension (as evidenced by single-peakedness), then a transitive outcome is guaranteed. So if a society is homogeneous in this sense, there will typically be Condorcet winners, at least on issues of *minor* importance. This fact will not prevent civil war, but it will at least ensure that the civil war makes sense.

A number of other kinds of restrictions on preference orders, D_i, that guarantee that D will produce a transitive outcome have been identified. Like single-peakedness they minimize disagreement over the dimensions of judgment. Consider "value-restrictedness," which is an obvious development from the forward and backward cycles of (5-2). One property of those cycles (observable by inspection) is that each alternative in X appears in first place in some D_i, in second place in another, and in third place in a third. So, if, for strong orders in D_i, some alternative is never first in a D_i, or never second, or never last—if, in short, an alternative is "value-restricted"—then no cycle can occur and transitivity is guaranteed.

A number of other such provisions for transitivity have been identified. They have been exhaustively analyzed by Peter Fishburn.[7] They are important because they indicate that quite a wide variety of rather mild agreement about the issue dimension guarantees a Condorcet winner. Furthermore, not all voters need display the agreement to obtain the guarantee. Richard Niemi has shown that the probabilities of the occurrence of top cycles, by calculations similar to those set forth in Display 5-1, reduce to tiny proportions (e.g., .02 to .04) when as few as three-fourths of 45 or 95 voters agree on the issue dimension while disagreeing on orders.[8] This result implies that agreement about dimensions probably renders uncontrived cyclical outcomes quite rare. So I conclude that, because of agreement on an issue dimension, intransitivities only occasionally render decisions by majoritarian methods meaningless, at least for somewhat homogeneous groups and at least when the subjects for decision are *not* politically important. When, on the other hand, subjects are politically important enough to justify the energy and expense of contriving cycles, Arrow's result is of great practical significance. It suggests that, on the very most important subjects, cycles may render social outcomes meaningless.

5.D. The Theoretical Invulnerability of Arrow's Theorem: Independence

Assuming that the practical significance of Arrow's theorem increases with the political importance of the subject for decision, it is then reasonable to inquire whether the theorem is too demanding. Does it overstate the case by stressing the possibility of intransitivity and its consequent incoherence when perhaps this is too extreme an interpretation?

To weaken the force of Arrow's theorem, it is necessary to question the conditions of either fairness or logicality. Most of the fairness conditions seem intuitively reasonable—at least to people in Western culture—so most of the attack has been focused on logicality. One fairness condition, independence, has, however, often been regarded as too strong.

The independence condition has at least three consequences:

1. It prohibits utilitarian methods of choice (for reasons discussed in section 4.I).

2. It prohibits arbitrariness in vote-counting, such as lotteries or methods that work in different ways at different times.

3. It prohibits, when choosing among alternatives in a set S, which is included in X, reference to judgments on alternatives in $X - S$.

It seems to me that one can defend the independence condition for each of these consequences. As for consequence 1, since interpersonal comparisons of utility have no clear meaning, the prohibition of utilitarian methods seems quite defensible, although a weaker form of Condition I might accomplish the same result. With respect to consequence 2, earlier in this chapter it was shown that arbitrary counting is just as unfair as violations of Conditions U, P, and D. It is difficult to imagine that any weaker form of Condition I would accomplish what I does, because the arbitrariness must be prohibited for any set.

Most attention has been given to consequence 3, because many people believe that judgments on alternatives in $X - S$ are germane to judgments on S itself.[9] In a presidential preference primary, for example, choice among several candidates may depend on judgments of still other candidates. For example, in the 1976 Democratic primaries, in thinking about a decision between Carter and Udall as if they covered the whole spectrum of party ideology, a mildly left-of-center voter might prefer Udall. But if the voter thought about Jackson also, so that Udall appeared as an extremist, that same voter might have preferred Carter to Udall. So "irrelevant" alternatives (here, Jackson) may really be "relevant."

The question is whether there should be some formal way to allow judgments on the "irrelevant" alternatives to enter into the choice. And the difficulty in answering is: How can one decide which nonentered candidates are relevant? Why not allow consideration of still other, even a hundred, irrelevant alternatives? But if no irrelevant alternatives are considered, then y might beat x; but with such consideration, if there is no Condorcet winner, x might beat y. Thus meaning and coherence depend on variability in the voting situations (on the size, that is, of X and S) as much as on voters' judgment.

There seems, unfortunately, no wholly defensible method to decide on degrees of irrelevance.[10] In the absence of such a method, Condition I seems at least moderately defensible. Furthermore, while some might argue about the desirability of consequence 3, Condition I seems necessary because consequence 2 is indispensable for fair decision.

5.E. The Theoretical Invulnerability of Arrow's Theorem: Transitivity

If the fairness conditions survive, then the only condition left to attack is transitivity. The sharpest attack is to assert that transitivity is a property of humans, not of groups. Hence the individual relation, R_i, should be transitive, but it is simple anthropomorphism to ask that the social relation, R, be transitive also.[11] Still, there is some reason to seek transitivity for outcomes.

Without transitivity, there is no order; and without order, there is no coherence. Social outcomes may in fact be meaningless, but one would like to obtain as much meaning as possible from social decisions. So the obvious question is: Can one, by modifying the definition of coherence, obtain some lesser coherence compatible with fairness? Unfortunately, the answer is mainly negative.

The social relation, R, which generates a weak order in Arrow's logicality condition, combines social preference, P, and social indifference, I. And R is useful for the purpose Arrow had in mind—namely, social judgments involving comparisons and ordering of all feasible social policies, such as distributions of income. Suppose, however, that one does not require quite so general a result. For purposes of making a social choice, which is the interest in this book, one does not need to impose a complete order on the whole set X merely to find a best alternative in X.

We can think of a best element in X as one that is chosen over or tied with every other alternative.[12] The best alternative is then the choice from X or $C(X)$.[13]

A requirement, weaker than transitivity, that nevertheless ensures the existence of one best alternative is *quasi-transitivity*—that is, the transitivity of P, but not of R or I. This means that, if $x P y$ and $y P z$, then $x P z$; but if the antecedent does not hold (e.g., if $x I y$), then the consequent need not hold either. For example, quasi-transitivity allows (as in note 12) $y P z$, $z I x$, and $x I y$, which is clearly intransitive in both R and I, although it is enough to establish that the choice from $X = (x, y, z)$ is $C(X) = (x, y)$.

Another, even weaker requirement for a choice, is *acyclicity*, which is the requirement that alternatives in X can be arranged so that there is no cycle.[14] It turns out that, by using the logical requirement of acyclicity rather than transitivity, it is possible to find social choice that satisfies all of Arrow's fairness conditions as well as the revised condition of logicality. A. K. Sen offers an example of such a method: For a set $X = (a, b, \ldots,)$, let a be chosen for $C(X)$ over b if everybody prefers a to b and let a and b both be chosen if not everybody prefers a to b or b to a.[15] This rule satisfies Condition U because all individual orders are allowed. It satisfies Condition P because it is based on the principle of unanimity. It satisfies Condition I because the choice between any pair depends only on individual preferences on that pair, and it satisfies Condition D because the only way a can be better socially than b is for everyone to prefer a to b. Finally, it is always acyclic. So even if one cannot guarantee an order with fair procedure, it appears that one can at least guarantee a best choice.

Unfortunately, however, something very much like dictatorship is required to guarantee quasi-transitivity or acyclicity. Quasi-transitive social outcomes can be guaranteed only if there is an oligarchy.[16] (An *oligarchy* is a subset of choosers who, if the members agree, can impose a choice, or, if they do not agree, enables all members individually to veto the choice.) If one modifies Condition D from no dictator to no vetoer, then even a quasi-transitive social outcome cannot be guaranteed.[17] As for acyclicity, Donald Brown has shown that acyclic choice requires a "collegium" such that alternative a is chosen over b if and only if the whole collegium and some other persons prefer a to b. Thus, although a collegium cannot unilaterally impose a choice, unlike an oligarchy it can always at least veto.[18]

Furthermore, if one strengthens Arrow's conditions just a little bit by requiring not just the monotonicity that enters into Condition P, but a condition of positive responsiveness (Condition PR), then quasi-transitivity again involves dictatorship. (Monotonicity requires merely that, if a voter raises her or his valuation of an alternative, the social valuation does not go down. In contrast, positive responsiveness requires that, if a voter raises her or his valuation, society does so as well, if that is possible.) It is then the case that any quasi-transitive social result that satisfies Conditions U, P, I, and PR must violate Condition D if there are three alternatives; and, furthermore, someone must have a veto if there are four or more alternatives.[19]

Weakening transitivity into some logical condition that requires only a social choice but not a full ordering does not gain very much. This brief survey indicates there is a *family* of possibility theorems of which Arrow's theorem is a special case. And in the whole family there is still some kind of serious conflict between conditions of fairness and a condition of logicality. In general, the only effective way to guarantee consistency in social outcomes is to require some kind of concentration of power in society—a dictator, an oligarchy, or a collegium. So fairness and social rationality seem jointly impossible, which implies that fairness and meaning in the content of social decisions are sometimes incompatible.

5.F. The Theoretical Invulnerability of Arrow's Theorem: Conditions on Social Choice

Of course, one can abandon entirely the effort to guarantee some kind of ordering for social "rationality," whether it be transitivity or merely acyclicity. One can simply provide that a social choice is made and impose no kind of ordering condition. The reason, however, that transitivity or even less restrictive ordering conditions are attractive is that they often forestall manipulation by some participants either of agenda or of sets of alternatives to obtain outcomes advantageous to the manipulator. As Arrow remarked at the conclusion of the revised edition of *Social Choice and Individual Values,* "the importance of the transitivity condition" involves "the independence of the final choice from the path to it."[20] "Transitivity," he said, "will ensure this independence," thereby ensuring also that the preferences of the participants (rather than the form of or manipulation of the social choice mechanism) determine the outcome. He went on to point out that both Robert Dahl and I had described ways in which intransitive social mechanisms had produced "unsatisfactory" results. So Arrow concluded that "collective rationality" was not merely an "illegitimate" anthropomorphism, "but an important attribute of a genuine democratic system." Consequently, if one gives up on social transitivity or some weaker form of ordering, one is in effect abandoning the effort to ensure socially satisfactory outcomes.

To ensure satisfactory outcomes without imposing an anthropomorphic collective rationality, one might impose consistency conditions on the social choice mechanism—conditions that could have the same effect of forestalling manipulation that transitivity does, but that would not attribute to society the ability to order possessed only by persons. Hopefully, one would thereby avoid all the problems of the possibility theorems put forth by Arrow and his successors. Unfortunately, however, it turns out that these consistency conditions also cannot be satisfied by social choice mechanisms that satisfy the fairness conditions. Consequently, although the problem can be elegantly restated in terms of choice rather than ordering, the main defect of the methods of amalgamation is unaffected by the new language. Just to say, for example, that $x\,P_1\,y$ and $x\,P_2\,y$ lead to $C(x, y) = x$ rather than to say that they lead to $x\,P\,y$ does not solve the problem of amalgamation. Some kind of inconsistency is ineradicable.

Consistency requirements on choice have been discussed in two quite different ways, which, however, turn out to be substantially equivalent in this context. I will discuss both ways here, despite their equivalence, because their verbal rationales are complementary.

A. K. Sen and subsequently many others have imposed on social choice conditions of logicality that were originally devised as standards for individual choice behavior. This procedure has the advantage of relating consistency in groups to consistency in persons, but it is subject to the same charge of anthropomorphism that was leveled against the use of ordering conditions. Charles Plott, however, has devised a consistency condition for social choice itself, one that could not easily be applied to persons but captures the spirit of Arrow's insistence that the final choice ought to be independent of the path to it. It is interesting and remarkable that Sen's and Plott's conditions turn out to be closely related and almost equivalent.[21]

Looking first at Sen's conditions, let S and T be sets of alternatives in $X = (x_1, x_2, \ldots, x_m)$ and let S be a subset of T. Sen's conditions are restrictions on the choice sets from these two sets of alternatives, $C(S)$ and $C(T)$:

1. *Property α*: For sets S and T, with S a subset of T, if x is in both $C(T)$ and S, then x is in $C(S)$.

2. *Property $\beta+$*: For sets S and T, with S a subset of T, if x is in $C(S)$ and y is in S, then, if y is in $C(T)$, so also is x in $C(T)$.

The meaning of these conditions is easily explained: Property α requires that, if the choice from the larger set is in the smaller set, then it is in the choice from the smaller set as well.

To see the rationale of α, consider a violation of it: A diner chooses among three items on a menu, beef (B), chicken (C), and fish (F), which are the set $\{B, C, F\}$. The diner chooses beef (B); then the restaurant runs out of fish (F). The new menu is the set $\{B, C\}$, whereupon the diner chooses chicken (C) in violation both of property α and of apparent good sense.[22]

Property α guarantees consistency in choices as the number of alternatives is *contracted* because in going from T to S the choice does not change if it is in both sets. Property $\beta+$, on the other hand, guarantees consistency in choices as the number of alternatives is *expanded*. It requires that, if any element in the smaller set is the choice from the larger set, then all choices from the smaller set are choices from the larger set. Thus, in going from S to T, if any choices from S continue to be chosen from the larger set, all such choices continue to be chosen.

The rationale of $\beta+$ can be appreciated from a violation of it: For a seminar with students $S = (a, b, c, d)$, a teacher ranks d best. Then another student enrolls making $T = (a, b, c, d, e)$, whereupon the teacher ranks c best. Doubtless student d discerns an inconsistency and believes that if he is the best or among the best in S and if some other member of S is best in T, then he (d) ought to be among the best in T also.

As I have already noted, property α and property $\beta+$ apply as well to individuals as to society. Plott, however, attempted to embody Arrow's notion of "independence of the final result from the path to it" directly in a condition on *social* choice. Plott justified his condition, which, appropriately, he called "path independence," thus:

> *the process of choosing, from a dynamic point of view, frequently proceeds in a type of "divide and conquer" manner. The alternatives are "split up" into smaller sets, a choice is made over each of these sets, the chosen elements are collected, and then a choice is made from them. Path independence, in this case, would mean that the final result would be independent of the way the alternatives were initially divided up for consideration.*[23]

The definition of *path independence* is that, for any pair of sets S and T, the choice from the union of the sets is the same as the choice from the union of the separate choices from each set.[24] Manifestly, if S and T are any ways of breaking up the set of alternatives, X, then to equate the choices from their union with the choice from the union of their choice sets is to say that it makes no difference to the final outcome how X is divided up for choosing.

Path independence (PI) can be broken up into two parts—$PI*$ and *PI:

1. $PI*$ is the condition that the choice from the union of S and T be included in or equivalent to the choice from the union of their choice sets.

2. *PI is the converse of $PI*$. Specifically, *PI is the condition that the choice from the union of the choice sets of S and T be included in or equivalent to the choice from the union of S and T.[25]

It is a remarkable and important fact that $PI*$ is exactly equivalent to property α.[26] Furthermore, a choice function satisfying property $\beta+$ satisfies *PI, so that, though not equivalent, *PI is implied by $\beta+$.[27]

These standards of consistency in choice turn out to be quite similar in effect to ordering principles.[28] Although property α does not guarantee transitivity, it does guarantee acyclicity in choices from X. So also, therefore, do PI and $PI*$. Consequently, social choice methods satisfying these conditions are dictatorial or oligarchic, just as are those satisfying ordering principles.

On the other hand, property $\beta+$ does not guarantee even acyclicity when choices from X are made in a series of pairwise comparisons. Consequently, methods satisfying $\beta+$ and *PI do not imply dictatorship or oligarchy or any other kind of concentration of power. If one is willing to give up consistency in contracting alternatives—and this is quite a bit to give up—then reliance on simple consistency in expanding alternatives might be a way around all the difficulties discovered by Arrow. Unfortunately, however, methods of choice satisfying $\beta+$ and *PI violate another fairness condition—namely, unanimity or Pareto optimality.[29]

Suppose a choice is to be made by three people with these preference orders: (1) $x\,y\,z\,w$, (2) $y\,z\,w\,x$, (3) $z\,w\,x\,y$. This leads to a cycle in simple majority rule, $x\,P\,y\,P\,z\,P\,w\,P\,x$, so that the choice set is all the alternatives: $C(w, x, y, z) = (w, x, y, z)$. But everyone prefers z to w, although there is a path by which w can be chosen. Let $S_1 = (y, z)$ and $C(S_1) = y$; $S_2 = (x, y)$ and $C(S_2) = x$; $S_3 = (x, w)$ and $C(S_3) = w$. Using S_1 at step 1, S_2 at step 2, and S_3 at step 3, w is selected even though z, eliminated at step 1, is unanimously preferred to w. This result is generalized by Ferejohn and Grether.[30] It tells us that, even if we rely solely on an expansion consistency condition and thus avoid concentrations of power, we still do not achieve fairness. So, in a quite different way, we are back where we began. Nothing has been gained except an elegant formalism that avoids anthropomorphizing society.

5.G. The Absence of Meaning

The main thrust of Arrow's theorem and all the associated literature is that there is an unresolvable tension between logicality and fairness. To guarantee an ordering or a consistent path, independent choice requires that there be some sort of concentration of power (dictators, oligarchies, or collegia of vetoers) in sharp conflict with democratic ideals. Even the weakest sort of consistency ($\beta+$ or $*PI$) involves a conflict with unanimity, which is also an elementary condition of fairness.

These conflicts have been investigated in great detail, especially in the last decade; but no adequate resolution of the tension has been discovered, and it appears quite unlikely that any will be. The unavoidable inference is, therefore, that, so long as a society preserves democratic institutions, its members can expect that some of their social choices will be unordered or inconsistent. And when this is true, no meaningful choice can be made. If y is in fact chosen—given the mechanism of choice and the profile of individual valuations—then to say that x is best or right or more desired is probably false. But it would also be equally false to say that y is best or right or most desired. And in that sense, the choice lacks meaning. The consequence of this defect will be explored in the ensuing chapters.

6

The Manipulation
of Social Choices:
Strategic Voting

The possibility of a lack of meaning in the outcome is a serious problem for social judgment and social choice. It forces us to doubt that the content of "social welfare" or the "public interest" can ever be discovered by amalgamating individual value judgments. It even leads us to suspect that no such thing as the "public interest" exists, aside from the subjective (and hence dubious) claims of self-proclaimed saviors.

Serious as are such (probably irresolvable) epistemological and ontological questions, it seems to me that the simple practical consequences for social choices are much worse. These consequences are either that power is concentrated in society or that any system of voting can be manipulated to produce outcomes advantageous to the manipulators or at least different from outcomes in the absence of manipulation. If we assume that society discourages the concentration of power, then at least two methods of manipulation are always available, no matter what method of voting is used: First, those in control of procedures can manipulate the agenda (by, for example, restricting alternatives or by arranging the order in which they are brought up). Second, those not in control can still manipulate outcomes by false revelations of values.

Both methods assume a static world, with the number of participants and alternatives fixed. Hence sometimes a profile of preferences cannot be manipulated by anyone. For example, if all participants are unanimous, no one has a motive to manipulate; and, given a voting system satisfying the Pareto condition, it is impossible to manipulate anyway. But in a dynamic world, where the sets of participants, N, or of alternatives, X, can vary, some kind of manipulation is probably possible with any profile. For example, in an X with m elements, even if everyone prefers x_i to the $m - 1$ other alternatives in X, still when X is enlarged to X' containing some x_{m+1}th element, unanimity may vanish and the potential for manipulation may appear.

6.A. The Elements of Manipulation

By limiting the discussion initially to the static case with fixed N and X, it is easy to illustrate the possibilities of manipulation with simple majority voting and the amendment procedure, although in principle similar possibilities exist—even in the static case—for *all* procedures. Suppose there are four alternatives, $X = (w, x, y, z)$, z is the status quo, and three roughly equal factions have this profile:

Faction 1: $w\ x\ y\ z$

Faction 2: $x\ y\ z\ w$

Faction 3: $y\ z\ w\ x$

In the abstract, this profile produces a cycle $w\ P\ x\ P\ y\ P\ z\ P\ w$; so all alternatives tie. But, given the amendment procedures, appropriate control of the agenda produces particular (though different) winners. Suppose faction 3 can control the agenda (perhaps by controlling an agenda-making body like the Rules Committee of the U.S. House of Representatives). Then, by posing its first choice, y, as the original motion with x and w as amendments, faction 3 can make y win in a decision process that proceeds in this way:

Step 1: x vs. w; w wins (with 1 and 3)

Step 2: w vs. y; y wins (with 2 and 3)

Step 3: y vs. z; y wins (unanimously)

Hence $C(w, x, y, z) = y$. Suppose, however, faction 2 controls the agenda-making body. Then by posing x as the original alternative with y and w as amendments, faction 2 can make x win:

Step 1: w vs. y; y wins (with 2 and 3)

Step 2: x vs. y; x wins (with 1 and 2)

Step 3: x vs. z; x wins (with 1 and 2)

So $C(w, x, y, z) = x$. Faction 1 cannot make w, its first choice, win because w loses to z, faction 1's least-desired choice. But faction 1 can, of course, make either x or y win, both of which faction 1 prefers to z. So every faction can produce a preferred choice by control of the agenda. Whether x, y, or even z wins thus depends not only on participants' preferences, but also on the chance of which faction controls the agenda.

It is true that, if the procedure included an ultimate fourth step in which the survivor at the penultimate step was placed against each of the others, then that survivor would also lose—and z would win by default.[1] This is not necessarily a desirable outcome, however, because z loses unanimously to y and by two-thirds to x. The more elaborate procedure renders manipulation slightly more difficult, but it may lead to a *worse* outcome—and, of course, manipulation by false revelation of preferences is not prevented at all.

Let us look, then, at strategic voting, which is available even to those less powerful people who do not control the agenda. Suppose faction 3 does make y the original motion and presumptive winner. Can factions 1 and 2 do anything in response? Indeed, members of faction 1 can, for example, vote strategically as if their valuations were $x\,w\,y\,z$ (instead of $w\,x\,y\,z$, as they truly are). Then x would be the Condorcet winner:

Step 1: x vs. w; x wins (with 1 and 2 because 1 votes strategically)

Step 2: x vs. y; x wins (with 1 and 2)

Step 3: x vs. z; x wins (with 1 and 2)

Hence $C(w, x, y, z) = x$. Although faction 2 cannot alone stop y, members of 2 can, of course, urge faction 1 to do so.

Conversely, if faction 2 succeeds in making x the original motion and presumptive winner, members of faction 3 can thwart 2 by voting strategically, as if 3's valuations were $w\,y\,z\,x$ (instead of the true valuation, $y\,z\,w\,x$). The process will then be:

Step 1: w vs. y; w wins (with 1 and 3 because 3 votes strategically)

Step 2: w vs. x; w wins (with 1 and 3)

Step 3: w vs. z; z wins (with 1 and 3 because 3 reverts to the true valuation, $y\,z\,w\,x$)

So $C(w, x, y, z) = z$, which is faction 3's second choice and preferable to its last choice, x. Nevertheless, 3 cannot guarantee victory for z because faction 1, observing 3's dissimulation at step 1, can also dissimulate at step 2, pretending to hold $x\,w\,y\,z$. So x will survive (with support from 1 and 2) and ultimately beat z (again with 1 and 2). Faction 1 will thus get its second choice, x, rather than its last choice, z, which would be chosen if 1 did not strategically counter 3's strategic voting.

The social choice depends, therefore, not only on the values of participants, but also on whether *any* of them falsely reveal those values, and, if any do, on *which ones* do so.

It may be thought that strategic voting is mainly characteristic of majoritarian procedures. But it is just as easy with positional methods such as the Borda count. Then, for the same profile,

Faction 1: $w\,x\,y\,z$

Faction 2: $x\,y\,z\,w$

Faction 3: $y\,z\,w\,x$

the Borda sums are: $w = 4$, $x = 5$, $y = 6$, $z = 3$; so y wins. But members of faction 1, preferring x to y, have only to rearrange their revealed order to $x\,w\,z\,y$, in which case $x = 6$, $y = 5$, $z = 4$, $w = 3$, and x wins.

Agenda control and strategic voting are often possible in the static world, with N and X fixed. In the dynamic world, with both sets variable, the possibilities of manipulation are enormously increased. Indeed, in the dynamic world, it is probably *always* possible to manipulate, provided participants are eager enough to change outcomes and hence willing to expend the energy necessary to create new alternatives or to introduce new participants.

Suppose, for example, there are two alternatives, a and b, and the status quo, z, and two parties, with this profile:

Party 1: $a\,z\,b$

Party 2: $b\,z\,a$

Party 1 has an absolute majority, 60 percent of the participants. Then with the amendment procedure, the social choice is, for certain, a. What can party 2 do to improve? Party 2 can either bring in more than 20 percent additional participants as supporters or bring in new alternatives that split party 1. Typically, the latter is the easier path. It amounts to a dynamic extension of agenda control, one that even allows losers to manipulate winners.

As in Display 6-1, let party 2 propose a new alternative, c, which splits party 1. In D^1, there is a cycle in $a\,b\,c$, so the status quo, z, will win if c is the original motion. In D^2, c is the Condorcet winner. Really clever leaders of party 2 can occasionally find some c that generates D^2, but many quite ordinary politicians can invent some c that generates D^1.

In lieu of expanding X with c, party 2 can instead trade votes, in effect commingling X with some $X' = (d, f, z)$ containing an alternative d favored more than a by group A of party 1, as in Display 6-2.

Assume party 2 would rather win on b than on f. Since members of group A of party 1 would rather win on d than on a, party 2 can offer to vote for d in choosing from X', in return for which members of group A of party 1 promise to vote for b from X. So $C(X) = b$ and $C(X') = d$. Defining $X^* = X \cup X'$, then vote-trading is simply coordinated strategic voting in X^*.

Altogether, then, in the static world of fixed N and X, there are many profiles permitting manipulation by agenda control and strategic voting. Even if such profiles do not exist in the static world, often, if not always, a dynamic development does permit manipulation. The dynamic version of agenda control is expansion of X with divisive alternatives, and the dynamic version of strategic voting is vote-trading. So it seems manipulation is almost always possible.

Is this a really general result? The answer is affirmative, as I will show for strategic voting in the rest of this chapter and for agenda control in the next chapter.

6.B. The Universality of Strategic Voting

Is strategic voting possible in *any* voting system, given an appropriate profile of individual values? Ever since Duncan Black pointed out the possibility in his original essay on the paradox of voting, social choice theorists have conjectured that the possibility of strategic voting is an inherent feature of voting methods.[2] Recently this conjecture has been proved, independently, by Allan Gibbard and Mark Satterthwaite.[3] Given an appropriate profile of preferences, any voting method can be manipulated strategically. That is, assuming there are "true" preference orders for voters, then there are occasions on which some voters can achieve a desired outcome by voting contrary to their true preferences.[4]

Display 6-1

Splitting the Larger Party with a New Alternative

D on $X = (a, b, z)$	
Party 1 (60%):	$a\ z\ b$
Party 2 (40%):	$b\ z\ a$

Note.   Alternative a wins.

A new alternative c in $X' = (a, b, c, z)$ is proposed such that the result is either D^1 or D^2 on X'.

	D^1 on X'	D^2 on X'
Party 1 (30%):	$c\ a\ z\ b$	$c\ a\ z\ b$
Party 1' (30%):	$a\ z\ b\ c$	$a\ z\ c\ b$
Party 2 (40%):	$b\ z\ c\ a$	$b\ c\ z\ a$

Number of Votes for the Alternative in the Row When Placed in Contest Against the Alternative in the Column

		For D^1		
	a	b	c	z
a	—	60	30	60
b	40	—	70	40
c	70	30	—	30
z	40	60	70	—

So a, b, c, and z cycle and z wins.

For D^2

	a	b	c	z
a	—	60	30	60
b	40	—	40	40
c	70	60	—	70 (Condorcet winner)
z	40	60	30	—

Gibbard remarked and Satterthwaite proved that this result is, in ef-fect, an application of Arrow's theorem. Like Arrow's theorem, it applies only to cases where there are three or more alternatives. (Simple majority voting on *two* alternatives is not manipulable, though the reduction of many alternatives to two is.) Still the Gibbard–Satterthwaite result is narrower than Arrow's theorem. The theorem on manipulation applies only to voting, not to amalgamation by other means such as markets. Since it does apply only to voting, it specifically does not allow for ties or for the choice of more than one winner.[5]

As Gibbard pointed out, however, voting is without meaning unless it produces a unique outcome. Consequently, the proof that strategic vot-ing inheres in all methods assumes that the method must lead to a unique choice. Similarly, it is quite easy to devise strategy-proof methods that use a chance device. (Gibbard's example is good: Everyone marks a ballot with a first choice among alternatives, and a decision is made by ran-domly picking one ballot. Then all are motivated to select their true first choices. If a voter selects otherwise, then, if his or her ballot is picked, the social choice will be less favorable than if the voter had selected honestly.) Although many such devices can be imagined, they all violate Arrow's independence condition in that, for a given profile, the social choice might be x with one chance selection and y with another. It seems appropriate, therefore, to exclude methods of amalgamation that use chance.[6] What remains are nontrivial voting methods, and these are all subject to manip-ulation by strategic voting.[7] The conclusion is, therefore, that any ordinal method of voting can be manipulated by individuals.[8] Furthermore, as will be shown in section 6.D, even demand-revealing voting, which was devised to preclude manipulation, is easily manipulable by minority coalitions. It seems, therefore, that some potential for manipulation is inescapable.

Display 6-2

Vote-trading on New and Old Alternatives

D on $X = (a, b, z)$	
Party 1, Group A (20%):	$a\ z\ b$
Party 1, Group B (40%):	$a\ z\ b$
Party 2 (40%):	$b\ z\ a$

Note. Alternative a wins.

D on $X' = (d, f, z)$	
Party 1, Group A (20%):	$d\ z\ f$
Party 1, Group B (40%):	$f\ z\ d$
Party 2 (40%):	$f\ z\ d$

Note.   Alternative f wins.

Vote trade: Party 2 promises to vote for d and group A of party 1 promises to vote for b. The result is:

Contest			
a	vs.	b	
Party 1, Group B	40%	Party 1, Group A	20%
		Party 2	40%
Total	40%	Total	60%

Note. Alternative b wins.

Contest			
d	vs.	f	
Party 1, Group A	20%	Party 1, Group B	40%
Party 2	40%		
Total	60%	Total	40%

Note. Alternative d wins.

6.C. Examples of Strategic Voting

Some writers have suggested that strategic voting is so difficult for most people that very little of it occurs. Evidence for or against this proposition is hard to come by because to know whether people vote strategically, one must know how their true values differ (if at all) from the values they reveal. The observer knows for certain only what is revealed, so half of the data for comparison are unavailable. Nevertheless, where one can make good guesses about true values, it appears that quite a lot of strategic voting takes place.

In Plurality Voting

One of the simplest kinds of strategic voting occurs in plurality systems, where supporters of third parties vote for their second choice in order to defeat the major party candidate they like the least. (See the examples in section 4.D.) Since this kind of strategic voting is one motive force behind Duverger's law ("The simple majority, single ballot system favors the two-party system.") and since Duverger's law, properly interpreted, seems almost invariably true, strategic voting of this sort must be very common in single-member district systems.[9]

In An Open Primary

One complicated strategy, sometimes recommended but, so far as I know, never used by enough voters to make a difference, is this: Given an open primary (wherein voters can participate in the primary election of any party they select at the time of the primary), given for party R two candidates, r_1 and r_2, and for party D one candidate, d, given that the chance r_1 beats d in the general election is 0.9 and that r_2 beats d is 0.4, then one recommended strategy for members of D is to vote for r_2 in the R primary, so that, if the prior estimates of probabilities are accurate, d will beat r_2 in the general election. (Similar possibilities exist in any double election or runoff system.)

This strategy assumes a profile somewhat like this, where R_i is a faction in R,

R_1 (15%) $r_1 \, d \, r_2$

R_2 (10%) $r_1 \, r_2 \, d$

R_3 (35%) $r_2 \, r_1 \, d$

D (40%) $d \, r_1 \, r_2$

and it anticipates voting thus:

Step 1: r_1 vs. r_2; r_2 wins (with R_3 and D or 75%)

Step 2: r_2 vs. d; d wins (with R_1 and D or 55%)

Something quite like this was recommended by Democratic activists in the Wisconsin Republican senatorial primary of 1956, where r_1 was the incumbent Senator Wiley, an Eisenhower Republican, and r_2 was Representative Glenn Davis, who was supported by the faction of Senator Joseph McCarthy. Not surprisingly, ordinary Democrats rejected this complicated and risky strategy, although a large number of them voted in the Republican primary for Senator Wiley, who won the primary with just less than 50 percent (there was a trivial third candidate) and who won the general election by a large majority.

That ordinary voters reject such a strategy (which may be followed by a few party activists) is sometimes cited as evidence that most people cannot vote strategically. In the instance cited, however, many Democratic voters apparently voted for Senator Wiley, that is for r_1 rather than for their true preference, d, which is also strategic voting—and, furthermore, probably more in accord with their desired result.

Assume, as in Display 6-3, appropriate probabilities of election outcomes and the following (possible but imaginary) cardinal utilities for the election:

	d (Maier)	r_1 (Wiley)	r_2 (Davis)
Democratic activists	1.0	0.2	0.0
Ordinary Democratic voters in Republican primary	1.0	0.8	0.0

Then *all* Democrats (activist and ordinary voters alike) who voted in the Republican primary voted strategically, although, having different values, they voted differently. In Display 6-3 is a calculation, based on imaginary prior expectations of outcomes, to show that both strategies are reasonable for different persons. If so, then—far from showing that strategic voting is rare—an election like this is in fact evidence that it is quite common. Many Democrats did vote for their probable second choice (Wiley) in order to eliminate for certain their probable third choice (Davis). Those activists who interpreted the outcome as evidence of nonstrategic voting merely attributed their own intense interest in electing a Democratic senator to ordinary voters who were probably instead intensely interested in rejecting McCarthyism.

The rationale for different choices by different kinds of Democrats among alternative strategies is set forth in Display 6-3. The rationales depend on the notions of prior probabilities and expected utility. There are three possible outcomes: $X = O_1$ (d wins), $X = O_2$ (r_1 wins), $X = O_3$ (r_2 wins). There are three possible actions for Democratic voters, set forth in column 1 of the Display: $A = a_1$ (vote for d [Maier] in the Democratic primary), $A = a_2$ (vote for r_1 [Wiley] in the Republican primary), $A = a_3$ (vote for r_2 [Davis] in the Republican primary). Each action, a_i, leads to a different arrangement of expectations about outcomes, the calculation of which is set forth in columns 2 and 3. The following assumptions underlie these probabilities.

For column 2:

> If Democrats vote in the Democratic primary, then in the uninvaded Republican primary r_1 (Wiley) would win with probability 0.3 and r_2 (Davis) with 0.7. (Presumably Davis had the lead over Wiley among Republicans.)

> If Democrats invade the primary to vote for Wiley, however, r_1 (Wiley) would win with probability 0.7 and r_2 (Davis) with 0.3. (Presumably strategically voting Democrats could render Wiley the most probable winner.)

> If Democrats vote for Davis (a highly improbably event), then r_1 (Wiley) would win with probability 0.1 and r_2 (Davis) with 0.9. (Presumably Democrats could render Davis an almost certain winner.)

In column 3, the assumptions are that, in general elections in head-to-head contests, the probabilities of victory are

r_1 (Wiley)	vs.	d (Maier)	
$p(r_1) = 0.9$		$p(d) = 0.1$	
0.9	$+$	0.1	$= 1$

r_2 (Davis)	vs.	d (Maier)	
$p(r_2) = 0.4$		$p(d) = 0.6$	
0.4	$+$	0.6	$= 1$

Display 6-3

Imaginary Expected Utility of Alternative Actions for Democrats in the 1956 Wisconsin Senatorial Primary

(1)	(2)	(3)	(4)	Activist Democrats		Ordinary Democrats	
				(5)	(6)	(7)	(8)
Alternative actions for Democrats	Voters' probabilities for outcome of Republican primary, given action in column 1	Voters' probabilities for outcomes of general election	Voters' probabilities for final outcomes for each action (Col. 2 · Col. 3)	Utility for outcome	Expected utility for outcome and alternative	Utility for outcome	Expected utility for outcome and alternative
a_1 Vote in Democratic primary	Wiley wins .3	Wiley wins .9	.27 Wiley wins	0.2	.054	0.8	.216
		Maier wins .1	.03				
	Davis wins .7	Maier wins .6	.42				
			.45 Maier wins	1.0	.450	1.0	.450
		Davis wins .4	.28 Davis wins	0.0	.000	0.0	.000
			1.00		.504 for a_1		.666 for a_1

a_2
Vote in
Republican
primary
for Wiley

Wiley wins .7 — Wiley wins .9 — .63 Wiley wins | 0.2 | .126 | 0.8 | .504
                — Maier wins .1 — .07

Davis wins .3 — Maier wins .6 — .18 Maier wins | 1.0 | .250 | 1.0 | .250
              — Davis wins .4 — .12 Davis wins | 0.0 | .000 | 0.0 | .000
                                1.00 | .376 for a_2 | *.754 for a_2

a_3
Vote in
Republican
primary
for Davis

Wiley wins .1 — Wiley wins .9 — .09 Wiley wins | 0.2 | .002 | 0.8 | .072
                — Maier wins .1 — .01

Davis wins .9 — Maier wins .6 — .54 Maier wins | 1.0 | .550 | 1.0 | .550
              — Davis wins .4 — .36 Davis wins | 0.0 | .000 | 0.0 | .000
                                1.00 | *.552 for a_3 | .622 for a_3

*Action with highest expected utility for category of voter.

The results in column 4 are several outcomes: O_1 (Wiley wins), O_2 (Maier wins), and O_3 (Davis wins). These are calculated by multiplying the probabilities along each path from a_i to the three possible outcomes associated with it. For example, along the top path $(0.3)(0.9) = .27$. Notice that, for each a_i, there is some probability for each outcome, O_i, and the sum of the probabilities for the outcomes is 1. For example, for a_1, $p_1(O_1) = .27$, $p_1(O_2) = .45$, and $p_1(O_3) = .28$ and $.27 + .45 + .28 = 1.0$.

It is not enough, however, to know the varying probabilities. Action a_3 gives the highest probability of d winning:

Probability of O_2 (Maier wins)	
a_1 (vote in Democratic primary)	.45
a_2 (vote for Wiley)	.25
a_3 (vote for Davis)	.55

Still, this action may not lead to the highest satisfaction. In order to estimate the anticipated satisfaction from the choice of an alternative action, one can multiply the probability of an outcome, given some action, a_i, times the value or cardinal utility ascribed to it by the Von Neumann–Morgenstern experiment, as previously imagined. Summing the result for all O_i for a particular a_i gives its expected utility.[10] Thus, *expected utility* is the measure of the satisfaction one anticipates from an action before one takes it, given, of course, all the assumptions one makes about the probable effects of the action on the occurrence of alternative outcomes.

The usefulness of the notion of expected utility is simply that one can calculate the expected utility of alternative actions and then select the action that provides the highest expected utility. In the instant example, the expected utilities of the several actions for activist and ordinary Democrats are easy to compare (the asterisks indicate the largest utility in the column):

Action	Expected utility	
	For activist Democrats	For ordinary Democrats
a_1	.504	.666
a_2	.376	.754*
a_3	.552*	.622

Clearly, neither should in this example choose the "naive" strategy of voting for Maier, the first choice. Activists should choose a_3, voting strategically for r_2 (Davis); ordinary Democrats should choose a_2, voting strategically for r_1 (Wiley). These are, of course, relatively easy and straightforward strategic choices, and a large but indeterminate number of Democrats did in fact vote strategically.

In Union Elections

There are instances of highly complicated strategic voting by select groups of voters. One such example, analyzed by Howard Rosenthal, involves voting by proportional representation in union elections in France.[11] Strategic voting is possible—and perhaps frequent—in all systems of proportional representation. A voter may truly order the parties or candidates x_i, $i = 1, \ldots, n$, like this, $x_j P x_k P x_h$, but still vote for x_k rather than for x_j because, for example, of a belief that x_k will be more likely to enter a governing coalition. The strategy used by union "militants" is, however, much more complex and is designed to discomfit the leaders of opposing unions. Rosenthal cites evidence that this strategy and a defense against it are used in a number of French labor unions.

Voting is for lists, offered by competing unions, for membership on committees in firms. Each union may offer a list, with names ordered as its leaders choose (typically with the most important leaders highest), of as many candidates as there are seats on the committee, though to apply the strategy here discussed the union must offer more candidates than it expects to win. Even small unions often offer a full list, presumably to demonstrate their legitimacy. Each voter can vote for one list, although voters can strike out names on it, thereby losing votes. The votes for a candidate are the number of votes for the list less the number of times the candidate's name is stricken. The votes for the list are the average of the votes for its candidates. Seats are then assigned to unions by the highest-average method (see Chapter 2, note 2), the first seat assigned to a union being in turn assigned to the candidate on its list with the most votes.

If leaders of union A anticipate some "wasted votes"—that is, if they expect to win k seats whether they get v or $v - \epsilon$ votes—, then they can have a few of A's militants vote for union B's list, striking out as many of the top names on B's list as A's leaders expect B to elect. Assuming the members of union B vote sincerely for the entire B list, A's militants will thus have reduced the vote for B's main leaders, thereby electing presumably less effective spokespersons for B. But the leaders of union B have a defense: They can arrange for B's militants to strike out all but the top names on B's list, those whom B's leaders hope to elect. If the militants of both unions vote strategically, then that union succeeds which has the greatest absolute number of militants engaged in the strategy.

This seems to me a remarkable instance of strategic voting, requiring a high degree of both information and discipline. That it occurs as frequently as it apparently does is strong evidence that strategic voting is widespread.

In the U.S. House of Representatives

Since the three foregoing examples of strategic voting do not display the process in complete detail, I will conclude with an example from the U.S. House of Representatives, where it is easy to see the motives for and the complexity of strategic voting and where many observers were convinced that some members gained a lot by voting contrary to their true and well-known tastes.[12]

This example involves a bill in 1956 to authorize grants to help school districts with construction costs. Because schools were then becoming overcrowded with the children of the post war baby boom, there was an obvious argument for this bill, especially since it involved only construction, not maintenance, and thus partially avoided the divisive issue of funds for sectarian schools, an issue that had stymied federal aid to education for the previous eight years. Consequently, there was probably a substantial majority in favor of the authorization, even though it meant a sharp break from the tradition of local financing. Nevertheless, the question was complicated because school desegregation also entered in. An amendment, offered by Adam Clayton Powell, a black representative from Harlem, provided that grants could be given only to states with schools "open to all children without regard to race in conformity with requirements of the United States Supreme Court decisions"—a reference to the 1954 decision in *Brown* vs. *Board of Education,* holding racially segregated schools unconstitutional.

There were, thus, three alternatives before the House:

a. The bill as amended by Powell's amendment

b. The original unamended bill

c. The status quo—that is, no action

With three alternatives instead of just two (that is, instead of just alternatives *b* and *c*), some who favored the status quo were able to vote strategically to generate a cycle. And, under the non-neutral amendment procedure, if a cycle exists, the status quo wins.

Since there were only two roll calls on the three alternatives, there is not enough information to specify complete preference orderings. But there is enough data from other roll calls in 1956 and 1957 and from the debate to show that some people probably voted strategically and that there were enough of them to generate a cycle.

The two roll calls were (1) a vote on the Powell amendment, which passed, and (2) a vote on final passage of the bill, which failed. These votes can be summarized as in Display 6-4.[13]

From the data, it is easy to calculate the social choices for alternative a vs. alternative b and for alternative a vs. alternative c. The vote on the Powell amendment pits a against b so that yea means a vote that $C(a, b) = a$, while nay means a vote that $C(a, b) = b$. Since the yeas won, $C(a, b) = a$ (by 229 to 197).

Similarly, the vote on final passage pits a against c so that yea is a vote that $C(a, c) = a$, and nay is a vote that $C(a, c) = c$. Since the nays won, $C(a, c) = c$ (by 227 to 199).

To establish the choice between b and c, we can infer, first of all, that those who voted yea on final passage preferred b to c. There are three ways that a (the amended bill) stands ahead of c (the status quo):

$a \, b \, c$ and $b \, a \, c$: These orderings mean that school aid, with or without the Powell amendment, is preferred to no aid.

$a \, c \, b$: This ordering means that school aid is preferred to the status quo only if the Powell amendment is attached.

Display 6-4

Voting on Aid to Education

	Final passage		
	Yea	Nay	Total
Powell Amendment			
Yea	132	97	229
Nay	67	130	197
Total	199	227	426

Nothing in the ideological circumstance of 1956 rendered the latter ordering likely, especially since the Powell amendment won. So I conclude that the 199 who voted for final passage had either $a\,b\,c$ or $b\,a\,c$ and thus all preferred b to c. In addition, some members, mostly Southern Democrats, almost certainly ordered $b\,c\,a$, which means that they wanted school aid with desegregation but would forgo the aid if desegregation were required. Eighteen Democrats—15 from the South and border—who voted against final passage of the bill with the Powell amendment and who were still in the House in 1957 when another school construction bill without the Powell amendment came up—voted in 1957 in support of school construction. Hence, it appears that at least 18 of those who voted for c against a nevertheless preferred b to c. So I conclude that, since 199 had $a\,b\,a$ or $b\,a\,c$ and at least 18 had $b\,c\,a$, $C(b, c) = b$ (by an imputed vote of 217 to 209). This leads to a cycle: a beats b, b beats c, and c beats a.

Although one cannot know for sure the motives or true tastes of the 97 members (all Republicans) who voted yea on Powell and nay on final passage, a substantial amount of evidence indicates that they voted strategically. Certainly the Democratic leadership believed they did. Representative Bolling of Missouri read into the *Congressional Record* a message from former President Truman:

> *The Powell amendment raises some very difficult questions. I have no doubt that it was put forward in good faith to protect the rights of our citizens. However, it has been seized upon by the House Republican leadership, which has always been opposed to Federal aid to education, as a means of defeating Federal aid and gaining political advantage at the same time. I think it would be most unfortunate if the Congress should fall into the trap which the Republican leadership has thus set. This is what would happen if the House were to adopt the Powell amendment. The result would be that no Federal legislation would be passed at all, and the loser would be our children of every race and creed in every State in the Union.[14]*

Truman is suggesting that there are four positions on the subject:

1. Pro school aid: Mostly Northern Democrats and some Republicans who recognize that passage of the Powell amendment would alienate Southern supporters of the bill, which will thus fail. Consequently, this group, even though it might ideologically prefer a to b, orders the bill ahead of the Powell amendment, $b\,a\,c$, because it wants the bill.

2. Pro Powell amendment: Mostly Northern urban Democrats with a substantial number of blacks in their districts, who, though favoring school aid, clearly favor a more than anything else. This group orders $a\,b\,c$.

3. Segregationist Democrats, mostly Southern, who would like school aid but will reject it if it entails desegregation. This group orders *b c a*.

4. Anti–school aid Republicans, whose ordering is *c a b* if they oppose segregation, *c b a* if they favor segregation.

Truman's assertion is that the true position of members in category 4 is *c b a*, but they are pretending to hold *c a b* in order to defeat the bill. He assumes that, if members in 4 voted the tastes he has imputed to them, the process would go like this:

Step 1: *a* vs. *b*; *b* wins with 1 (*b a c*), 3 (*b c a*), and 4 (*c b a*)

Step 2: *b* vs. *c*; *b* wins with 1 (*b a c*), 2 (*a b c*), and 3 (*b c a*)

However, since people in group 4 are going to vote strategically, the process will actually go like this:

Step 1: *a* vs. *b*; *a* wins with 2 (*a b c*) and 4 (*c a b*, which Truman believes is strategic)

Step 2: *a* vs. *c*; *c* wins with 3 (*b c a*) and 4 (*c a b* or *c b a*)

Just because Truman and Bolling—intense partisans—attribute tastes to their enemies, it does not follow that the attribution is correct. Conceivably, every one of the 97 Republicans believed in the order *c a b*, in which case they were unfairly maligned by Truman because they voted according to their true values. If so, the cycle, which clearly existed, was entirely accidental and owed nothing to strategic voting. There is some support for this interpretation because Republicans had, in an earlier tradition, supported blacks' aspirations more than had Democrats, and in 1956 President Eisenhower was attempting to revive that tradition. On the other hand, there is some evidence this cycle was contrived:

Item: Several members in category 4 gave speeches favoring both integration and school aid, which implies either *a b c* (like group 2) or *b a c* (like group 1). Yet they actually voted for *c* against *a*. This suggests that they were influenced to vote as part of a unified maneuver.

Item: At least 12 members in category 4 soon afterward voted against various civil rights provisions of other bills, which suggests that their true opinions were, as Truman believed, *c b a*.

That some strategic voting occurred seems extremely likely. Whether it was enough to generate the cycle, we cannot know. Only 32 of the 97 had to vote strategically to contrive the cycle, however, and I think it likely that at least 32 did so.

6.D. The Consequences of Strategic Voting

Strategic voting, if successful produces an outcome different from the "true amalgamation," however defined, of the values of the members of the group.[15] Of course, just what the "true amalgamation" is depends, as was shown in Chapter 4, on the voting system in use. But, given an agreed-upon constitution for voting, there is some specific outcome produced by voting in accord with one's true tastes. That specific outcome—the "true amalgamation"—is precisely what strategic voting displaces.

Whether this displacement is good, bad, or indifferent depends on one's standards. For example, in the election of 1912 (see section 4.D), if Taft voters had voted strategically, Roosevelt, who was, possibly, the social choice by both the Condorcet criterion and the Borda method, would have been elected. If one believes those methods better than plurality voting, then strategic voting would have produced a social gain; still the Wilson supporters and the Taft supporters, who did *not* vote strategically, probably would not have thought so. In the case of the Powell amendment, construction would probably have been authorized in the absence of strategic voting. That would have been a social gain for the majority that wanted new schools more than anything else, including of course, those who would have used the schools to deny civil rights. On the other hand, it would have been a social loss for the majority that opposed federal invasion of school financing or did not want to perpetuate racism in schools. It is hard to say whether one majority is "better" than another.

In general I see no way to evaluate the consequences of strategic voting. In majority decisions between pairs of alternatives, strategic voting (given perfect information) leads to the selection of the Condorcet winner—if one exists—or of some alternative in the top cycle. Sincere voting in this procedure, however, may lead to a less-desired choice.[16] But this is just one procedure; in others—for example, positional methods—sincere voting may lead to "better" results. All we know in general is that the outcome of strategic voting differs from the outcome of sincere voting.[17]

6.E. Vote-trading

The most extreme version of strategic voting is vote-trading, which is coordinated strategic voting on two or more issues. Like strategic voting by individuals or ideologically unified groups, vote-trading requires that traders vote contrary to their true tastes on some issues. That is, when trading on motions x and y, person 1 votes sincerely on x and strategically on y while person 2 votes strategically on x and sincerely on y. Like strategic voting also, vote-trading can improve the outcome for individuals and possibly for a majority as well. And finally, again like strategic voting, vote-trading can also produce the worst possible outcome, wherein each trader—and everybody else—is worse off.

It is not always possible to trade votes, as I have already pointed out. For example, if the same absolute majority passes two motions, no trade is available. For a trade to occur, there must be, for two voters (or groups of voters) and two issues, a situation in which person (or group) 1 is

Pivotal on the winning side on issue x (pivotal in the sense that, by changing sides, person 1 changes the outcome on x)

On the losing side on issue y and more interested in obtaining his or her (or their) preferred outcome on issue y than on issue x

and conversely for person (or group) 2. When these conditions are met, person 1 can change sides on x and thus help person 2 get what he or she (or the group) most wants and person 2 can change sides on y and thus help person 1 get what he or she (or the group) most wants. Both persons (or groups) will then be better off. These conditions are, however, restrictive, so trading is not always possible.

When vote-trading can occur, it vastly expands the possibilities of strategic voting. On a motion, x, there are exactly two positions: (1) support, which will be written x, and (2) opposition, or "not x," which will be written $\bar{x}$. Under simple majority voting on a pair of alternatives, x and $\bar{x}$, the choice between the alternatives is ambiguous only in case of a tie. If either x or $\bar{x}$ wins, that choice cannot be upset by strategic voting simply because one is better for a majority than the other. But if another motion, y, with possible choices, y and $\bar{y}$, is joined with the consideration of x, there are four possible choices: $x\,y$, $x\,\bar{y}$, $\bar{x}\,y$, and $\bar{x}\,\bar{y}$. And with four alternatives strategic voting is, of course, possible.

Let us introduce a notation and assume simple majority voting:

$q_x = C(x, \bar{x})$, so q is the choice between passing and defeating x, assuming sincere voting.

$Q^* = q_1, q_2, \ldots, q_m$, for m motions, so Q^* is the social choice from sincere voting on each motion separately.

$Q = C(x y \ldots, x \bar{y} \ldots, \ldots, \bar{x} y \ldots, \ldots, \bar{x} \bar{y} \ldots)$ for m motions, so Q is the social choice among passing all, passing some and defeating others, and defeating all.

One can then point out that, although q is stable in the sense that it cannot be overturned by strategic voting, Q^* may not be the same as Q because of vote-trading and Q is not stable because it may be overturned by vote-trading. Of course, Q is most obviously unstable if the relation, P, of *social* preference is cyclic—if, that is, $xy\, P\, \bar{x}y\, P\, x\bar{y}\, P\, \bar{x}\bar{y}\, P\, xy$.[18] But Q is also, in a limited way, unstable, even if Q is a Condorcet winner.

Consider, first, a cyclic situation, with three voters and two motions, as in Display 6-5. Clearly, if voters vote sincerely, $C(x, \bar{x}) = \bar{x}$ (because voters 2 and 3 prefer $\bar{x}$) and $C(y, \bar{y}) = \bar{y}$ (because voters 1 and 3 prefer $\bar{y}$) and q_x and q_y are individually stable. Hence $Q^* = \bar{x}\bar{y}$, but Q^* need not be the social choice because Q is unstable in the cycle: $xy\, P\, \bar{x}\bar{y}\, P\, \bar{x}y\, P\, x\bar{y}\, P\, xy$. Indeed $C(xy, x\bar{y}, \bar{x}y, \bar{x}\bar{y}) = (xy, x\bar{y}, \bar{x}y, \bar{x}\bar{y}) = Q$, which means that the outcome may be *any* of the possible ones. Voters 1 and 2 can trade, so each gets his second best, xy. (That is, 1 votes sincerely for x and strategically for y, while 2 votes strategically for x and sincerely for y.) But voter 3 can perhaps upset this outcome, which she most dislikes, by trading with 2. If 2 agrees to abandon his trade with 1, to continue to vote sincerely for y, and to change his strategic vote for x to a sincere vote for $\bar{x}$, then 3 can vote sincerely for $\bar{x}$ and strategically for y, thus producing $Q = \bar{x}y$, which both like better than $Q = xy$. And so on around the cycle. What outcome will eventually occur is just a matter of where trading happens to stop. So anything can happen and Q is wholly unstable.

It is a remarkable fact that Q is unstable even if there is no cycle. In an example in Display 6-6, adapted from Thomas Schwartz, under sincere voting $Q^* = \bar{x}\bar{y}$ and furthermore $\bar{x}\bar{y}\, P\, x\bar{y}\, P\, \bar{x}y\, P\, xy$ so there is no cycle.[19] But Q may be unstable. Voters 1 and 3 may trade in an attempt to produce $Q = xy$. That is, 1 promises to vote sincerely for x and strategically for y while 3 promises to vote strategically for x and sincerely for y. Assuming 2 votes sincerely for x and 4 votes sincerely for y, then the outcome is $Q = xy$ (because 1, 2, and 3 voted for x and 1, 3, and 4 voted for y). Of course this can be upset by a trade of 2 and 4 to return to $Q = \bar{x}\bar{y}$, which both prefer to xy (that is, 2, 4, and 5 vote for $\bar{x}$ and $\bar{y}$).

Display 6-5

A Cyclic Situation for Vote-Trading

In each column is the ordinal ordering for that voter of outcomes on x and y. The most highly valued outcome is at the top of the column, the least highly valued at the bottom.

Voter 1	Voter 2	Voter 3
$x\bar{y}$	$\bar{x}y$	$\bar{x}\bar{y}$
xy	xy	$\bar{x}y$
$\bar{x}\bar{y}$	$\bar{x}\bar{y}$	$x\bar{y}$
$\bar{x}y$	$x\bar{y}$	xy

By sincere voting, the outcome is $\bar{x}\bar{y}$ because voters 2 and 3 vote for $\bar{x}$ and voters 1 and 3 vote for $\bar{y}$. Since $\bar{x}\bar{y}$ is less preferred than xy by 1 and 2, they can agree to vote for x (strategically for 2) and y (strategically for 1) to produce xy.

Display 6-6

The Instability of Vote-Trading Even with a Condorcet Winner

Voter 1	Voter 2	Voter 3	Voter 4	Voter 5
$x\bar{y}$	$x\bar{y}$	$\bar{x}y$	$\bar{x}y$	$\bar{x}\bar{y}$
xy	$\bar{x}\bar{y}$	xy	$\bar{x}\bar{y}$	$x\bar{y}$
$\bar{x}\bar{y}$	xy	$\bar{x}\bar{y}$	xy	$\bar{x}y$
$\bar{x}y$	$\bar{x}y$	$x\bar{y}$	$x\bar{y}$	xy

The Condorcet winner is $\bar{x}$ (by 3, 4, and 5) and $\bar{y}$ (by 1, 3, and 4). But 1 and 3, both of whom prefer xy to $\bar{x}\bar{y}$, may trade to produce xy.

Depending on where the trading stops, the Condorcet winner may lose. In general, however, if there is a Condorcet winner in $(xy, x\bar{y}, \bar{x}y, \bar{x}\bar{y})$, and if voters have perfect information, then members of the majority supporting the Condorcet winner in Q can, by individual *sophisticated voting* (that is, by voting in anticipation of votes and trades by others) force the choice of the Condorcet winner.[20] And, of course, that same majority can also enforce the Condorcet winner by a coalition. Still, if information is imperfect and trading is costly, it may be hard for the majority to counter minority trades. And if so, even the Condorcet winner may be strategically upset.

Even demand-revealing voting, which was invented to render strategic voting impossible by individuals, is subject to manipulation by coalitions in a way comparable to vote-trading.[21] (See Chapter 3, note 18.) Since votes are cast in terms of money, vote-trading is by exchange of money. An example is set forth in Display 6-7, where voter 1, for example, can conspire with voter 3 to upset the "honestly revealed" victory for y.[22] The method is intended to prevent this because each voter is supposedly motivated by the tax to vote his or her true tastes. If voter 1, for example, increases his reported valuation of x to $7 to make x win, his tax would be $5 or his marginal contribution to victory for x. (That is, z, the winner without 1's vote, is valued by others at $5 and x is valued by others at zero. To make x win, voter 1 must bid more than $5. Hence the tax is $5 − 0 = $5, or 1's marginal contribution.) Since $5 is all that x is worth to 1, it is apparently pointless for him to exaggerate his valuation of x. So, with truthful valuation, each voter gets a net value of $1 from the choice of y, as in Part A of the Display.

But if x were to win, voter 1 could make $5, part of which he would use to bribe voter 3, say, to make x win. Thus it is not pointless to trade votes. If voter 1 gives voter 3 a bribe of $2.50 to report a valuation of, say, $4 for x (which eliminates the tax), then x wins, each makes $2.50 by vote-trading, and both are indeed better off. Other coalitions are possible (for example, to make z win), but it is always possible for at least two voters to be better off from the choice of x or z than from the choice of the "true" winner, y.

In this example, vote-trading makes a majority better off. This is, however, an unusual (even bizarre) method of voting, and the improvement may be untypical of ordinary methods. Nevertheless, under ordinary procedures, vote-trading can sometimes improve outcomes for a majority. Schwartz offers a good example, which is set forth in Display 6-8.[23]

Without trading, voters 1 and 3 choose $\bar{x}$ and voters 1 and 2 choose $\bar{y}$, so $Q^* = \bar{x}\bar{y}$. Yet $Q = xy$ is the Condorcet winner (preferred by 2 and 3 to Q^*) and the social order is transitive: xy P $\bar{x}\bar{y}$ P $\bar{x}y$ P $x\bar{y}$. The Condorcet winner cannot be reached by sincere voting; but, if voters 2 and 3 trade (with 2 voting strategically [yea] on y and 3 strategically [yea] on x), then both x and y pass and a majority is clearly better off.

On the other hand, vote-trading can produce outcomes that are universally undesirable—outcomes, indeed, that everyone is strongly motivated to reach but that make everyone worse off than sincere voting. This occurs when issues are voted on serially and when the costs for losers are large—a common situation in most legislatures. The root of this disaster is that vote-trading imposes an external cost on nontraders.

If we think of an external cost as the cost a person suffers through no action of his or her own (like the cost to the pedestrian who suffers from auto exhaust), then the nontrading voter (who is changed from a winner to a loser by others' trading) innocently suffers a cost externally imposed. Conceivably the gains a member makes on trades might outweigh any external costs. But just as conceivably, the sum of the external costs may exceed the gains from trade. If that happens to everybody, then everybody is worse off from trading.

This kind of outcome seems especially characteristic of contemporary legislatures, which so often spend more than they tax, thereby generating inflation that hurts everybody. They do so because by vote-trading they create small benefits such as subsidies, public works, and fixed prices; yet the inflation that the excess cost of all these benefits creates is suffered by everybody.

Steven Brams and I have worked out a highly simplified example of such self-destructive trading, using cardinal utilities, three voters ($i = 1, 2, 3$), and three pairs of issues (x and y, w and z, and t and v) that are voted on serially so that trades made on prior issues cannot be undone at the time of later trades. A different member is left out of the trading on each pair of issues. The detail is set forth in Display 6-9.[24] Considering just motions x and y, $Q^* = xy$ and the sum of the utilities for each voter, U_i, from sincere voting will be:

$$U_1(x, y) = 1 + 1 \quad\ = 2$$

$$U_2(x, y) = 1 + (-2) = -1$$

$$U_3(x, y) = (-2) + 1 = -1$$

Display 6-7

Strategic Manipulation with Demand-Revealing Voting

A. Truthful Voting (Without Vote-Trading)

Voters	Valuation of alternatives			Other voters	Sum of valuations without i's valuation			Tax* on i	Net benefit from choice of y (Valuation less tax)
	x	y	z		x	y	z		
$i = 1$	$5	2	0	2, 3	$0	4	5	$1	$2 - 1 = $1
$i = 2$	0	2	0	1, 3	5	4	5	1	2 - 1 = 1
$i = 3$	0	2	5	1, 2	5	4	0	1	2 - 1 = 1
Sum	$5	6	5						

Note. Alternative y wins.

*The tax is i's marginal contribution to making the winning alternative (here y) at least tie with any other. Thus, without voter 1, z wins. So 1 pays a tax of [(valuation of z without 1's valuation) less (valuation of y without 1's valuation)] or $5 - 4 = $1.

B. Strategic Voting (with Vote-Trading)

Voters	Valuation of alternatives (False by voter 3)			Other voters	Sum of valuations without i's valuation			Tax** on i	True benefit from choice of x	Bribe by voter 1	Net benefit
	x	y	z		x	y	z				
$i=1$	$5	2	0	2, 3	$4	4	4	0	$5	$-2.50	$2.50
$i=2$	0	2	0	1, 3	9	4	4	0	0	0	0
$i=3$	4	2	4	1, 2	5	4	0	0	0	+2.50	2.50
Sum	$9	6	4								

Note. Alternative x wins.

**Voter 1 is not assessed a tax because, without 1's valuation, x and z tie. Voters 2 and 3 are not assessed because x wins without 2's or 3's valuation.

Display 6-8

Vote-Trading Improves the Outcome for a Majority

Voter 1	Voter 2	Voter 3
$\bar{x}\bar{y}$	$x\bar{y}$	$\bar{x}y$
xy	xy	xy
$\bar{x}y$	$\bar{x}\bar{y}$	$\bar{x}\bar{y}$
$x\bar{y}$	$\bar{x}y$	$x\bar{y}$

Without trading, $\bar{x}\bar{y}$ wins. If 2 and 3 trade, xy wins and xy is better than $\bar{x}\bar{y}$ for both 2 and 3.

Of course, 2 and 3 can trade, 2 voting (strategically) for $\bar{x}$ and (sincerely) for $\bar{y}$ and 3 voting (sincerely) for $\bar{x}$ and (strategically) for $\bar{y}$. Then $Q = \bar{x}\bar{y}$ and the sum of the utilities will be:

$$U_1(\bar{x}\bar{y}) = (-2) + (-2) = -4$$

$$U_2(\bar{x}\bar{y}) = 2 + (-1) \quad = 1$$

$$U_3(\bar{x}\bar{y}) = 2 + (-1) \quad = 1$$

Thus, 2 and 3 have a net gain of two units and 1 a net loss of six units. Considering just this pair, x and y, voters 2 and 3 have a powerful motive to trade and so presumably they do so. As x and y are settled and voters go on to w and z, voters 1 and 2 now trade and 3 suffers an external cost. So also with t and v: 1 and 3 trade and 2 suffers. The net effect of all the trading is as follows:

	Outcomes			
Voters	$\bar{x}\bar{y}$	$\bar{w}\bar{z}$	$\tilde{t}\tilde{v}$	Total
1	-4	$+1$	$+1$	-2
2	$+1$	$+1$	-4	-2
3	$+1$	-4	$+1$	-2

Display 6-9

The Paradox of Vote-Trading:
Cardinal Utilities for Outcomes on Motions

Voters	Preferred outcome	Cardinal utility Motion wins	Cardinal utility Motion loses	Preferred outcome	Cardinal utility Motion wins	Cardinal utility Motion loses
		Motion x			Motion y	
1*	x	1	-2	y	1	-2
2	x	1	-1	$\bar{y}$	-2	2
3	$\bar{x}$	-2	2	y	1	-1
		Motion w			Motion z	
1	w	1	-1	$\bar{z}$	-2	2
2	$\bar{w}$	-2	2	z	1	-1
3*	w	1	-2	z	1	-2
		Motion t			Motion v	
1	$\bar{t}$	-2	2	v	1	-1
2*	t	1	-2	v	1	-2
3	t	1	-1	$\bar{v}$	-2	2

*Nontrader on the pair of motions.

Had these voters been able to foresee the sorry consequences, they would perhaps have exercised greater self-control, avoided trading, and produced:

Voters	Outcomes xy	wz	tv	Total
1	$+2$	-1	-1	0
2	-1	-1	$+2$	0
3	-1	$+2$	-1	0

They would all have been better off with sincere voting than with strategic voting. But, given that these are serial events, voters would not dare pass up a possible trade. Suppose a voter, trying for the sincere outcome, refused to trade. Then 1, for example, would refuse trades on w and z and t and v. If 2 and 3 trade on x and y, however, the result is

| Voters | Outcomes | | | |
	$\bar{x}\bar{y}$	wz	tv	Total
1	-4	-1	-1	-6
2	$+1$	-1	$+2$	$+2$
3	$+1$	$+2$	-1	$+2$

So 1 would be worse off for not trading, when others traded, than if he too had traded at every chance. Hence 1 has a strong motive to trade, even though he knows it will hurt. Of course, 1 might persuade others to agree not to trade; but, as in any cartel, agreement is difficult to enforce because great advantages accrue to those who break the agreement. Since the positions of the players are identical over the three pairs of issues, universal trading is to be expected, *even though everyone knows it will make everyone worse off.*

There is, of course, one way to avoid this devastating outcome. Some pair, say 2 and 3, can form a coalition to trade when they can with each other and vote sincerely otherwise. Then the members of the pair each gain two units and the outsider loses six. Coalitions of this sort are possible if the voters have perfect information about utilities and about the actual issues that will arise, and if the costs of organization are less than the possible net gains.[25] But in the real world of legislatures, future issues are unknown and, even if guessed at, the payoff to other members on these potential future issues is doubtless obscure. Hence when members trade on x and y, they may not know that w and z will arise. Moreover, in legislatures of more than a few members, party discipline—that is, coalitional cohesion—over time is difficult and expensive to maintain. In decentralized governments like the United States it is impossible. Since members of a coalition (party) depend for reelection almost entirely on people in their home districts rather than on other members of the legislature, leaders of a legislative coalition can neither reward nor punish its members. Hence while people may not hurt themselves by vote-trading in the small-group laboratory, they are quite likely to do so in the real world.

To summarize the discussion of vote-trading, I want to make these observations:

1. Vote-trading enormously expands the potential for strategic voting in legislatures.

2. One manner in which vote-trading works is by generating cyclic situations where none existed before.

3. Vote-trading is also possible regardless of whether Q is a Condorcet winner; vote-trading may even produce another outcome when there is a Condorcet winner, although with perfect information and costless trading the Condorcet winner can always be chosen.

4. Cases exist in which vote-trading improves Q for a minority and even for a majority. Possibly more frequently in the real world, cases also exist in which vote-trading makes more people worse off than are made better off. And there are doubtless occasions in which vote-trading makes *everybody worse off.*

6.F. The Ineradicability of Strategic Voting

Strategic voting is an ineradicable possibility in all voting systems. It is not possible for me to estimate how frequently chances to vote strategically occur; but I am sure they are frequent in popular elections and, by reason of vote-trading, almost always present in legislatures. And even if parties are disciplined in order to prevent vote-trading, still vote-trading doubtless occurs inside cabinets and committees.

The factual question of whether people take advantage of these opportunities is difficult to answer. To identify strategic voting requires that we know both the voter's true values and the voter's actual expression of the values in a vote. From direct observation we can know only the latter. We must infer the former from other and softer evidence. Nevertheless, considering the real-world examples I have offered, it does seem likely that strategic voting occurs quite frequently.

If it does, I conclude that the meaning of social choices is quite obscure. They may consist of the amalgamation of the true tastes of the majority (however "majority" and "amalgamation" are defined), or they may consist simply of the tastes of some people (whether a majority or not) who are skillful or lucky manipulators. If we assume social choices are often the latter, they may consist of what the manipulators truly want, or they may be an accidental amalgamation of what the manipulators (perhaps unintentionally) happened to produce. Furthermore, since we can by observation know only expressed values (never true values), we can never be sure, for any particular social choice, which of these possible interpretations is correct.

Many philosophers, partially aware of these difficulties, have argued that strategic voting and vote-trading ought to be prohibited. This is shortsighted, of course, because sometimes strategic voting reveals Condorcet winners that would otherwise lose.[26] But since strategic voting does often produce "worse" situations, it is frequently condemned. When it was pointed out to Borda that strategic voting could distort outcomes, he replied, "My scheme is intended only for honest men."[27] Unfortunately, we have no test for honesty. If a man *tells* me his vote reflects his true tastes, how can I prove he perjures himself?

Dodgson (Lewis Carroll) had a clearer view than Borda. Seeing that strategic voting "makes an election more a game of skill than a real test of the wishes of electors," his solution was that "all should know the rules by which this game may be won."[28] Thereby he displayed the correct belief that strategic voting *cannot* be eliminated. What he did not recognize, but what we now know, is that strategic voting renders the meaning of *all* social choices obscure. I emphasize *all* because we never can know, on any particular outcome, how much or what kind of strategic voting occurred.

7

The Manipulation of
Social Choices:
Control of the Agenda

Strategic voting is usually unobservable, and its incidence is therefore not calculable. In contrast, agenda control, another kind of manipulation, is often obvious, and its incidence can in principle be estimated. This incidence is surely very high, for the consequences of agenda control are apparent in some degree in the content of almost all social choice. The significance, variety, and pervasiveness of agenda control are partially revealed simply by a categorization of the kinds of controls exercised. One category is control by formal leaders.

In any organized decision-making body, committee, legislature, or whole government, one function of leaders is to guide the operation of the body. For a body as ad hoc as a jury, the judge instructs, setting limits to the agenda; for a committee, a chairperson or agenda committee guides the order of business; for a legislature, partial control resides in chairpersons (speakers), party and coalition leaders, agenda committees (such as rules committees), executives (premiers and presidents) who propose bills; and so on for nations, corporations, universities, and other bodies. Despite institutional variations, the leaders in every such body must select alternatives among which decisions will be made, and they must select the procedures for coming to a choice. Typically, of course, leaders work within customs, constitutions, and other constraints; typically, also, they have some freedom of choice.

Often leaders are constrained by procedures that allow the whole body itself to change leaders' selections. This means, simply, that in voting bodies there is a way for backbenchers to seize control and become leaders themselves. Thus, party leaders may endorse candidates, but the final decision on nominations is made in primary elections or conventions. A chairperson may rule on whether a motion is in order, but the ruling is often subject to appeal to the floor.

Despite these restrictions, however, leaders' control of agenda is ordinarily not challenged. One reason is that most bodies have customary
criteria of fairness, and most leaders abide by them. For example, they
accept for consideration alternatives they oppose when it is apparent some
members are in favor of them. They use customary routines, bending
them perhaps, but seldom devising new routines blatantly designed to get
their own way. In the absence of extreme "unfairness," therefore, leaders'
control is seldom challenged. But there is a subtler reason for this lack of
conflict: To challenge leaders on agenda and procedures is to challenge
their leadership itself. So, unless there is an intent to dethrone or displace
them, leaders usually have some, though constrained, control of the content of the set, X, of alternatives and of the process by which a choice is
made from it.

Thus one category of methods of agenda control is defined in terms
of leaders' opportunities to dominate. There is another category, however,
that admits control by ordinary members: They can generate new alternatives. Leaders officially define X, but the definition is in terms of what the
surrounding culture suggests, and ordinary members can determine the
content of that culture. This method of control is, of course, open to
leaders also; but typically it is the method used by nonleaders, mainly
because it is the only one easily open to them. Furthermore, nonleaders
are often losers on recent agenda and so have a compelling motive to
generate a new agenda on which they have a chance, at least, to win.

To summarize: Agenda control consists on the one hand of chosen
leaders actually leading and on the other hand of nonleaders developing
new alternatives. This chapter consists of a brief survey of the infinite
variety subsumed in these two categories.

7.A. The Universality of Agenda Control

If, given a profile of preference, there is some outcome potentially in
a strong equilibrium (in the sense that, for the set Y of all possible alternatives, some alternative is a first-place choice for a majority of voters);
and if voters have enough information to know that such an outcome
could be arrived at, then it is probably difficult to manipulate an agenda.
(Later in this chapter I will sometimes use "equilibrium" in a weaker
sense to mean merely a Condorcet winner from a set, X (which is a subset
of Y) such that this winner, under sincere voting, can beat each other
alternative in X individually, but not all others in X simultaneously.)

Since the conditions for a strong equilibrium are difficult to fulfill, manipulation of the agenda is not usually precluded because of the distribution of tastes. For example, with majority voting, there is often a Condorcet winner without an absolute majority of first-place preferences in $X = (a, b, c)$, as in this profile:

	D
1	a b c
2	b a c
3	c a b

This condition, of course, admits strategic voting. Although I do not know of any way, by individual manipulation, to beat an absolute majority in the static case (where X is fixed) with majority voting, it is easy enough to do so in the dynamic case (where X is not fixed), by vote-trading. One can enlarge X and thereby transform D^1 into D^2:

D^1			D^2		
1	2	3	1	2	3
ab	ab	$\bar{a}b$	abc	$ab\bar{c}$	$\bar{a}bc$
$a\bar{b}$	$\bar{a}b$	$\bar{a}\bar{b}$	$\bar{a}bc$	$ab\bar{c}$	$\bar{a}b\bar{c}$
.	.	.	.	.	.
.	.	.	.	.	.
.	.	.	.	.	.

Although in D^1 ab seems invulnerable, in D^2 persons 2 and 3 can trade to produce $\bar{a}b\bar{c}$. Likewise, in Borda voting even an absolute majority is vulnerable to agenda control, as in profile D,

	D
D_1–D_3:	a b c
D_4, D_5:	b a c

with these point sums: $a = 8, b = 7, c = 0$. Here a wins with 8 points and beats each other alternative in pairwise contests with 3 or 5 points.

If an additional alternative, d, is added to X to make it X', and if D becomes D',

D'	
$D'_1-D'_3$:	$a\ b\ d\ c$
$D'_4,\ D'_5$:	$b\ d\ a\ c$

with these point sums—$a = 11$, $b = 12$, $c = 0$, $d = 7$—then the winner is changed from a to b.

Equilibrium is thus a highly restrictive notion, probably rarely satisfied in nature. Of course, it is satisfied if X has just two members and no additions are allowed, (this is why simple majority voting is attractive). But such an X is usually the result of narrowing down a larger set, Y, not itself in equilibrium. Even if a given profile over a larger Y does have an equilibrium outcome, leaders still can manipulate the agenda to prevent its adoption if voters do not know this outcome exists. This is one reason why ordinary members like, and leaders dislike, straw votes, opinion polls, and test votes. Such trial runs often reveal equilibria, if they exist, and, once revealed, they cannot be prevented. Fortunately for leaders it is often difficult to conduct trial runs, and thus leaders may procure a nonequilibrium outcome simply because voters never discover that an equilibrium potentially existed.

Since, therefore, the conditions that preclude manipulation (that is, equilibrium *and* information about it) are difficult to fulfill, manipulation must usually be possible. Furthermore, it is possible under *any* method of voting. We know that no fair method of voting can satisfy the logical criterion of path independence. This criterion (see section 5.F) is the requirement that, regardless of how alternatives are divided up for a serial decision process, the same choice will result from all possible divisions.[1] Since no nonoligarchic method of voting satisfies this criterion, in any democratic procedure that operates by successive reduction of alternatives manipulation of the agenda is possible simply by choosing one division of alternatives into subsets for selection rather than another division. Furthermore, even for positional methods that operate on the entire set X simultaneously, expansion of the number of alternatives to form X' permits inconsistencies in subset expansion that also violate path independence. Consequently, just as the inability of any fair method of voting to guarantee social acyclicity permits strategic voting, so the inability of any fair method to guarantee path independence permits agenda manipulation. Since manipulation can occur under *any* method of voting and *most* profiles of preference, we can assume that it does occur sometimes.

7.B. Examples of Agenda Control

From the earliest recorded history of voting bodies we know that some kind of manipulation has been standard practice. In the Athenian assembly, choice by lot was often substituted for choice by election because, with nonsecret voting, great men controlled their clients' choices. This crude manipulation was common until the end of the nineteenth century in popular elections and is still the basis of party discipline (as it is euphemistically called) in legislatures.

Much more interesting than mere physical control of the voter is control of the agenda in such a way that voters are constrained to vote as the manipulator wishes. This kind of control, though ancient and universal, is not always easy to observe. So I will here set forth two examples of conscious control of the agenda, one by Pliny the Younger in the Roman Senate, the other by Charles Plott and Michael Levine in a contemporary laboratory.

In the Roman Senate

Pliny the Younger tells of an instance of both kinds of manipulation, and Robin Farquharson used that tale as the continuing example throughout his *Theory of Voting*. Pliny presided over a case in the Roman Senate concerning the fate of the freedmen of a consul found killed in his house. The consul's slaves had already been condemned to death, and traditional law required execution of the freedmen also; but in this case there was reason for leniency because the consul may have been a suicide, or, if he was murdered, the freedmen may have acted from "obedience" rather than from "malice."

There were three factions in the Senate: A, for acquittal, which was a plurality but not a majority; B, for banishment; and C, for condemnation to death. Pliny favored acquittal. If he had put the question in the customary way, pairwise on guilt or innocence, B and C would have voted together, acquittal would have been eliminated, and then, in choice between banishment and death, A and B would have voted together and the ultimate outcome would have been banishment. Pliny foresaw that outcome and chose, therefore, to put the three alternatives simultaneously, requiring each senator to vote for just one, in the hope that A's plurality would result in acquittal. As it happened, the leader of faction C foresaw this consequence and strategically aligned his party with B so that, evidently, banishment prevailed.[2] Thus, the presiding officer's attempt at controlling the agenda was foiled by the strategic voting of an opponent—convincing evidence that knowledge about manipulation is nearly as old as voting bodies themselves.

Pliny did not recognize the frequency of manipulation, partly because the Senate had just been reactivated under Emperor Trajan and partly because no science of politics then existed by which knowledge of such behavior could be systematized. Today it is different. A substantial part of the commentary on legislatures by political scientists concerns techniques for controlling agendas by presiding officers (for example, speakers, of whom the American prototype was Speaker "Czar" Reed, and party leaders and premiers, who preside in fact if not in name), by agenda committees (such as rules committees, cabinets, and even more substantive bill-writing committees), and by extra-legislative bodies that write bills and select topics for legislation (for example, specialized bodies like the Office of Management and Budget in the United States and the Treasury in Great Britain and diffuse bodies like the bureaucracy, parties, and lobbies).

It would be burdensome here to repeat or even summarize that huge literature. It is enough to point out its immediate relevance to this discussion. Nevertheless, I will describe in some detail an experiment on the control of an agenda, which is especially interesting because it throws light on a difficult epistemological question that often arises in reflection on natural events.

In a Contemporary Laboratory

In reflecting on the example from Pliny, it might be argued that banishment would have resulted in any case because it was the Condorcet winner and that the assertion about manipulation is merely *my* attribution of intent based on *my* interpretation of the motion and the voting. A similar difficulty arose in section 6.C, where the observer could not be absolutely certain that the cyclic outcome on school construction was in fact contrived. Since all historical interpretation of manipulation requires an attribution of motives, an attribution that cannot be directly validated, it is always possible to assert that apparent manipulation is the product not of actors' conscious intent, but of observers' overactive imagination. If, however, one can display instances in which experimenters consciously and successfully used different agendas on identical profiles of preference to produce different outcomes, then one has more confidence in historical interpretations. Such an experiment was conducted almost exactly for these reasons by Charles Plott and Michael Levine.[3]

They came to the problem out of a practical interest in influencing the composition of a new fleet of aircraft for a flying club. One of them, who was chairman of the agenda committee, had interests somewhat different from the interests of most members. While nearly everybody wanted a fleet composed basically of moderate-cost (type E) or more expensive (type F) four-seat planes, he wanted in addition a secondary fleet of two (or at least one) moderate-cost six-seat planes (type C) and no type A, an expensive six-seat plane. After carefully estimating the tastes of members based on earlier discussions and questionnaires, Plott and Levine devised an agenda that serially narrowed consideration in such a way that A's were eliminated and C's survived: The chosen fleet was seven planes—five E's and F's and two C's. They believed that their agenda had an influence because a questionnaire subsequently sent to the members at the meeting revealed that the Condorcet winner was a fleet of six E's and F's, and one A.

Nevertheless, in the absence of certain knowledge about the pre-decision profile of preferences, they could not be absolutely assured that they had influenced the outcome. To settle their doubts, they then carried through a data-generating experiment in which they used different agendas for partitioning a set of five (wholly abstract) alternatives, $X = (1, 2, 3, 4, 5)$, for committees with exactly the same induced preferences. The goal of the experiment was to show that they could use four agendas to produce four different social choices from X in four identically motivated human groups. The experiment was successful enough to show fairly conclusively that conscious manipulation could change outcomes.

The agendas consisted of partitioning X into two complementary subsets, S and $\overline{S}$, of partitioning each of these into complementary subsets, etc., until a single alternative was reached. For example, one agenda might be:

Step 1: Choose between {2, 4} and {1, 3, 5}.

Step 2a: If {2, 4} is chosen, choose between {2} and {4}.

Step 2b: If {1, 3, 5} is chosen, choose between {1, 5} and {3}. If step 2a is used or if {3} is chosen at step 2b, the process is complete. Otherwise go on to step 3.

Step 3: If {1, 5} is chosen at step 2b, choose between {1} and {5}.

This agenda and another are depicted schematically in Figure 7-1. Altogether, with five alternatives, 105 distinct partitioning agenda are possible

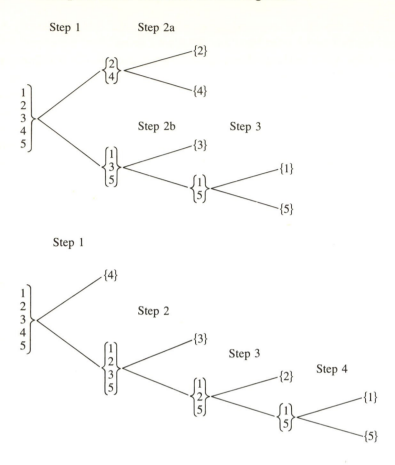

Figure 7-1 Two possible agendas.

(not counting 30 others that could be constructed for the amendment procedure).

Although actual subjects (college students) in each trial were different, the same profile of preferences was induced in each group by the promise of a money payment for the choice of each alternative. For example, person 1 in each group was told to expect

$$\left.\begin{array}{l} \$6.00 \\ \$7.00 \\ \$5.00 \\ \$8.00 \\ \$ \ .50 \end{array}\right\} \text{ if the group chose alternative } \left\{\begin{array}{l} 1 \\ 2 \\ 3 \\ 4 \\ 5 \end{array}\right.$$

Display 7-1

Payoffs in Dollars in the Plott-Levine Experiment

Person	Alternative				
	1	2	3	4	5
1	6.00	7.00	5.00	8.00	.50
2	6.00	7.00	5.00	8.00	.50
3	6.00	7.00	5.00	8.00	.50
4	6.00	7.00	5.00	8.00	.50
5	6.00	7.00	5.00	8.00	.50
6	6.00	7.00	5.00	8.00	.50
7	7.50	7.75	6.75	5.75	.25
8	7.50	7.75	6.75	5.75	.25
9	7.50	7.75	6.75	5.75	.25
10	7.50	7.75	6.75	5.75	.25
11	7.50	7.00	6.00	8.00	.50
12	8.00	7.50	7.00	6.00	.50
13	8.00	7.50	7.00	6.00	.50
14	8.00	7.50	7.00	6.00	.50
15	7.00	5.50	7.50	6.50	.25
16	7.00	5.50	7.50	6.50	.25
17	7.00	5.50	7.50	6.50	.25
18	7.00	5.50	7.50	6.50	.25
19	7.00	5.50	7.50	6.50	.25
20	7.00	5.50	7.50	6.50	.25
21	7.00	5.50	7.50	6.50	.25

Source. Charles Plott and Michael Levine, "A Model of Agenda Influence on Committee Decisions," *American Economic Review,* Vol. 68 (March 1978), pp. 146–160.

The entire schedule of payoffs for the 21 members is set forth in Display 7-1. Assuming each person votes sincerely, in pairwise contests, for the alternative paying more for him or her, the Condorcet winner is alternative 1, which beats 2 by 11 to 10, 3 by 14 to 7, 4 by 14 to 7, and 5 by 21 to 0. Alternatives 2, 3, and 4 cycle because 2 beats 3 by 14 to 7, 3 beats 4 by 14 to 7, and 4 beats 2 by 14 to 7. Alternative 5 always loses.

But, of course, even in pairwise contests, voters can vote strategically; so the Condorcet winner need not really win, unless all voters have perfect information and all use it to vote strategically. In the more complicated serial partitions of Figure 7-1, there is even less likelihood of choosing the Condorcet winner. So the next step in construction of the experiment is to predict the choice under any given agenda (all 105 of them), assuming that each voter knows *only* his or her own payoffs. This prediction requires assumptions about the way voters behave. Plott and Levine suggest three rules of behavior, all of which appeared to be used by some subjects:

> Rule 1: Sincere strategy. Vote for the set, S or $\overline{S}$, that contains the alternative with the highest payoff.
>
> Rule 2: Avoid-the-worst strategy. Vote for the set, S or $\overline{S}$, that does *not* contain the alternative with the lowest payoff.
>
> Rule 3: Highest-expected-value strategy. Vote for the set, S or $\overline{S}$, in which the alternatives have the highest average value.

Notice that these strategies do not necessarily lead to the same action by a voter. For example, if $S = (1, 4, 5)$ and $\overline{S} = (2, 3)$, voter 1 should choose S by rule 1 and $\overline{S}$ by rules 2 and 3. Which of these—and other—strategies are actually used is, of course, an empirical question. So Plott and Levine estimated probabilities, from data gathered in pretesting,

1. That S would be chosen over $\overline{S}$ when all three rules prescribed S or one (or two) prescribed S and the other one (or two) were ambiguous in that it (they) prescribed indifference between S and $\overline{S}$

2. That S would be chosen when one rule prescribed S, another $\overline{S}$, and the third was ambiguous

3. That S would be chosen over $\overline{S}$ when rule 1 prescribed S and 2 and 3 $\overline{S}$

Etc., through all nine possible cases.

Using this empirical data, they calculated, for each agenda, first the probability that S would be chosen over $\overline{S}$ by majority rule and then the probability that some y in X would be finally chosen. This number, $P(y/a)$, the probability y is chosen given a particular agenda, a, they called the "strength of the agenda for y." They then selected four agendas each with unit strength (that is, maximum strength), $P(y/a) = 1$, for $y = 1, 2, 3, 4$. Thus they would, if they succeeded, induce the subjects to choose four different alternatives with four different agendas and identical preference profiles.

The actual experiment was conducted in the following way. On each trial, 21 subjects assembled in a classroom were given detailed written instructions, including, for each, his or her own payoffs but no one else's. They were told that each person's reward would depend exclusively on the group choice of an alternative, that payoffs were different for different people, and that, while they should discuss which alternative to choose, they should under no circumstances reveal quantitative information about their own payoffs. A student chairman, uninformed about the purpose of the experiment, presided. He explained a typical predetermined agenda with its series of questions like "Do we want to consider further only the numbers 1 and 2 or only the numbers 3, 4, and 5?" He explained the rules of debate, closing debate, and voting, and he led the group through a practice agenda. Finally the group selected a winner according to the agenda for that trial.

The four agendas are shown in Figure 7-2. The predicted path is indicated with a boldface arrow, →, the predicted outcome with an asterisk, *, and the actual path (with vote record) with a sharp, #. Notice that, to predict for all contingencies, a boldface arrow is provided for each pair of sets, S and $\overline{S}$, even though it is *not* predicted that subjects would ever be in a position to choose between S and $\overline{S}$. As can be seen at the second and third stages of trial 2, the completeness of the prediction turned out to be useful.

As the figure shows, the predicted outcome was actually chosen on trials 1, 3, and 4. On trial 2, the Condorcet winner (alternative 1) was chosen, though alternative 4 was predicted. Plott and Levine attribute this failure to the fact that, early in the discussion, the chairman allowed a straw vote, which revealed that 5 was least preferred by everyone. Plott and Levine believe that this changed the agenda to that of trial 2'. Once S and $\overline{S}$ were changed by the straw vote before step 1, the path predicted by the "new" agenda was then followed. If one accepts this explanation, they succeeded completely; if not, then they succeeded three times out of four.

Richard Freedman and I repeated this experiment, but with only 11 subjects per trial, somewhat smaller payoffs, and similar agendas. We obtained similar results—three successes out of four. And our one failure had exactly the same explanation—a straw vote that enabled the group to arrive at the Condorcet winner when we did not intend that they should.

These results on controlling outcomes impress me deeply. They depend, probably, on the subjects' lack of perfect information. Given some quantitative information from the straw vote, they managed in both the experiment and its repetition to find the Condorcet winner. But in the world outside the laboratory, information is almost never perfect because

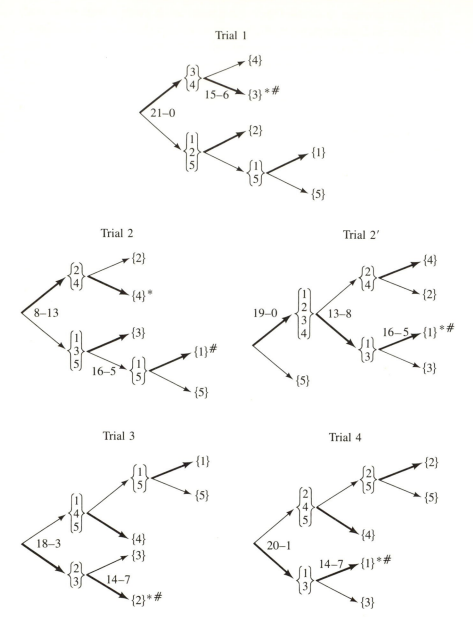

Figure 7-2 Agendas and outcomes. (Adapted from Plott and Levine, "A Model of Agenda Influence on Committee Decisions," *American Economic Review,* Vol. 68 (March 1978), pp. 146–160.)

rewards from choices are typically expressed ordinally, not cardinally, and almost never in dollars. My conclusion is, therefore, like Plott and Levine's, that it is demonstrably possible for social choices to be determined not by the true values of voters but by the manipulation by agenda-makers. If manipulation can occur so easily in the laboratory, we have good reason to believe it occurs in the larger world, where, indeed, allegations of manipulation are frequently uttered.

7.C. The Paucity of Equilibria

In the discussion in section 5.B of the frequency of profiles with and without a Condorcet winner, it was implicitly assumed that alternatives were discrete objects. If so, then the creation of new alternatives would often be difficult, especially in decision-making bodies having a rule that amendments must be germane to the main motion or in popular elections conducted under rules that favor the main parties. Although it is true that political alternatives often appear discrete, it may still be more realistic to think of them as continuous. Indeed Duncan Black's original idea that alternatives could be expressed as curves in two-dimensional space implies, by the very use of curves, that alternatives are continuous variables. Similarly, although Kenneth Arrow's theorem is proved with discrete mathematics, his verbal interpretation of alternatives as "social states," the objects of choice in his model, also implies continuous alternatives. He defined a "social state" as

a complete description of the amount *of each commodity in the hands of each individual, the* amount *of labor to be supplied by each individual, the* amount *of each productive resource invested in each type of productive activity, and the* amounts *of various types of collective activity [emphasis added].*[4]

Note that every component of a social state is an amount and so continuous—apart from the lumpiness of some commodities.

Some alternatives are unquestionably continuous. A common subject of parliamentary motions is an appropriation or a tax rate, and money is for all practical purposes a continuous variable in alternative motions involving x dollars, $(x + \epsilon)$ dollars, and so on. In a less obvious way *all* sentences are embedded in a continuum. One of the significant assumptions of structural linguistics is the idea that a language can express an infinity of propositions. If so, then between a pair of sentences one can insert a third, intermediate in meaning. On a motion to declare war, the choice is not just between "war" or "peace." Amendments are possible: to declare war unless the enemy pays tribute, or unless an apology is uttered, or unless a sign of friendship is given, and so on. In that sense, propositions are continuous.

A quite separate tradition that utilizes and reinforces this belief in the continuity of alternatives is the spatial model of party competition. In Downs' model with only one dimension of judgment, voters' ideal points are arranged on an ideological scale and parties are shown to write platforms located at the median point of the scale, as in Figure 3-1, in section 3.G.[5] Since a platform is a sentence identifying a particular point on a line, this model amounts to an assertion that propositions are continuous. As this model was developed, especially for the case of n dimensions of judgment, the assumption of continuity was embedded even more deeply in it.[6]

One important feature of continuity is that it is relative to one or more dimensions. This feature is wholly realistic because survey researchers repeatedly find that voters appear to judge candidates and issues by one or more dimensions of concern. They say that they like candidate A better than candidate B "because A favors *more* [a quantitative word]" defense or inflation or employment or some constellation of such issues. Thus the very language of popular political discourse suggests that voters themselves impose the dimensions that admit continuity in the real world of political choice.

This continuity in a world of several dimensions is of utmost importance for strategic manipulation. It is this feature that allows for the easy multiplication of alternatives, that generates a wide variety of individual orderings, and that thereby creates situations of disequilibrium in which the chance of the existence of a Condorcet winner is reduced to practically zero.

Disequilibrium in Three Dimensions

Historically, the first discussion of disequilibrium was by Duncan Black and R. A. Newing, whose fundamental model is set forth in Figure 7-3, part A and part B.[7] Horizontal dimensions, x and y, are standards of judgment, and the vertical dimension is the order of preference. In the xy plane, the point, A, which is directly beneath the peak of the single-peaked hump (an analogue of the single-peaked curve), is the individual's ideal point—that is, the combination of amounts of x and y that the person prefers over any other possible combination. Since the hump is single-peaked, the farther away a point is from A on a ray, k, the less desired it is because it is beneath a lower point on the surface of the hump. Thus, $A\, P_i\, G\, P_i\, F$ in the figure. All the points at the intersection of the hump with the xy plane are an indifference curve, c, in the sense that any point on the curve is as good as any other for person i. Other indifference curves, c', can be reflected in the xy plane from parallel planes, like $x'y'$.

Assume there are three voters, 1, 2, and 3, and let Figure 7-3B consist of indifference curves for persons 1 and 2. Given the point, H, at the intersection of indifference curves for person 1 (ideal point at P_1) and person 2 (ideal point at P_2), any point, L, in the overlapping portion is preferred by both 1 and 2 to H because L is on an indifference curve closer for each person to P_1 and P_2 respectively. If there is any possibility of a majority decision consisting of persons 1 and 2 (out of 1, 2, and 3), that decision point must lie on a locus of points connecting the tangents of indifference curves around P_1 and P_2 as the dashed line in Figure 7-3C, often called the *contract curve* because it is where 1 and 2 can agree.

To appreciate agreement on this curve, assume persons 1 and 2 initially agree on some point, off the curve, say H in Figure 7-3C. Then, the pair can move to point K on the curve because (1) there is no cost to person 1 because H and K are on the same indifference curve for 1, and (2) there is a gain for person 2 because K is on a curve closer to P_2 than is H. Thus, when off the contract curve, one person, at least, can always be made better off with no cost to the other person. Hence, it is expected that agreements between 1 and 2 will lie on the contract curve.

To see if there is a Condorcet winner, we need to consider a third person's ideal point, P_3, in Figure 7-3D. It is apparent that no Condorcet winner exists in Figure 7-3D. For example, consider the contract curve between persons 1 and 3, or simply $P_1 P_3$. If P_1 itself is tested, 2 and 3 vote against it, for any point on $P_2 P_3$. If P_3, 1 and 2 defeat it for any point on $P_1 P_2$. If it is H, then 2 and 3 prefer, say, K; and so on, so no point on $P_1 P_3$ can get a majority. Similarly for $P_1 P_2$ and $P_2 P_3$. There are cases, however, in which some point might win by a majority, as in Figure 7-3E, where P_3 lies on $P_1 P_2$. In this case P_3 is a majority winner. (Notice, for example, if P_3 is put against any point closer to P_1 on $P_1 P_2$, then 2 and 3 will vote for P_3. Or if P_3 is put against H, then 1 and 3 will vote for P_3.) This argument assumes sincere, not strategic, voting. Even so, a Condorcet winner must be very rare indeed.

Gerald Kramer applied essentially this analysis to all the conditions for the existence of a Condorcet winner discussed in section 5.C—single-peakedness and value restrictedness, among others.[8] He assumed a multidimensional continuum and mathematically useful and humanly acceptable restrictions on utility functions. Then he showed that no Condorcet winner exists if there is even a modest divergence of tastes. These Condorcet winners cannot prevent voting paradoxes in the two-dimensional case unless there is something approaching a unanimous preference profile—for example, a majority of voters with exactly the same ideal

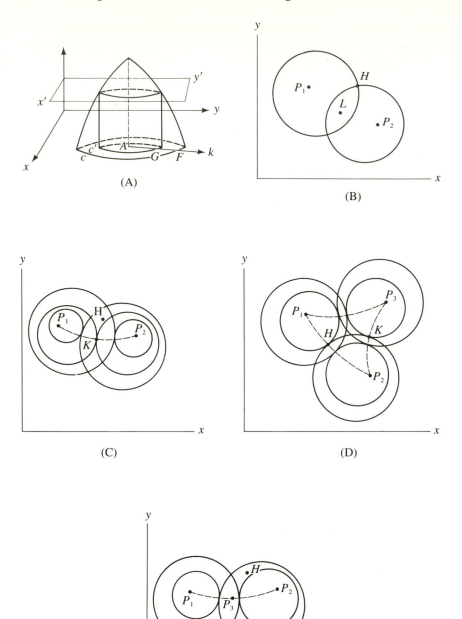

(A)

(B)

(C)

(D)

(E)

Figure 7-3   Multidimensional equilibria.

point. Continuous variables in two or more dimensions thus eliminate, for all practical purposes, the majority-rule conditions that seemed so promising in Chapter 5.

Conditions for Equilibrium

Reopening the discussion started by Black and Newing, Plott looked for a majority-rule equilibrium (of sincere voting) given continuous variables in two or more dimensions; that is, he sought a general definition of a point such as P_3 in Figure 7-3E. He found one in an extension of Black and Newing's suggestion for the three-person case.[9] A local equilibrium, μ, exists for m voters on a social choice in n dimensions, if the following sufficient conditions are satisfied:

1. Indifferent persons abstain from voting.

2. If n is odd, where n is the number of voters who are not indifferent, the equilibrium, μ, is the ideal point for one voter (or an additional even number of voters). If n is even, μ is the ideal point for no voters or an even number of voters.

3. The remaining voters can be divided into pairs, h and j, such that h and j are diametrically opposed around μ in the sense that, if they could move the equilibrium point as they wished, they would move it in exactly opposite directions in n-dimensional space. Furthermore, the contract curve between the ideal points for h and j, P_h and P_j, passes through μ.

This equilibrium may be thought of as an n-dimensional median, an analogue of the median that in one dimension is the equilibrium for single-peaked curves. It can be visualized for the five-person, two-dimension case as in Figure 7-4. The ideal points, P_{1-5}, are so marked and μ and P_3 coincide. The contract curves between P_1 and P_2 and P_4 and P_5 pass through μ. As can be seen, if some point, a, were set against μ, then a majority of 2, 3, and 5 would choose μ. As the number of voters increases, the difficulty of the pairing doubtless increases, so that majority-rule equilibria must be extremely rare in this model.

But perhaps they are not rare in the world, but only in the model, where the equilibria are "local" (that is, restricted to some defined neighborhood in the space) rather than "global" (that is, effective for the entire space), where there are only particular kinds of utility functions (such as differentiable ones), and where there is absolute majority rule. Unfortunately, one cannot escape this conclusion so easily. Much subsequent work

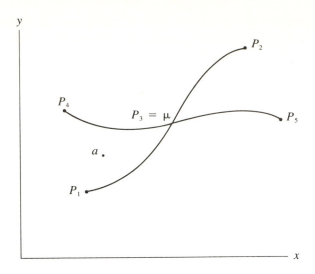

Figure 7-4   Majority-rule equilibrium, five persons, two dimensions.

has generalized the model considerably and thus made it more realistic without in any way reducing the presumption of rarity. McKelvey and Wendell, integrating and elaborating this work, show that, for a wide variety of utility curves (including nondifferentiable ones), a median, μ, at the unique intersection of contract curves among paired diametrically opposed voters is a sufficient condition for a Condorcet winner.[10] Furthermore, the existence of a median, μ, is a necessary condition for equilibrium if each utility curve by itself is single-peaked.[11] Finally, the existence of μ is a necessary and sufficient condition for a global equilibrium in the form of a Condorcet winner if utility curves are differentiable. So the present state of knowledge suggests that majority-rule equilibria must be very rare, given continuous variables in n dimensions, which, in my opinion, is a thoroughly realistic model of the world.

Complete Disequilibrium

Although cyclic outcomes "almost always" exist in this general model of majority rule, one might hope that the cycles would be confined to a small area in the space, so that there would be a "few" cycling alternatives, all of which, however, are socially preferred to everything else in the space. Then, in spite of intransitivities, the small top cycle would be socially better than the large set of worse outcomes. Unfortunately this is no way out of the social incoherence of almost universal disequilibrium. McKelvey and Schofield have shown, in quite different ways, that this escape from instability will not work.

In a remarkable discovery, McKelvey has shown that, for a wide class of differentiable utility functions, once "transitivity breaks down, it *completely* breaks down, engulfing the whole space in a single cycle set. The slightest deviation from the conditions for a Condorcet point (for example, a slight movement of *one* voter's ideal point) brings about this possibility."[12] Hence, not only is a Condorcet winner unlikely, but also, when one does not exist, *anything* can happen. There is no "small" set of probable outcomes.

McKelvey's argument runs as follows: There is a set of points, $P(x)$, which is the set of all points that can be reached by majority rule from point x.[13] (To reach some point r in $P(x)$, let y beat x by majority rule in a pairwise contest, let z beat y similarly, and so on until r beats $r - 1$.) The set $P(x)$ can be either all points in the multidimensional space or a smaller set. If it is a smaller set, then it must have a boundary and the boundary points must satisfy the symmetry conditions of the constrained Plott equilibria, which are special cases of the symmetry conditions of the Plott equilibria.[14] Since we already know such equilibria are rare, it is likely that such a boundary is extremely rare. Hence intransitive cycles of social choice almost always exist and almost always include the *whole* space. In short, in the absence of an equilibrium, *anything* can happen.

Norman Schofield approaches the problem differently, but comes to the same result.[15] His analysis begins with the observation that, for any point, x, in a multidimensional issue space, some indifference curve for each participant passes through x. Given these indifference curves, he defines the set of points, $P_M(x)$, as the set of points in the neighborhood of x that are preferred to x by some winning coalition, M. Putting all the coalitions, M, together in the set, W, of winning coalitions, Schofield defines $P_W(x)$ as the set of points in the neighborhood of x that are preferred to x by *any* winning coalition. If there are some points, y, that cannot be included in $P_W(x)$ by some path ($y P_M z, \ldots, w P_M x$, when M is any winning coalition)—that is, if there are some points, y, that x can defeat no matter what—then there may be an equilibrium at x. If, however, all points in some arbitrary neighborhood of x can by some sequence of majority coalitions defeat x, then equilibrium at x is impossible. Furthermore, if for any particular set of individual ideals and indifference curves, there is even just one point x for which equilibrium is impossible, then every point in the entire space is included in the majority-rule cycle. Effectively, this means that, unless the individual preferences are highly similar—so that all winning coalitions are similar—social choices are certain to be cyclical.

Although this condition does not in itself indicate the likelihood of cyclical outcomes, Schofield has shown that, if the issue space has at least as many dimensions as one more than the number of persons necessary for a minimal winning coalition, then the system is, for certain, cyclical. Of course, all political issues of a distributive nature (for example, "Who gets what?") have at least as many dimensions as participants in the sense that each participant is concerned, among other things, with the amount distributed to him or her. For that huge category of issues, perhaps most of human concerns, disequilibrium is, therefore, certain.

Since McKelvey's and Schofield's theorems are similar in tone, it seems likely that majority rule is almost always in disequilibrium. The inference one therefore draws from the foregoing analysis is that, for the amalgamation of an extremely wide variety of individual value structures (that is, utility functions) by majority rule under fair procedures, intransitivities almost always exist and cycles include the whole space of political possibilities. This means that wide swings in political choices are possible and expected. Topsy-turvy revolution is as certainly predicted as incremental change.

Our ordinary experience indicates, however, that there is some stability in political life: Issues persist and similar outcomes repeat themselves. There must be more to the world, therefore, than the almost complete disequilibrium suggested by the Black and Newing, Plott, McKelvey, and Schofield analyses. How can one fit incremental change and stability into this model?

7.D. Practical Stability and Theoretical Instability

To begin with, disequilibrium does not prohibit incremental change. A theory of disequilibrium tells us only that change will occur; it says nothing about whether it will be incremental or catastrophic. Indeed, it seems likely that most of the apparent stability we see in the world, such as generation-long periods of dominance by one political party, is really incremental disequilibrium in which party composition changes slightly while always maintaining some cyclicity of values.

Theories of disequilibrium, however, do not require that change be incremental. The difference between theories of disequilibrium and theories of equilibrium is that the former admit revolution (although they do not necessarily predict it) and the latter do not. We know, however, revolution is not infrequent. Even the United States, the oldest of modern democracies (originating in the 1770s), has had one bloody and devastating civil war. Since revolution occurs and is admissible in a theory of disequilibrium but is inadmissible in a theory of stability, it follows that some kind of theory of disequilibrium is a priori empirically superior to a theory of equilibrium. The advantage of theories of disequilibrium is that they admit both long periods of apparent stability (often indistinguishable from incremental change) and episodes of catastrophic revolution.

For another thing, these theories of disequilibrium concern values, preferences, or tastes, not constitutions and political structures. It may well be that the stability and continuity we observe in the world come mainly from institutions that, by reason of their interference with and restriction on majority rule, render majority-rule disequilibria less likely to influence and affect natural outcomes.

Indeed, Kenneth Shepsle has investigated institutions in just this way.[16] He observed that many institutions have the effect of forcing participants to approach political questions in just one dimension. Voting bodies often have single-peaked profiles on each of several dimensions but are in disequilibrium when these dimensions are combined in multidimensional issue space. Thus it follows that any institutional arrangement that forces consideration dimension by dimension may induce an equilibrium, even though an abstract general equilibrium does not exist. Many institutions—for example, committee systems in legislatures, rules restricting amendments, and agenda-setting devices—do indeed divide up the decision-making process into a set of decisions on single dimensions. Hence, institutionally engendered equilibria are often observed in the real world.

It should be noted, however, that these real-world equilibria, which depend on constitutions as much as on voters' tastes and values, are often subject to attack because they enforce an equilibrium that tastes would not allow. Hence they frustrate majorities; and if majorities are frustrated by institutions, these majorities may change the institutions. Thus, in the U.S. House of Representatives, the appropriations system developed in the period from the 1930s to the 1960s probably provided for frequent equilibria through the policy and structure of the appropriations committee. But the frustrations engendered in House members by the rules restricting outcomes led to the post-Watergate reforms that destroyed many of the restrictive rules and probably reduced sharply the frequency of equilibria.

Finally, many institutions in the real world force the reduction of the set of alternatives to exactly two—for example, the two-party system (and the method of plurality voting in single-member districts on which the two-party system seems to depend). In the choice between two alternatives, there is a majority winner. Since the individual tastes for one of the two parties appear to be fairly constant, the values thus institutionally restricted and incorporated in the political system may indeed provide for considerable stability. Thus, in the United States, one of the two parties has appeared dominant for fairly long periods (Jeffersonian Republicans from 1800 to 1825, Democrats from 1832 to 1854, Republicans from 1861 to 1930, Democrats from 1933 to 1980). This stability is more apparent than real, however, not only because it masks a large amount of incremental disequilibrium (as indicated in Chapter 2 by the fact that about 40 percent of the presidential elections have involved significant third-party candidates), but also because (as will be illustrated in Chapter 9) there is always an intense struggle, beneath the apparent stability, to induce a genuine disequilibrium of tastes.

We have, therefore, a number of good reasons, exogenous to the world of tastes and values in social choice theory, for the observed social stability. An equilibrium of tastes and values is in theory so rare as to be almost nonexistent. And I believe it is equally rare in practice. But individuals in society are more than ambulatory bundles of tastes. They also respect and are constrained by institutions that are intended to induce regularity in society. And it is the triumph of constraints over individual values that generates the stability we observe. But tastes and values cannot be denied, and they account for the instability we observe.

Although stability probably roots in institutions, Gerald Kramer has attempted to explain stability in terms of social choice equilibria, using a model of electoral competition between two parties acting in a multidimensional space of policies.[17] In this model, parties compete for voters over an infinite series of elections (or preelection time periods), offering platforms as points in the space. The voters respond by supporting the platform closest to their ideal points (using a conventional, rather restricted measurement system to determine "closeness"). In this simple majority system, one of the two platforms is chosen, the winning party enacts it, and the losing party picks out another platform (point in space) to maximize its chance of winning. Assuming it finds such a platform, the parties alternate in office.

Kramer calls the succession from winning platform to winning platform a *trajectory*. Then he defines a set for possible equilibria: the minmax set. For alternatives x and y, $n(x, y)$ is the number of votes by which y beats x. Some particular y gets the most votes against x, and that number of most votes is $v(x)$.[18] Assuming cyclicity, x will not beat all y, so $v(x) > n/2$. Nevertheless, some x, say x', comes closest to winning, in the sense that the value for $v(x')$ is the smallest of all $v(x)$—that is, it is the minmax number, $n*$.[19] The difference between $n*$ and $n/2$ is the measure of how close a society comes to having a majority winner.

Kramer's notion of equilibrium, then, is this: If parties seek to maximize votes, then the trajectory of successive platforms leads to the set of all $n*$ (the set of all alternatives with the minmax number). That is, the trajectory leads, perhaps by a path on which there are backward steps, to the alternatives closest to being majority winners. When the trajectory arrives at the set of $n*$, equilibrium exists. This equilibrium is not unique—except when the number of voters is infinite—but it may be a "small set" as against the "whole space" of McKelvey and Schofield.

Does Kramer's elegant model save us from devastating disequilibrium? Unfortunately, I think not because at least three of its assumptions are extremely unrealistic. One is the assumption of two parties. As was shown in Chapter 3, simple majority voting is attractive, but two and only two parties in both unrealistic and unfair. Another unrealistic assumption is that parties always maximize votes. Sometimes they do, as possibly happened for the winning party in the 1972 and 1964 presidential elections. But much more frequently one or both parties do not successfully deter factions from breaking off; Display 2-1 shows this failure in over 40 percent of the presidential elections. This failure to deter the breakoff of factions is evidence that parties do not care about maximizing votes or pluralities but rather care simply about winning with enough votes to ensure election.[20] So when old parties break up, they are, for certain, not maximizing votes. Hence the assumption of vote maximization is highly unrealistic, but crucial to the mathematical argument for the convergence of the trajectory to the set, $n*$, of alternatives closest to winning.

A third unrealistic assumption is that dimensions do not change, even though the model is otherwise dynamic. If one allows platforms to change, then surely dimensions should change too. And if that happens, then trajectories have to start over. Given dynamism in dimensions, it seems probable that no trajectory would ever get very far in the convergence to $n*$. In addition, trajectories are likely to be deflected by parties' occasional efforts, just mentioned as the opposite of the second assumption, to minimize (not maximize) votes toward the minimal winning size, the so-called size principle.

No one doubts that there is occasional stability in the real world. Sometimes this stability is more apparent than real, for there are cycles of similar alternatives and the disequilibrium moves from one outcome to another by increments so minute that political life seems stable even though it is not. But sometimes also the stability is real, and it is imposed by institutions not the product of preferences and values. If we consider only values, then disequilibrium seems inherent in majority rule. *Anything* can happen—incremental change or revolution.

Of course when institutional stability is imposed on what would otherwise be a disequilibrium of tastes, the imposed equilibrium is necessarily unfair. That majority which would, were it not institutionally restrained, displace the current outcome is denied the opportunity to work its will. In that sense institutional stability (such as the responsible two-party system discussed in Chapter 3) is unfair and is sure to cause frustration. Perhaps this frustration in turn ultimately brings about great changes, such as the disruption of long-standing alliances, rewriting of constitutions, and even violent revolution.

7.E. The Fragility of Equilibria: An Example of the Introduction of New Alternatives to Generate Disequilibrium

McKelvey interpreted his discovery that cycles cover the whole space to mean that a chairperson, with complete information and a taste for sophisticated voting, could, with appropriate agenda, lead the society to choose *any* alternative she or he most desired. As such, this model is, for majoritarian voting, a theoretical explanation of agenda control. It does not, however, explain the efforts of either Pliny or Plott and Levine, for they manipulated by procedures not contemplated in McKelvey's model.

It seems to me, however, that much the more significant practical consideration raised by McKelvey and Schofield is the extraordinary *fragility* of equilibria. Just a little bit of change in the situation—by strategic voting or by introducing another alternative—opens up a whole new world of political possibilities. I will conclude this chapter with an illustrative instance of just that fragility, and then in the next chapter I will set forth a general interpretation of political disequilibrium.

My concluding illustration concerns the history of the motions that ultimately became the Seventeenth Amendment (about the direct election of U.S. senators).[21] Originally this issue appeared to be one of discrete alternatives on one dimension (that is, for or against amending the Constitution). Furthermore, an equilibrium of single-peaked curves probably existed. But clever parliamentary tacticians—ordinary backbenchers, not leaders—generated other alternatives in at least two other dimensions, one a dimension of party loyalty, the other a dimension of racism. Consequently, they destroyed the equilibrium (if it existed) and generated cycles from which no motion would be chosen. This is what the fragility of equilibria permits, and this is what makes the dynamic disequilibrium of majority rule so significant a feature of all democratic life.

Toward the end of the nineteenth century, there began to be considerable agitation for direct election of senators, agitation deriving from quite diverse sources. One powerful source was Southern white populist racism. As a means of eliminating the influence of black voters, Southern white populists had invented the device of nominating Democratic candidates in primary elections from which blacks were excluded. Since Democrats had a considerable majority in Southern states, this meant that only white officials would be elected. The primary election, however, was a dubiously valid device as applied to U.S. senators, who were supposed to be elected by state legislatures. Adoption of direct election nationally was, then, an attractive means of strengthening racist institutions locally. Another source was the progressive movement in the North, with its emphasis on direct citizen participation. A third source was a movement for good-government reform supported by middle-class reformers repelled by the corruption of state legislators in electing senators.

It would seem that a coalition of such strange bedfellows would be both an absolute majority and an irresistible force—and of course it was in the end. But for about twenty years it was successfully opposed by an *almost* immovable object—the distaste of a minority of sitting senators for submitting to the sexennial torture of a popular canvass. At first those senators simply ignored resolutions regularly passed by the House, which seemed to delight in embarrassing the Senate. But by 1902 the Senate could no longer ignore the pressure, and the proposed constitutional amendment was considered in committee in substantially the form it now has: "the Senate of the United States shall be composed of two Senators from each State elected by the people thereof, for six years." This sentence may well have been an equilibrium outcome, if not in 1902, at least by 1905 or 1906, had not a remarkably inventive parliament man, Chauncey DePew of New York, disrupted the equilibrium with the following proposed addition:

The qualifications of citizens entitled to vote for United States Senators and Representatives in Congress shall be uniform in all States, and Congress shall have the power to enforce this article by appropriate legislation and to provide for the registration of citizens entitled to vote, the conduct of such elections, and the certification of the result.[22]

The DePew amendment, though it perhaps seems innocuous today, was highly devisive, for it was then interpreted as a "force bill," a bill to authorize the president to send the army into the South to register blacks and enforce their voting rights—in short a revival of Reconstruction. White supremacist Southern Democrats who were enthusiastic for the constitutional amendment without the DePew amendment would be bitterly opposed to the constitutional amendment if the DePew amendment were attached to it. And attached it would be, for at that time the one point of ideological unity for the Republican party was support for black aspirations. Hence, even those Republicans who very much wanted the constitutional amendment were obliged by party loyalty and their strong antiracist sentiments to favor the DePew amendment. The opposition to the DePew amendment consisted of Southern Democrats, of Northern Democrats who were for the most part tolerantly sympathetic to Southern racism, and of a few progressive Republicans who put electoral reform above party loyalty. In 1902 and 1911 these were simply not enough to defeat DePew.

The issue never got to the floor in 1902, but it did get there in February 1911, when there was much more support for reform. This time the progressive proponents of reform protected their Southern allies against the DePew maneuver by adding a proviso to guarantee white supremacy: "The times, places, and manner of holding elections for Senators shall be prescribed by the legislatures thereof [i.e., the states]." The opponents of direct election moved to delete this sentence. The motion to delete was identified as the Sutherland amendment, and it was a negatively stated version of the DePew amendment. There were thus three alternatives:

a. The resolution to amend the Constitution, as amended by the Sutherland amendment

b. The original resolution to amend the Constitution (including the clause to protect Southern racism)

c. The status quo

The vote on the Sutherland amendment put a against b, and the Sutherland amendment passed 50 yea to 36 nay. So the social choice was $C(a, b) = a$. The vote on passage of the amended resolution, which put a against c, was 54 yea (for a) and 34 nay (for c). Since the resolution to amend the Constitution required two-thirds yeas (here, 59), the motion failed. So the social choice was $C(a, c) = c$.

To finish out the pairings and thus to show that the introduction of a new alternative involving new dimensions generated a cycle, b and c must be compared. Presumably all 54 who voted for the amended resolution also favored the original resolution (b) over the status quo (c). So presumably also did at least 10 Southern Democrats who had originally insisted on the proviso deleted by the Sutherland amendment and who ultimately voted against the amended resolution (that is, for c against a). Together these are 64 out of either 86 or 88, easily enough to pass the constitutional amendment. So the social choice is $C(b, c) = b$. Hence follows this cycle: a beats b, b beats c, and c beats a. In the non-neutral amendment procedure, c wins when a cycle exists. Hence, a fairly small minority, probably no more than 24, won because they generated a cycle with a new alternative with new dimensions.[23] This is not, I believe, an isolated example of manipulation, but a typical instance of electoral and democratic politics, as I will show in the next chapter.[24]

8

The Natural Selection
of Political Issues:
An Interpretation of
Political Disequilibrium

The General Possibility Theorem—and all it implies about the manipulation of outcomes from voting and about the politically even more devastating consequences of the frequent (indeed, typical) nonexistence of equilibrium under majority rule—raises extremely difficult problems for political theory and political philosophy. Yet simultaneously those same implications do permit a new and deeper understanding of the process of politics. We now can understand what always before has seemed an impenetrable mystery—namely, the motive force for the perpetual flux of politics.

In an effort to comprehend this flux, theorists have put together all sorts of reductionist theories that purport to explain changes in popular taste but explain nothing about the effect of tastes in politics. Thus, Marxists, for example, say change is entirely a matter of technological innovation. More humane but equally dogmatic writers say change is all a matter of new systems of philosophy. (Recall Keynes' remark: "The ideas of economists and political philosophers, both when they are right and when they are wrong, are more powerful than is commonly understood. Indeed the world is ruled by little else.")[1] Still others, more cosmic, look for change in the forces of nature, the weather, sun spots, or even in events outside the solar system. It is possibly true that all these things affect tastes, though we know almost nothing about how tastes and values are in fact formed and influenced.

Still, knowing that tastes change does not tell us anything about how politics changes. To understand political events we need to understand how tastes get incorporated into political decisions. This is precisely where the flux of politics occurs, and it is precisely where an explanation is needed. Previous theorizing about changes in tastes and values has mostly been reductionist. Hence it has been aimed at explicating the internal history of these tastes and values, and it also has been based on the assumption that their effects on politics are automatic. Because of this reductionist feature, these theories by-pass the political mobilization of tastes. Yet it is exactly this mobilization that is the center of political life, the very thing that *political* theories should explain. In this sense a vast number of supposed explanations of politics (economic, technological, ideational, astrological, and others) are simply irrelevant to politics. They explain the origin, not the operation, of tastes.

Now, however, we can explain the mystery, the perpetual flux of politics, in terms of the mobilization and amalgamation of tastes. Political evolution is now at least explicable, if not predictable. The force for evolution is political disequilibrium, and the consequence of disequilibrium is a kind of natural selection of issues. We do not know what will win in any given situation, but we do know why winners do not keep winning forever.

All methods of amalgamation involve illogicalities in choice, which is the fundamental basis for disequilibrium. If, furthermore, choice is made over continuous alternatives by voting, especially by majority rule, then disequilibrium is an almost certain consequence. Disequilibrium is in turn the setting for a natural selection of issues, and this natural selection in turn ensures that no winner will win forever. We cannot say when one issue will be displaced by another, thus bringing new leadership to succeed old leadership; nor can we say which new issue will be the vehicle for new leaders. But we can describe the process of natural selection and display the motives that make it inevitable. This description and display is the subject of this chapter.

8.A. Disappointments with Disequilibria

The hope of identifying a political equilibrium dies hard because the failure to identify is a disappointment both scientifically and philosophically. It is beginning to be evident, however, that the wisest course for a science of politics is to abandon the search for equilibria and try to understand what the world is without them. Nevertheless, there is intense intellectual resistance to such a course because of the disappointments involved. By way of introduction to the new understanding of political dynamics, therefore, I will devote this initial section to a discussion of just how deep these disappointments are.

Concerning first the scientific disappointment, social scientists have always been eager to identify and describe equilibria. And for good reason. The usual definition of *equilibrium* is the ultimate state of a process toward which its internal forces propel it and at which these forces are so balanced that it remains in this ultimate state. One property of such an equilibrium is that, if the process is adventitiously disturbed, it again moves toward that ultimate state when the disturbance disappears. The classic social example is the structure of prices, which is, in the competitive equilibrium, a state of balance about willingness to trade all commodities. If one price is fixed by some outside force (such as a government), the effect ripples through the system until a new balance of prices is achieved. Once the fixing is undone, all prices again readjust, other things being equal, to what had been the original price structure.

Even less deterministic notions of equilibrium have this same property of returning to the balance when an external disturbance is removed. For example, nonunique equilibria consist of several possible ultimate states toward one of which, however accidentally targeted, internal forces propel and from which, once reached, there is no expectation of departure. The only difference in the nonunique cases is that there exists a *set* of ultimate states. If the process is diverted from one of them, it returns, when the disturbance is removed, to some one of those ultimate states, though not necessarily to the one it was originally in or targeted toward. The classic example here is the game with a solution containing several possible outcomes. If driven off the target of one outcome, the play moves, when permitted, toward the same outcome or toward another one in the solution (the particular outcome being determined by "irrelevant" factors such as the course of the play and the personalities of the players).

In either kind of equilibrium the important feature from the scientific point of view is the tendency of the process, even after disturbance, to move toward one or one of several ultimate states. Given this property, the scientist who has identified and described an equilibrium can confidently predict social outcomes. Knowledge of equilibria is therefore knowledge of the future and carries with it the power of the seer.

In terms of specifically political equilibria in a democratic setting, the hope, from a scientific point of view, of finding political equilibria is that one might isolate political phenomena from the complexity of the whole social and biological world and, simply by understanding that abstracted process, might then predict political outcomes. The political facts in a democratic process are, of course, relatively simple: participants' values and the constitutional structures wherein these values are amalgamated. Hence, if equilibria exist, prediction (and explanation) would also be relatively simple, thereby conforming to the scientific ideal of slicing the world up into self-contained pieces in order to predict and explain each piece by itself. The achievement of that ideal depends, however, on the pieces in fact being self-contained, and in the political case it depends specifically on the political process being independent of the morass of participants' perceptions and personalities, which are features of the world entirely outside the political abstraction.

The absence of political equilibria means that outcomes depend not simply on participants' values and constitutional structures, but also on matters such as whether some people have the will or wit to vote strategically, whether some leader has the skill, energy, and resources to manipulate the agenda, or whether some backbencher—in a committee or out—has the imagination and determination to generate a cyclical majority by introducing new alternatives and new issues. These are matters of perception and personality and understanding and character. The fact that the absence of equilibrium makes them relevant to prediction means that the power that comes from scientific knowledge is well nigh unobtainable for political abstractions. Of course, then, there is much scientific disappointment over the results described in Chapters 5, 6, and 7.

There is much philosophical disappointment also. Political disequilibrium means that political forces (individual values and the operating features of constitutions) are insufficient to account for political outcomes. This insufficiency means in turn that democratic political outcomes are not simply a mechanical, impersonal, unbiased amalgamation of individual values, but rather are an amalgamation that often operates quite personally and unfairly, giving special advantages to smarter or bolder or more powerful or more creative or simply luckier participants, counting their values for more than other people's. Given disequilibrium, therefore, the democratic ideal of equal participation cannot be regarded as always achievable. And, furthermore, the notion that political outcomes are the will of the people must be revised to say that they are the will of the smarter, bolder, more powerful, more creative, or luckier people. Consequently, there is a philosophical (or ideological) disappointment along with the scientific.

Simply because these disappointments exist, however, we cannot deny political disequilibrium in democracy or any voting bodies. The theory of disequilibrium is too powerful and the describable instances of disequilibrium too many to dismiss it with a shrug. Instead, we are obliged, I believe, by both the theory and the facts to look at the political world anew, as if disequilibrium is indeed its salient characteristic. What kind of world, we must ask, do we have then?

That is the kind of new look at politics I propose for this chapter.

8.B. Voting Disequilibrium: What It Means to Lose

The main feature of disequilibrium in voting is the deep dissatisfaction of many people with the outcome. To appreciate the depth and extent of this dissatisfaction, it is instructive to compare the concept of losing in several contexts, economic and political. Let us consider first the economic context, especially within the competitive equilibrium.

Losing Economically

At the beginning of a time period there are traders with initial endowments; during the time period all feasible trades are made; and at the end the market is in equilibrium. At this stage in this voluntary system, everybody is better off because, by definition, no trade occurs unless the traders improve their positions. This situation is Pareto optimal in the sense that no additional trades can be made that will make the traders better off. (That is, any new trade would make one trader better off only at the expense of making another worse off. Assuming voluntary trading, the trader who would be worse off does not agree to the new trade, which is why the process has come to balance.) Furthermore, this competitive equilibrium is the best that the market as a whole can do, for every possible coalition of traders has achieved at least as much as its members could expect to achieve, given their initial endowments. (In game-theoretic terms, this is an outcome in the core, which, if it exists, is the solution of a game in which every player and every coalition achieves at least its minimal value.)[2]

Although everybody is better off in the competitive equilibrium, it does not follow that everybody is satisfied. Some are unhappy because of accidents—human errors and natural disasters leading to bankruptcy or natural windfalls leading to great wealth. But here I do not consider accidents simply because they are accidents. Others are unhappy because—as in the case of unemployment—they are excluded from economic participation. Such exclusion is always temporary unless it is politically enforced (as, for example minimum-wage laws exclude the unskilled or union contracts exclude blacks). So I also do not consider the political manipulation that makes markets unfair.

Even in the highly idealized equilibrium that remains, however, where, ignoring luck and political oppression and assuming intelligence, everybody is better off, some people are still dissatisfied. In the definition of Pareto optimality, people are better off relative to where they started.[3]

And some people may have started off badly, either poor or having chosen a declining trade. Furthermore, in the operation of the market some poor people may become just a little better off while some rich people may become very much better off. Or scions of old wealth may see themselves far surpassed by the nouveau riche. Pareto optimality does not necessarily mean that inequalities or profound unfairness are either created or erased; it merely means that, relative to a given initial endowment, everybody is better off in some amount, however small. One can thus be deeply dissatisfied with the operation of a market either because it preserved an unfair initial distribution or because it generated an unfair final distribution. The same potential dissatisfaction is equally characteristic of solutions in the core. That every coalition achieves the value implicit in its initial endowments is not particularly satisfactory if the initial endowments are themselves thought to be unfair.

However real and politically significant is the resentment of a poverty not alleviated by the operation of the market, still the market does not make people worse off, unless—as in the case of unemployment—they are politically excluded from participation. Since exclusion is temporary unless politically imposed, losing in the market is a remarkably mild kind of losing compared with losing in politics. Losing politically is typically much worse than losing economically.

Losing Politically

Losses of roughly the same scale are worse in a political context than in an economic context. For both individual citizens and the whole society, losing a war and being pillaged, harried, and murdered is worse than chronic unemployment and poverty. For economic groups and regional coalitions, losing a series of elections so that government policy generally is tilted against the losers is worse than losing jobs and business contracts.

Nineteenth-century journalists called economics the "dismal science." They overlooked politics, which by its fundamental nature is far more dismal. In politics, there are almost always losers and losing usually involves not being better off. It is the expectation of this fact that makes politics dismal.

To begin with, some kinds of political situations are, in game-theoretic terms, zero-sum, which means that the winner gains exactly what the loser loses. (Two-candidate elections are a good example: The winner gains office and the loser misses it.) It is apparent that such games cannot have a core; that is, unlike the market equilibrium, not all coalitions can obtain their initial expectations. Suppose that there are three minority factions, any two of which can elect one of the two candidates, and suppose that each of the successful factions gains from its participation in the choice. Then the successful candidate can be elected by a coalition of (1 and 2) or (1 and 3) or (2 and 3). It is apparent that one faction cannot win and thus cannot achieve its initial expectation. To lose in this circumstance is to lose all, although of course one can always hope to win another day.

Zero-sum situations may occur infrequently in politics, except for two-candidate elections. Nevertheless, a similar kind of losing is a common feature of non-zero-sum political situations. Suppose that, although the political game is not in the technical sense zero-sum, it is still the intent of each possible winner to impose some kind of external cost on the losers. Then, no matter who wins, there exists a loser who is the worse off for having participated in the political system.

Before the Civil War era, for example, there were three main political positions on slavery: (1) to extend by national decision the geographic area in which slavery was permitted, (2) to restrict the area of slavery by national decision, (3) to make local decisions on the subject, not national ones. It is apparent that the adoption of any of these three precludes, indeed denies, the other two. If position 1 is chosen, then position 2 is directly contradicted on slavery and position 3 is directly contradicted on the level of decision. Similarly for position 2. As for position 3, its adoption denies both 1 and 2 with respect to the level of decision and either 1 or 2 with respect to the nature of the decision. Thus, no matter what position wins, adherents of the other two positions will suffer and will indeed be worse off than if the status quo—local decision—is maintained. But one of the three positions was *certain* to occur. Hence some unspecified people were *certain* to win, and other unspecified people were *certain* to lose.

Many political situations—perhaps most—are very similar to this. The fundamental reason for this fact is that political or moral scarcity is more deeply punishing and more profoundly dissatisfying than economic scarcity. Economists make much of scarce resources, but they mean thereby no more than that resources are limited with respect to human wants at the moment. (This is not, as is sometimes said, the assumption that wants are insatiable or that "more is better"; rather it is just an assumption that at the moment there is not enough land, labor, and capital to produce everything that people would currently like to have.) Economic scarcity forces the use of a rationing device such as market prices or planning allocations. It means that those who cannot pay for a resource or who cannot persuade a planning body to allocate it to them cannot use it.

But that is all it means. Simply, those who do not have must go without. Economic scarcity does not also require that the nonpossessor suffer additional punishment for nonpossession, nor does it mean that the nonpossessor is legally prohibited from gaining possession. Economically, it is enough that the poor go hungry; politically and morally the poor may—perhaps, must—also be publicly ridiculed for starving and permanently condemned to starvation.

Political or moral scarcity arises when contradictory values are believed by some participants in the political system to be universal. The believers in a putatively universal value wish the value to be applied and enforced generally, even on nonbelievers. Nonbelievers resist because they are unwilling that it be enforced and are able to prevent its enforcement. Then follows a contradiction. The putatively universal value cannot actually be universal because its adherents cannot secure its universal acceptance. Scarcity is the absence of the universality of acceptance because of the unwillingness of people who accept one value to be guided by a conflicting value. For a moral or political position to have worth in society (that is, to be scarce), some people (for instance, those who are hurt by it or lose by it) must reject it.

For example, just prior to the Reformation, relatively few people in Europe cared about political enforcement of religious orthodoxy, although they enjoyed and believed in killing Muslims. In that sense there was very little political value in Christian belief in Europe. Once the Reformation aroused in people on all sides the desire to impose their distinct religious beliefs locally, religions became universal ideals. Simultaneously, they became politically scarce, simply because not everyone was willing to be converted.

For another example, when abortion could be induced only at great risk to the life of the pregnant woman, it was uncommon and hence not a subject of intense moral and political concern. In the last century or so, owing to advances in sanitation and surgery, abortion has become easy, relatively safe, and common. Contradictory values have developed around the practice (for example, "Abortion is murder." and "A woman has a right to control her body."); and, by reason of this dispute, these values have become both universal and scarce.

There is a huge number of such issues in the contemporary world, issues over which some people are prepared even to kill others. Nearly everywhere civil liberties and enforced military service are such issues.

And in all places where significant racial, religious, linguistic, and even cultural minorities exist, issues between the minority and majority generate universal political values and political scarcity.

But of all the kinds of political and moral scarcity extant, that having to do with manipulating markets and money is the most common. Those who want to rig markets and income distribution to their own advantage typically assert that their kind of business or their social state is more desirable or more deserving than others. Naturally, not everyone agrees with such assertions of special economic rights, thus rendering them scarce. These assertions are, of course, propaganda devices to rig markets and economic outcomes, but they are typically presented as universal political and moral values.

An assertion of the general virtue of rural life on the family farm justifies farm subsidies. An assertion of the general moral value of the economic health of communities (tied in, typically, with arguments about "infant industries," "defense needs," and "regional unbalance") justifies tariffs, subsidies, and noneconomic government contracts. An assertion about the general moral value of helping the unfortunate justifies a huge variety of welfare subsidies such as social security. An assertion about the general moral value of a "fair wage" justifies excluding some laborers from the market in order to lessen competition for others. Assertions about the general justice of rewarding inventors, investors, or consumers justify monopolies (almost all of which are granted or maintained by governments and regulation). Assertions about the general moral value of labor peace and "fair" bargaining power justify the cartelization of labor in unions. Assertions about the moral repugnance of the spoils system justify grants of permanent tenure to civil servants. Etc.

Almost all politically imposed special economic privileges and market manipulations depend on assertions of a universal morality. Because these assertions, when acted upon, make some people *worse* off, they are not universally acknowledged. Hence these political values are scarce in the sense that some people reject them.

Just as economic scarcity requires some method of allocation (namely, the market), so does political and moral scarcity. The method is governmental authority, which prescribes which of conflicting moral beliefs will be acted upon, or socially enforced. Thus the outcome of a voting decision in a political context is, typically, to choose which of politically scarce values to enforce. And the act of enforcement in the face of scarcity requires not only that the losers forfeit the values they believe in but also that they abide by, if not accept, the values they despise.

Thus, to lose on issues of political and moral scarcity (which issues are the stuff of politics) is much worse than to lose in the market. One must suffer outcomes in which one is economically or emotionally deeply deprived. Truly, it is politics, not economics, that is the dismal science.

8.C. Voting Disequilibrium: The Quantity and Quality of Political Dissatisfaction

To consider the kind and amount of dissatisfaction with outcomes of voting, I will here attempt to estimate these features from a survey of the varieties of outcomes.

The least dissatisfaction exists when the outcome is unanimous. Unfortunately the subjects of such decisions are usually trivial. It may be true that members of a group are unanimous on the subjects that brought them together in the first place, though this unanimity seldom exists for very large groups like nations and even on such fundamental subjects as whether the nation ought to continue to exist. But people usually do not vote on these important questions where unanimity is conceivable. When they do so vote, the operation is largely ceremonial and does not typically involve a political decision.[4] On the other hand, when decisions do appear to be both political and unanimous, usually nobody cares very much about the outcome. Examples are the 90 percent or so of legislation passed by Congress by unanimous consent, which is unanimous because the subjects are politically trivial.[5] So although unanimity guarantees minimal dissatisfaction, one expects very little dissatisfaction on low-salience issues.

Absolute majorities of first-place votes, which are necessarily in strong equilibrium, tend to minimize the number of dissatisfied persons, but other conditions may affect the degree of dissatisfaction. Given an outcome in the core, as might happen if a legislature distributes a windfall by cutting taxes, even losers are to some degree content. Zero-sum situations, on the other hand, mean an empty core. And in all cases, zero-sum or not, involving moral scarcity, losers lose badly.

A Condorcet winner, even without an absolute majority of first-place votes, is in equilibrium if voters vote sincerely. This means more people are satisfied than not. But some winners do not get their first choice, and relative dissatisfaction is greater, other things being equal, than with an absolute majority. Of course, Condorcet winners also involve the dissatisfaction inherent in moral scarcity. Situations with Condorcet winners under sincere voting are subject to manipulation that may vastly increase dissatisfaction. With strategic voting, for example, an alternative favored only by a minority may be adopted. Suppose there are three motions and c is the status quo. Voting by amendment (a vs. b, survivor vs. c) on profile D

$$
\begin{array}{ll}
\multicolumn{2}{c}{D} \\
\hline
D_1: & a \; c \; b \\
D_2: & c \; a \; b \\
D_3: & b \; a \; c \\
\hline
\end{array}
$$

yields a as the winner. But 2 can make c win by altering D_2 to cba, thus generating a cycle. This revised outcome is, of course, vulnerable to attack by 3, who can alter D_3 to abc so a has an absolute majority; but if 2 succeeds, then a majority (1 and 3) is dissatisfied in the sense that both of them prefer the loser a to the winner c. The depth of their dissatisfaction varies by whether the issue involves moral scarcity.

A similar situation arises when cycles exist naturally. If procedures force a decision, as in ordinary elections and amendment procedures, then, in the absence of manipulation, an alternative opposed by a majority is certain to be chosen, thereby maximizing the number of dissatisfied persons. If the issue also involves moral scarcity, the dissatisfaction is maximal.

This survey of the quality and quantity of losing leads to these conclusions:

1. Even in equilibrium, substantial though minority dissatisfaction is to be expected. But, for reasons already discussed, equilibrium is itself a rarity if alternatives are continuous in multidimensional space. And even with discrete alternatives, important issues are not likely to be in equilibrium. Hence, one can expect majority dissatisfaction as the typical situation in political decisions.

2. Furthermore, this dissatisfaction is typically intensified by the fact that political issues involve matters of moral scarcity. Politics thus truly is what David Easton described as the "authoritative allocation of values."[6] Unfortunately, Easton's formulation masks the awful fact of moral scarcity and fails to reveal that the values thus allocated to benefit some simultaneously punish others.

3. In a world of disequilibrium under majority rule where the subjects of decision are morally scarce—that is, in the world of politics—the main feature of life is continuing and intense dissatisfaction for a *majority* of participants.

8.D. The Consequences
of Dissatisfaction:
A Model of Political Change

The various members of the majority of dissatisfied losers, who may have little in common except their distaste for the status quo, have a compelling motive to upset the current outcome. Indeed, political life in a democracy—or indeed in any voting body—consists of continual efforts to dislodge the temporary authorities who have authoritatively but temporarily allocated despised values. The losers do this in two ways: First, within current dimensions of politics, they generate new alternatives that may be able to beat the current winner. The existence of global cycles assures us this is possible. Second, by inventing new dimensions of politics, they create new political structures in which an old equilibrium, if it exists, is upset. In practice, these activities are probably so much alike that they can be distinguished only by observers, not by participants. The reason for distinguishing between them is simply to note that losers have a method of displacing outcomes in equilibrium as well as the more typical and frequent outcomes in disequilibrium.

All this adds up to a model for political change with three components:

1. *Voters in a voting body, from committee to nation in size.* Each voter perceives alternatives in a limited number of dimensions—two or three, perhaps. In any given situation, however, the number of dimensions perceived by all voters may be numerous (perhaps more dimensions than voters), and these dimensions overlap among voters in many and various ways. Voters do not ordinarily create either alternatives or dimensions; but commonly they are receptive to leaders' suggestions of both, and they are able to accommodate quickly to a new space or a new pattern in an old space. Voters are fickle: They can accept new versions of the world in which old leaders are losers and old losers are new leaders.

2. *Leaders in a voting body.* Mere members of a voting body are transformed into leaders by reason of creating and urging new dimensions, new platforms, and new policy alternatives. Success in persuading the acceptance of new alternatives is what makes a leader, and the failure of a leader to persuade voters to support his or her alternatives is what unmakes a leader. Assuming that leaders obtain special satisfaction from the alternatives they create as well as from the positions they occupy, a motive exists for constant competition for leadership. This motive is the driving force behind political change.

3. *The interaction between leaders and voters.* Leaders in voting bodies may be likened to entrepreneurs in a market. Entrepreneurs succeed by offering new products, and so it is with leaders. Of course, entrepreneurs often fail, offering products no one wants. So also with voting leaders: New alternatives, new issues, are like new products. Each one is sponsored as a test of the voting market, in the hope that the new alternative will render new issues salient, old issues irrelevant, and, above all, will be preferred by a majority to what went before. This is the art of politics: to find some alternative that beats the current winner. Such an alternative almost certainly exists, given disequilibrium. But given that the opponents of the current winner may agree on nothing but their opposition, it is difficult to find a way to put together a coalition that beats it. Yet politicians constantly do so.

8.E. The Natural Selection of Issues

The difficult task of putting together a winning coalition is the constant occupation of would-be political leaders. The fundamental dynamic of political life is their restless search for the issues and alternatives around which a new winning coalition can coalesce. Assuming that leaders and citizens interact in the way just described, prospective leaders must as a matter of course raise new issues—of all sorts and just about all the time. A new issue, expressed in terms of a specific alternative, may appear initially as a proposal to help in the election of a particular candidate or in the passage or defeat of a particular bill. If that alternative appears unattractive, then it is dropped, probably never to be heard of again. But if it should attract some response, it is started on a life of its own. It no longer belongs exclusively to the person who invented it. Anybody can take it up, and it often happens, especially when an alternative catches on, that opponents seize an inventor's alternative and use it to forward their own cause. Furthermore, it can no longer be expected to retain its original form. If the alternative makes a new issue salient, then other related alternatives exploiting the issue quickly appear. The array of alternatives exchanges elements, thus presenting the society with an infinity of new alternatives.

None of this happens by magic, of course. Each step of the proliferation is carried forward by a politician with an interest. This is why a new issue is raised by one person, why it is stolen by another, why still others jump on the band wagon, why still others combine the alternatives in novel ways. In this way, the market for alternatives is very much like the market for products in which proliferation is motivated by the desire of producers to make money.

In another sense, however, the market for alternatives is quite unlike the market for goods. Entrepreneurs and politicians are alike in motive and method, but consumers and voters are quite different. Given budget constraints, buyers choose among goods mainly on the basis of clearly defined and specific needs, only secondarily on the basis of taste. One buys a lamp in order to light a room but chooses the design because of aesthetic concerns. Voters, however, respond to needs that are often ill defined. They know they want to be better off. But, although many platforms are offered as a means to make them better off, the objective connection between particular platforms and the actual solution of voters' problems is seldom clear. Consequently voters' choices have a much larger component of style as distinct from need than do buyers' choices. Even altruism—sometimes apparent, sometimes real—may, for example, play a significant role in voting, though seldom in buying.

Consequently, although the entrepreneur can be guided in picking products by objectively known human needs, the politician has less objectively verifiable knowledge about his or her "market." In this situation the politician must try out alternatives more or less randomly. Furthermore, although artifacts are usable in any society, values expressed in political alternatives are always relative to the culture of a particular society. The content of culture is moreover always rather vague, so, in still another way, politicians as a whole must behave fairly randomly in generating alternatives.

The world of political issues can thus be better compared to the world of organic nature than to markets. New issues are produced, more or less randomly, just as genetic recombinations are constantly produced, more or less randomly. Some few of the animal and vegetable recombinations find a niche in the environment and survive and flourish; most of the recombinations fail. So it is also with issues. Most find no significant audience and fail; but some are responded to enthusiastically and flourish, even to the point of completely reshaping the environment in which they arose.

Thus, the rise and fall of issues is a process of natural selection, in which politicians, like genes, seek to survive and flourish. We know very little about the course and direction of that process. We can chart the history of biological evolution. We can show that over time more complex creatures appear (although, of course, very simple creatures persist). We know details about the process, such as the fact that highly specialized species stand little chance of surviving a change in habitat. Still we cannot see any clear direction in the process, and it seems likely there is none. Indeed, if a biologist possessed of all current knowledge about the principles and processes of evolution but no details of evolutionary history were transported back 100 million, 500 million, or 1, 2, or 3 billion years, it is doubtful that at any point the biologist's predictions of the future course of organic development would be correct, although the biologist *might* make better guesses at 100 million years ago than at 3 billion. So it is with the history of political issues. No seers have ever existed, although sometimes well-informed people have made pretty good guesses about the short-run future.

If there is any significant difference in the procedure of natural selection among creatures in the biological world and natural selection among issues in the political world, it is that the past lays a heavier hand on the course of biological evolution than on political evolution. A species does not disappear unless the environment changes markedly; issues do not have long lives and may disappear even though social conditions remain fairly stable. In this sense, the natural selection of issues is somewhat more random than the natural selection of species.

8.F. Structural Regularities in Natural Selection

To admit that disequilibrium is the characteristic state of politics and that the rise and decline of issues is a random process does not mean that it is impossible to generalize about regularities in the process. Biologists are able to generalize about regularities in organic evolution, and there is no reason why political scientists cannot generalize about similar regularities in political evolution. Features of the environment do affect the selection of both creatures and issues, and, for issues, the most salient features of the environment are institutions or constitutional structures, which have always been of great concern to political scientists. We know, for example, quite a bit about the way single-member district systems influence the development of issues and even something about the way proportional representation does; and we know quite a bit also about the way highly abstract institutions such as zero-sum elections and transferable and nontransferable utility generate structural equilibria.[7]

In less scientifically satisfying ways we know a great deal about political socialization and the vagaries of political opinion in governments with different constitutions—not just the contrast between democracies and absolutisms, but even the more delicate contrast among different kinds of democracies. Furthermore, all sorts of new questions are subject to investigation in light of the theory of natural selection. For example, it seems possible that different kinds of constitutions make for different rates of evolution of issues. There is no theory on this subject, and common sense is not a very good guide. All kinds of governments involve some amalgamation of preference, and even perverse tyrannies like Mao's are from time to time required to change direction in accord with popular values. It is not obvious, however, and would indeed be interesting to discover whether such tyrannies, because tyrannical, tend to slow down evolution more than other governments or whether, because perverse and capricious, tend to speed it up. Thus, to say that disequilibrium and natural selection exist is not to say that science is impossible. But it is to say that prediction of the rise and decline of particular issues is probably impossible.

9

Manipulation and the Natural Selection of Issues: The Development of the Issue of Slavery as a Prelude to the American Civil War

As an illustration of the public importance of manipulation of the agenda in a democracy and of the way the natural selection of issues works, in this chapter I will examine the creation of a new issue on a grand scale—namely, the issue of slavery, between 1819 and 1860. This history shows that new issues are rooted in the voting system, in the necessary existence of losers and of the opportunity they have to control the agenda in such a way as to become winners. By extension it indicates that great political events can be interpreted as part of the continuing effort by participants (either leaders or losers) to manipulate outcomes to their advantage.

The particular event here studied involves losers introducing new issues to generate cycles and disequilibrium, from which, with luck, they can emerge as winners. In this case the losers were ultimately successful: They did produce disequilibrium, and they did reshape American politics so that the fundamental coalitions during the latter part of the nineteenth century were quite different—and to the advantage of the previous losers—from the coalitions in the first part of the century. I want to emphasize, however, that this particular outcome was not entirely due to the wit and persistence of the losers. The outcome of efforts at manipulation is also conditioned by the external circumstances in which the manipulation occurs, the underlying values, the constitutional structure, and the state of technology and the economy. Numerous efforts are made at manipulation. Not all succeed. The choice of which ones do succeed is partially determined by these external circumstances. This is the significance of the process of natural selection.[1]

To delimit the subject of this chapter, I emphasize that I do not inquire into the cause of the Civil War.[2] Rather I inquire into the reason for one necessary condition of that war—and probably of all civil wars—namely, the existence of an issue that occasioned some degree of territorial separation of the disputing factions. My interest in the inquiry is not, however, in explaining the Civil War as an event or the slavery issue as a phenomenon, but rather merely to illustrate, with an event of supreme political importance, how manipulation works on the grand scale of national politics, how disequilibrium is generated over a long time-span, and how the natural selection of issues occurs in the gross social world in rough analogy to natural selection in the gross organic world.

9.A. The Appearance of Slavery as a National Political Issue

The initial status quo on slavery, incorporated in the Constitution and the initial actions under it, was an acknowledgment of the existence of slavery as decided by the states internally and by the United States within territories. This status quo persisted for a generation without significant challenge, and during that time slavery was not a salient political issue. Then political losers raised it, presumably as a way to generate disequilibrium from which they might improve their position by detaching some of the winners' support.

From 1800 to 1860, the United States was usually governed by that hardy intersectional coalition of agrarian expansionism: Jeffersonian Republicanism and Jacksonian Democracy. That coalition was built on the initial status quo, which included a tacit approval of slavery, and most of its major leaders were slaveowners. Nevertheless, several essential components of the coalition—the Middle Atlantic states and later the states of the Northwest Territory (Ohio, Indiana, Illinois, Michigan, and Wisconsin)—were free territory. Hence to raise the issue of slavery was to threaten that dominant coalition, whose parts could agree on slavery only so long as they ignored it. Therein lay both the difficulty and the opportunity for opponents.

The issue was difficult to raise because it threatened a winning majority, most of which would ignore it for the sake of winning. But because it was potentially so divisive it was probably the best opportunity the continuing losers had. Ultimately, they were able to raise it in a way that wholly disrupted the dominant coalition, generated a cyclical majority that was resolved by the Civil War, and set the scene for a new coalition on a new theme that dominated American politics for even longer than the Jefferson-Jackson coalition had.

Manipulating the social agenda with a new issue that generates disequilibrium allows old losers to become new winners. This is what happened with the slavery issue. It was introduced with that purpose, turned out to work, and was selected from among other issues just because it did work.

9.B. Slavery as an Issue from the Ratification of the Constitution Through the Missouri Compromise

The initial status quo in the Republic involved recognition of the legality of slavery, where established, with almost no controversy on the subject. The Congress of the Articles of Confederation never sought to legislate about domestic institutions of member states, but it did, of necessity, govern the territories and produced (apparently without much dispute) the Northwest Ordinance of 1787, which prohibited slavery in that area. In the constitutional convention slavery did occasion much discussion and one important compromise, although the great compromise was between the large and small states. By the slavery compromise, on the one hand the Constitution did not prohibit navigation acts and on the other hand the importation of slaves was prohibited after 1808 and slaves were to be counted as three-fifths of a person for purposes of apportioning representatives. This agreement implicitly recognized the legality of slavery as the status quo. Thereafter slavery did not enter national politics as an issue in any significant way until 1819.

Of course, some people condemned slavery on moral grounds. Even in the constitutional convention, liberals such as Gouverneur Morris and Rufus King, as distinct from Southern and Northern conservatives, condemned slavery on grounds of morality rather than expediency. And quite a few Northern politicians, especially Federalists, whose party was mainly confined to the North after 1800, resented the fact that nonvoting slaves were counted for apportionment. Federalist resentment, however, was directed not at slavery itself but at the advantage it gave to Republican politicians. Probably most Federalists would simply have preferred that slaves not be counted at all, without caring much whether slavery continued to exist.

In 1819, however, a bill to admit Missouri occasioned a proposed amendment prohibiting slavery in the new state. What may well have been intended as no more than a local maneuver very swiftly caught on nationally. Anti-Missouri rallies were organized all over the Northeast.

State legislatures instructed congressmen to vote for the amendment. Newspapers carried on a dramatic debate. Jefferson wrote that the issue terrified him "like a firebell in the night"—as it should, for *his* coalition was under attack. Prophecies of war and secession became journalistic commonplaces.[3]

Why, one might ask, did slavery suddenly become a salient issue, 200 years after it was initially introduced in Virginia and 30 years after the framers of the Constitution, without serious dispute, accepted it as the status quo? This question is all the more difficult because the Missouri agitation was a brief episode, soon settled, and the issue was not seriously revived in national politics for another 15 years. One can hardly argue there was any economic reason. Nothing happened in or around 1819 to change the relative economic significance of slave and free labor. Indeed, the very episodic feature of the event precludes an economic explanation. Nor can one argue that there was a profound humanitarian explanation. Antislavery sentiment had long existed, although the Missouri agitation provided a good vehicle for propagating it. Still no great change of the American heart occurred in 1819–1820, and the concern about slavery was easily inhibited for another decade. Lacking an alternative, we must, I believe, say that the precipitating force was political; and political it was, rooted in an effort by losers to manipulate the agenda to their advantage.

(By attributing the origin of the issue to political ambition, I do not imply that the motives were cynical or cheap. In a democracy, the function of a politician is to find an issue on which he or she can win, for thereby a politician expresses some part of the values of the electorate. Political opportunism is not evil, therefore, but is instead the engine of democracy.)

The immediate origin of the Missouri issue can fairly be attributed to the pettiest of politics. The motion to amend the Missouri bill was offered by James Tallmadge of New York. He was about to become a candidate for the state senate from New York City as an ally of DeWitt Clinton, the maverick Republican who had run for president with Federalist endorsement in 1812. Clinton and Tallmadge both had previously denounced slavery. Their opposition in New York was the Tammany faction, led by Martin Van Buren, then the chief New York supporter of the Republican intersectional alliance and of William Crawford of Georgia for president in 1824. Tallmadge had a special reason for raising the slavery issue against Van Buren: In New York City there were a significant number of free black voters, concentrated in marginal wards and typically Federalist in loyalty. Contemporary writers as well as recent historians have asserted that, as a result of his amendment, Tallmadge stood to gain blacks' votes.[4]

It is foolish, however, to attribute a huge social movement to the private ambition and local manipulation of one man. The interesting fact is that, even if the motion was initially a personal ploy, it aroused the entire North. Events like the Missouri agitation may be attributed to some individual advantage (as, for instance, Tallmadge's) or to a conspiracy (here the main conspirator often blamed is Rufus King); but such attribution is self-deluding, for the movement was far greater than one man or one conspiracy. It reflected the interest of a large public, and it is this interest that must be specified in order to explain the event.

In 1819–1820 the Federalist party was substantially eliminated as a political force. Only 15 percent of the House was then Federalist; and in 1816 Rufus King, the last Federalist candidate for president, carried only Massachusetts, Connecticut, and Delaware, 34 votes out of 225, or again 15 percent. The victory of the Republicans was so complete that James Monroe was reelected later in 1820 with only one dissenting elector.

The reasons for the decline of the Federalist party are easy to identify. From Washington's time onward, it had been infused with a commercial and somewhat aristocratic spirit at the very time the legal electorate was being slightly expanded to include all white males. (The states west of the Appalachians had all entered the Union with white manhood suffrage, and most of the original 13 states had by 1820 abolished property qualifications.) More significantly, the actual electorate was being enormously expanded by the Jeffersonian enthusiasm to use government for distributive advantages for farmers. Hence, Federalism was ideologically out of touch, while expansionist agrarian Republicanism captured the imagination of a society still over 90 percent rural. Furthermore, Federalism had been identified with treason because prominent Federalists (and only Federalists) were at the Hartford Convention of 1814. This convention was popularly interpreted as a step toward a separate peace and secession for New England. So, as the party with an old-fashioned ideology and a recent history interpretable as treason, Federalism was dying out. As it died, careerist politicians deserted it, even when they believed its ideology. By 1819 it was almost defunct.

Discredited the party might be, but its main economic content still had appeal. The desire for tariffs, internal improvements, and commercial development did not go away simply because its spokesmen were mute. And it was not just Federalists who wanted these things. Many who had drifted into the Republican camp—such as John Quincy Adams and Henry Clay—were eager for commercial development even though Republican orthodoxy frowned on it.

Consequently, there was a substantial class of losers on an issue of political and moral scarcity. Highly simplified, the issue was this: Should government encourage agrarian expansion or commercial development? To encourage the former meant, for example, that there would be no subsidies for the latter. (Characteristically, President Monroe in 1817 had refused national assistance for the Erie Canal.) To encourage commerce, on the other hand, meant that there would be policies such as tariffs, which would be costly to farmers. (Again characteristically, it was John Quincy Adams' Tariff of Abominations in 1828 that occasioned nullification in South Carolina.) So truly the great issue of the era was politically and morally scarce: To favor one side was to hurt the other. Furthermore, as Federalism declined, one side of that issue was losing badly. The triumphant Virginia dynasty, inspired as it was by Jefferson's vision of a republic of yeomen farmers, more or less consistently ignored commercial needs and interests.

There was a chance, consequently, for new leadership to put the case for commercial development, provided additional issues could be introduced that would slice up politics in different coalitions. One such issue was slavery, especially when expressed in the conventional free soil terms of the Northwest Ordinance. And so the anti-Missouri movement, once launched, attracted both old Federalists, like Rufus King, who led in the Senate, and Republicans disillusioned with the Virginia dynasty, like John Taylor of New York, who led in the House. These people, the losers of the moment, were trying out a new issue. As one recent student of the agitation remarked, "It is noteworthy that almost every prominent leader of the Missouri agitation was found in the Adams camp soon afterwards. . . . [T]he Missouri question played an important part in crystallizing what would be known as the National Republican party."[5] Generalizing, this is to say that the motive for the agitation was to find a new and disequilibrating program, a new agenda whereon dissident Republicans and old Federalists could combine to win.

So interpreted, there is nothing surprising about the sudden popularity of the slavery issue. Even with a huge Republican majority, there were still losers: One cannot have, for example, a policy against internal improvements without depriving those who want them. These losers needed new combinations of issues to win, and the Missouri agitation was a tentative step toward the manipulation of the agenda for just this purpose.

The logic of this manipulation is perfectly straightforward. If the dissidents could not beat Monroe on conventional agrarian issues, then they could introduce a new issue to split the intersectional alliance. The puzzlement expressed both then and now about the meteor-like development of the Missouri agitation can be erased with the understanding that this agitation was merely a normal incident in the search by losers for a platform from which to beat previous winners. It is comparable to the anti-Masonic movement a decade later and the nativist movement a generation later. Since the slavery issue promised to split the intersectional winning coalition, it was embraced with enthusiasm in 1819 and repeatedly thereafter until it generated cyclical majorities and civil war.

The anti-Missouri agitators were, however, losers in the nation as a whole, and they could not carry off victory the first time they tried. The leaders of the enduring Jeffersonian alliance, recognizing the strains the slavery issue would subject it to, produced a compromise: Maine and Missouri were to come in together; slavery was to be permitted in Missouri but prohibited north of the Missouri line in all the Louisiana Purchase. A good many Northern Jeffersonians—"doughfaces" as they were later called, meaning Northern apologists for slavery—voted for this compromise, and almost all of them were immediately defeated for reelection. Their defeat was a harbinger of what the slavery issue might become. But the compromise effectively buried the issue for the time being because the Republican establishment won and the anti-Missouri agitators lost.

9.C. From the Missouri Compromise to the Gag Rule

In the theory of manipulation, losers bring forth new issues to generate disequilibrium in hope of exploiting it to their advantage. But the losers on the Missouri Compromise had no motive to raise the slavery issue again for nearly a decade. Between 1820 and 1829, they sought the election and reelection of John Quincy Adams, who had won in 1824 by reason of a split among the Jeffersonians. His supporters, the commercial party generally, therefore had no motive to drive away any Southern votes. Similarly, the old Jeffersonians—turned Jacksonians after 1824—were dependent on the intersectional alliance and, even though temporarily losers, had no motive to discuss slavery. So the issue was not broached from 1820 to 1829.

Nor was it broached during most of Andrew Jackson's administration. Northern opponents of Jackson again had a motive to raise the question, but they were distracted by two developments. First, in the North anti-Masonry was an alternative issue to slavery. It drained the political energies of exactly those politicians in New England and New York who later promoted the slavery issue. Anti-Masonry failed and was discarded, just as nativism (the Know-Nothings) also failed as an alternative to the slavery issue in the mid-1850s. But while the natural selection of issues was selecting against anti-Masonry, the slavery issue could not be broached. Second, in the South the opponents of the Jackson alliance had for the first time since early in the century a strong organization based on economic issues. This was the beginning of Southern Whiggery, and it infused all of Jackson's opponents with the hope of an intersectional alliance of their own. Thus, the rise of the National Republicans, later the Whigs, turned politicians away from the slavery issue to conventional economic issues like the Bank of the United States.

On the other hand, although slavery was, for these reasons, not an issue during most of Jackson's administration, two things happened that prepared for its revival. One was that Jackson's opponents lost on both anti-Masonry and economic issues. The other was that Jackson more or less fortuitously isolated South Carolina, which then became a territorial center of slaveholding imperialism. Apparently deciding that he did not need South Carolina to win, Jackson effectively expelled John Calhoun and his coterie over the nullification issue.[6] In the next two elections South Carolina had its anti-Jackson political party, never incorporated into Whiggery. When South Carolina was welcomed back into the Democracy, it was as the center of proslavery fanaticism, which gradually took over most of the Southern wing. If, as some argue, the Civil War was a revolution by slaveholders, then a crucial step toward that outcome was the political isolation of South Carolina so it could develop the ideology of that revolution.[7]

The isolation was crucial to the development of the slavery issue also, for it gave abolitionists and Free-Soilers a concrete target. Had South Carolina been contained in the Jacksonian alliance, perhaps the Northern populists in that alliance would have been able to ignore the slavery issue. But after South Carolina in the 1840s effectively forced the commitment of the Southern Democracy to the defense of slavery, Northern Jacksonians were also forced to reconsider their loyalties.

Toward the end of Jackson's administration, therefore, the scene was set for a revival of the slavery issue. His opponents had failed on anti-Masonry and economic nationalism; so they began to test out the slavery issue again. It worked; and, from the mid-1830s until the end of the Civil War, it was never far from the center of American politics.

It has long been assumed that the spread of antislavery agitation in the 1830s resulted from secularizing religious enthusiasm. But many reform movements—temperance, penal reform, free education, women's rights—vied with antislavery as proto-political issues. Only one, however, was fully absorbed into politics. Why? One answer is that the evil of slavery was worse than the others and so quite properly received the attention it deserved. Another answer, less moralistic, is that abolition was in the air: Britain emancipated in 1833. Both answers imply that the issue was pushed into politics by social forces outside the political system, forces that would have made slavery an issue regardless of the structure of politics.

It has also been often argued that the antislavery agitation of the 1830s was an economic response to the swift increase in cotton planting in the 1820s and 1830s. The assertion is that, since cotton was especially adapted to and profitable with slave cultivation, this new agriculture threatened free labor and provided an economic motive for the antislavery movement. This explanation also locates the slavery issue outside of politics in a kind of economic or technological determinism.

Both these nonpolitical theories are suspect, however, because they entirely fail to explain the Missouri agitation. In 1819–1820 secularization of religion had hardly begun, and the cotton culture was still economically modest. Yet to explain the antislavery movement adequately one needs a theory that ties together both the agitation over Missouri and the agitation over the gag rule, which was the occasion for the rally of free soil and abolition.

Such is the argument offered here. In both eras the issue of slavery was attractive as a way to win office. It was peculiarly attractive politically to Northern Whigs in the 1830s because it played on the geographic strains in the Jacksonian coalition. I do not, of course, deny the genuine moral fervor of antislavery propagandists like William Lloyd Garrison or later Harriet Beecher Stowe. Nor do I mean to suggest that men like John Quincy Adams and Joshua Giddings, two leaders against the gag rule, were insincere opportunists. It is true, however, that Adams never mentioned slavery while he was president. And as late as 1858, Giddings refused to support suffrage for blacks in Ohio.[8] These facts suggest that these men were Whigs first and abolitionists second. Their moral concern was surely genuine, but idealism and political interest ran hand in hand. Given the large Jacksonian majority, only a new issue could split that majority. Slavery was such an issue, and fortunately the Northern Whig leaders who fought the gag could simultaneously promote Christian principles and party advantage.

Slavery was always an evil but not always a political issue. What made it a political issue was that, by reason of the structure of politics in the mid-1830s, it was to some people's advantage to place abolition on the political agenda.

The issue was introduced by a petition campaign launched by anti-slavery societies and propagandists, most of whom probably had no deep partisan attachment. The petitions took the form of prayers for abolition of the slave trade or slavery in the District of Columbia. Whig congressmen received them, encouraged more, and overwhelmed the House.[9] Without the concerted and deliberate encouragement and instigation of Whig congressmen the petition campaign would have come to nought. But they did encourage and instigate and their motive was, of course, obstruction.[10]

Democrats had two motives to refuse to receive and discuss the petitions, that is, to gag the petitioners and the congressional presenters. From the point of view of governing, Northern and Southern Democrats alike wanted to get on with "real" issues rather than waste time on slavery, which they regarded as a partisan distraction. From the point of view of Southern proslavery fanatics, the gag was necessary to silence abolitionist agitation, which obtained a certain legitimacy by focusing on a legitimate subject for national legislation—slavery in the District of Columbia. So they passed gag rules (rules prohibiting the acceptance of petitions for the abolition of the slave trade—or, later, slavery—in the District, a proper subject for federal legislation). These rules were then the focus of antislavery agitation from 1835 to 1842. The leader of the opposition to the gags was John Quincy Adams, who may, therefore, be judged to be the chief generator of the slavery issue that ultimately destroyed the Jackson coalition.

The issue was uncomplicated so long as Democrats ruled: Whigs simply secured and presented a continuing flood of petitions. But when in 1841 they took office, themselves an intersectional coalition—really a somewhat more commercial version of the Jacksonian coalition—Whigs did not know how to deal with the petitions. Those who were fully committed to breaking up the Democracy with the slavery issue simply continued their campaign. But those who wished to govern passed a gag rule (with Democratic help). The Whig gag produced a crisis, common enough in radical movements, in which it is necessary to discipline natural allies the better to attack the enemy.

There were three main events in the course of the discipline: Adams' censure, Giddings' reelection, and the Liberty party of 1844.

John Quincy Adams, bolder and bolder in denouncing slavery, eventually attacked the behavior and character of members of Congress. The Whig majority, seeing their national coalition subjected to the same strains the slavery issue had imposed on Democrats, sought in 1842 to censure him. His defense, the dramatic claim of constitutional rights by an old and great man, won the sympathy of the country and of Congress. The motion to censure was tabled. Also in 1842, however, Joshua Giddings of Ohio was censured for antislavery resolutions. He immediately resigned and was triumphantly reelected. He was quickly readmitted to Whig councils, probably, as Gilbert Barnes remarks, because his vote and the votes of other antislavery Whigs were needed on party issues.[11] From that point on, constant discussion of slavery could not be kept out of Congress. Finally in 1844, the Liberty party offered James G. Birney for president, and he got enough votes (drawing mainly from Whigs) to elect James Polk. (In New York Polk beat Clay by 6,000 votes while Birney had 16,000. With Birney's votes Clay could have obtained New York's 36 electors and beaten Polk by 141 to 136.) This was a salutary lesson to all Northern politicians, Democrats as well as Whigs. From then on, a large contingent in both parties would be prepared to adopt antislavery positions. This was the beginning of the end for both Whig and Democratic intersectional alliances.

9.D. The Wilmot Proviso

The point at which Northern Democrats clearly adopted an antislavery stance was at the offering of the Wilmot Proviso in 1846. The political background for this motion was Northern Democratic resentment that the North-South balance in the intersectional Democratic coalition had been tipped in favor of the South. Polk ran in 1844 on a platform of maintaining the balance by admitting both Texas and Oregon. But Texas came in before Polk took office, and Polk then compromised on Oregon, giving up what is now British Columbia. So, when the Mexican War began, with the prospect of even more slave territory in the Southwest, David Wilmot, a Pennsylvania Jacksonian, moved to prohibit slavery in land acquired from Mexico.

The Wilmot Proviso was offered first in August 1846 and then numerous times in 1847 and 1848. It always failed; but it laid the basis for the Free Soil party of 1848, which nominated, of all people, Martin Van Buren, who, from the Missouri Compromise until the end of his own presidency, had been the archetypal doughface, the Northern voice of proslavery Jacksonian populism. But as a Free-Soiler, in 1848, Van Buren drew enough Northern Democratic antislavery votes to give the election to the Whigs.

The people involved in the proviso controversy typify the strains in the Democratic party. Polk represented the old Jacksonian agrarian, populist imperialism and was a slaveholder, though not a fanatic defender of slavery. He believed that the slavery issue was not genuine and that both sides were simply opportunists. Fortunately, we have a candid statement of these opinions in a diary kept as a political reminder and never intended for publication.[12] I will quote several passages as evidence that one remarkably astute observer, intimately acquainted with events and personalities, honestly assessed the slavery issue as political opportunism on both sides. Polk may have been excessively cynical, but his remarks ring true, given that very few Free-Soilers were abolitionists or even very much interested in blacks. Let Polk speak for himself:

Mr. Hamlin [Hannibal Hamlin of Maine, later Republican vice president, 1861–1865] professes to be a [D]emocrat, but ... is pressing a mischievous course ... on the slavery question. ... The slavery question is assuming a fearful and most important aspect. The movement of Mr. King [Preston King, New York Democrat, managing the Wilmot Proviso], if persevered in, will be attended with terrible consequences to the country, and cannot fail to destroy the Democratic party, if it does not ultimately destroy the Union itself. Slavery was one of the questions adjusted in the compromises of the Constitution. It has, and could have no legitimate connection with the war with Mexico. ... It is a domestic and not a foreign question. ... Of course, Federalists [Polk's pejorative name for Whigs] are delighted to see such a question agitated by Northern Democrats because it divides and distracts the Democratic party and increases their [i.e. Whigs'] prospects of coming to power. Such an agitation is not only unwise but wicked [January 4, 1847, Vol. 2, p. 305].

Or the next year:

The agitation of the slavery question is mischievous and wicked, and proceeds from no patriotic motive by its authors. It is a mere political question on which demagogues and ambitious politicians hope to promote their own prospects for political promotion. And this they seem willing to do even at disturbing the harmony if not dissolving the Union itself [December 22, 1848, Vol. 4, p. 251].

Polk was just as cynical about the motives of the other territorial wing breaking off from the Democratic coalition:

I remarked to Mr. Mason that Mr. Calhoun had become perfectly desperate in his aspiration to the Presidency, and had seized upon this sectional question as the only means of sustaining himself in his present fallen condition, and that such an agitation of the slavery question was not only unpatriotic and mischievous, but wicked [April 6, 1847, Vol. 3, p. 458].

Polk resented the Whig delight at Democratic discomfort, but it was Northern Democrats, Polk's own political friends, who were causing him trouble. These Democratic Free-Soilers were not abolitionists. Wilmot himself, for example, was a conventional Jacksonian populist from a wholly rural Pennsylvania district.[13] He was against slavery in the territories because he was fearful of slave competition with free labor.[14] His concern was for whites, not for blacks. He was afraid that Polk's failure to maintain the North-South balance by losing part of Oregon would render the Northern Democrats vulnerable to Whig agitation. The Wilmot Proviso was the Democratic defense against the Whig antislavery agitation of the previous decade.

As Polk intuitively understood, the proviso generated disequilibrium. Early in August 1846, Polk conceived the Machiavellian plan for a quick victory over Mexico by buying off whoever might be in control of its army. He asked Congress for $2 million for that purpose.[15] To this appropriation Wilmot moved as an amendment the proviso prohibiting slavery in any territory acquired. The proviso was voted on eight times on August 8, 1846, but the largest and crucial vote was on a motion to lay on the table the motion to engross (that is, to make a fair copy), which was defeated by 79 to 93.[16] The details are in Display 9-1, where a vote nay is a vote in favor of the proviso.

All Southerners voted against the proviso; almost all Northerners, Whigs and Democrats alike, voted for it. In two ways this outcome involved disequilibrium. Let us identify the possible outcomes thus:

a. Appropriation without the proviso

b. Appropriation with the proviso

c. No action

Polk almost certainly ordered *a b c*. The Senate had already in secret session agreed with him.[17] So as a body it held either *a b c* or *a c b*. The House action showed a preference for *b*. Probably, Wilmot and Northern Democrats held *b a c* and Southern Democrats *a c b*. Northern Whigs, certainly a minority, were probably the only ones who placed *c* first: *c b a*. But *c* won. The House attached the proviso to the appropriation and sent it to the Senate several hours before adjournment. Senator John Davis, a Massachusetts Whig who favored *c* and who had voted against an earlier resolution on the appropriation (which passed by 33 to 19), then filibustered until the clock ran out. So *c*, probably the least-desired alternative, won—clearly an outcome in disequilibrium and, incidentally, one that probably prolonged the war that Davis opposed.[18]

Display 9-1

The Vote on the Motion to Lay on the Table the Motion to Engross the Wilmot Proviso

	North		Border		South		Total	
	Democrats	Whigs	Democrats	Whigs	Democrats	Whigs	Democrats	Whigs
Yea	7	2	8	8	46	8	61	18
Nay	51	39	—	3	—	—	51	42
Total votes	58	41	8	11	46	8	112	60
Total membership	77	58	10	12	53	13	140	83

Furthermore, there was almost certainly disequilibrium in the House itself on this motion. There were not enough votes to ascertain preference orders, but it is easy to guess what they were:

7	Northern administration Democrats	*a b c*
51	Northern Free Soil Democrats (Wilmot)	*b a c*
8	Border Democrats	*a b c* or *a c b*
46	Southern Democrats	*a c b*
2	Northern prowar Whigs	*c a b*
39	Northern antiwar Whigs	*c b a*
3	Border Whigs	*b a c* or *b c a*
16	Southern and border Whigs	*a c b*

If this guess is even approximately correct, *b* beats *a* (as happened), *a* beats *c* (which is reasonable because all Democrats, 60 percent of the House, supported the administration on the war), and *c* beats *b* (which is reasonable because favoring *c* is a majority consisting of all Southerners—Democrat or Whig—who despised the proviso and Northern Whigs who wished to impede the administration on the war). So there is a clearcut cyclical majority, which is of course complete disequilibrium.

Thus, the issue of slavery, first broached in 1819 as a means to break up the Jeffersonian intersectional coalition, actually did so in 1846. Although the Whigs both generated the issue when out of office and tried to suppress it when in office, they could not really succeed until Northern Democrats were so afraid of losing on Free Soil issues that they would also raise the issue that threatened their own coalition. This is what they did, however, in the Wilmot Proviso, which may thus be regarded as the final act in the construction of the slavery issue. From then on the issue would have a life of its own. The Kansas-Nebraska Act of 1854 and the Dred Scott case in 1857 would put slavery in the very center of politics. And in 1861 would come civil war, surely the product of this issue.

9.E. From the Wilmot Proviso to the Civil War

Although the issue was fully developed by 1846, much had to happen before the Jeffersonian-Jacksonian coalition could be finally split.

Some Northern Democrats broke off from the party in 1848, and Van Buren ran on the Free Soil ticket, thereby electing Whigs. As always, Whigs in office played down the slavery issue and produced the Compromise of 1850, while Democrats, chastened by defeat in 1848, closed ranks in 1852 to win with a huge majority. This election revealed to Whigs that they could not win as an intersectional alliance on conventional economic issues. Initially they tried nativism again—a kind of replay in 1854 with the American or Know-Nothing party of the anti-Masonic movement of 1831–1832. But they soon found that nativism had a limited appeal. So, in 1856, capitalizing on the Democratic error with the Kansas-Nebraska Act, they went back to the slavery issue. The Northern Whigs, the bulk of the party, discarded their Southern branch and drew in the Free Soil Democrats (like Wilmot). That coalition, now called Republicans, was able to get office in 1860 and to get a majority in the whole country by 1868, a majority that won much more than half of the time from 1868 to 1930.

The Republican success in 1860 was in a sense a replay of the disequilibrium of the Wilmot Proviso. Abraham Lincoln won by a plurality of about 40 percent. Since it seems likely that he stood second in very few voters' preference orders, one suspects that there may well have been a cycle in this case also. Knowing only first-place votes, I have tried to guess at the full preference orders of voters in each region who cast first-place votes for each of the four candidates—Abraham Lincoln, Stephen A. Douglas, John C. Breckinridge, and John Bell. In Display 9-2 are listed 15 of the 24 possible preference orders for four candidates, with estimates by party and section of the number of voters who held these orders. In the Display, each row contains a preference order followed by my estimate of the number of voters who held it. In the last column of each row is an explanation of how my guess was arrived at. Thus in row 1, the number 450,000 consists of one-fourth of the number of voters for Lincoln in New England, the Middle Atlantic states, and the Midwest, plus all of the voters for Lincoln in the South.

If my guesses are even roughly like the true situation, then Lincoln, Douglas, and Bell were in a cycle, and all three clearly defeated Breckinridge. So by majoritarian voting, we get:

Douglas P Lincoln P Bell P Douglas P Breckinridge

Using the Borda count or using approval voting with each voter casting three approval votes (highly unlikely in the circumstances), Douglas wins:

Douglas *P* Bell *P* Lincoln *P* Breckinridge

But using approval voting with each voter casting two approval votes, Bell wins:

Bell *P* Lincoln *P* Douglas *P* Breckinridge

Thus, with five methods of voting, Douglas wins twice, Bell once, Lincoln once (the method actually used), and they are in a cycle and hence tie once. Clearly, if my guesses are even roughly right, there was complete disequilibrium in 1860, which is how the slavery issue destroyed the Jeffersonian-Jacksonian coalition.

*   *   *

In this chapter I have tried to illustrate how losers manipulate the agenda by introducing new issues. The new issue breaks up the old majority and in the resultant disequilibrium the original losers have a chance to win. This is what happened with the slavery issue. It was raised by Federalists and dissident Republicans (the group that later became National Republicans and then Whigs) in 1819 and again in 1835 and after to put strain on the Jeffersonian-Jacksonian coalition. National Republicans and Whigs were not eager to raise it, however, when they held office or had a good chance for it (between 1820 and 1828, 1841 and 1845, 1849 and 1852). The issue matured when Whigs had sufficiently frightened Northern Democrats that they too became, defensively, enthusiastic Free-Soilers, as in the Wilmot Proviso episode, the Free Soil party, and ultimately the Republican party.

Nevertheless, there was no straight-line progression in the Federalist-Whig development of this issue. Not only did they ignore it when they too held national office on the basis of an intersectional coalition; but also they ignored it when the tried out other issues—anti-Masonry in 1830–1832, nativism in 1855–1856, and economic issues for an intersectional coalition in 1832–1835—and when they held office. The slavery issue gradually displaced these others by a kind of natural selection. It worked and the others did not. Anti-Masonry and nativism had rather too-local appeals to serve as the basis of a nationally successful party. And the Federalist-National Republican-Whig economic position of commercial development was based on a national coalition that was repeatedly demonstrated to be *smaller* than the Jeffersonian-Jacksonian coalition of agrarian populism. Failing all else, the slavery issue came to be chosen

Display 9-2

Possible Preference Orders in 1860, by Candidate of First Choice and by Region

	Preference orders			Number	Location
	1st	2nd	3rd	4th		

#	1st	2nd	3rd	4th	Number	Location
1.	L	D	Bl	Bk	450,000	One-fourth New England, Mid-Atlantic, and Midwest Lincoln voters All Southern Lincoln voters
2.	L	Bl	D	Bk	1,414,000	Three-fourths New England, Mid-Atlantic, and Midwest Lincoln voters All Border and Western Lincoln voters
3.	D	Bk	L	Bl	173,000	One-third New England and Mid-Atlantic Douglas voters
4.	D	Bk	Bl	L	489,000	One-third Mid-Atlantic and Midwest Douglas voters One-half Border and Western Douglas voters All Southern Douglas voters
5.	D	L	Bk	Bl	83,000	Two-thirds New England Douglas voters
6.	D	L	Bl	Bk	318,000	One-sixth Mid-Atlantic Douglas voters One-third Midwest Douglas voters One-fourth Border and Western Douglas voters
7.	D	Bl	L	Bk	319,000	One-sixth Mid-Atlantic Douglas voters One-third Midwest Douglas voters One-fourth Border and Western Douglas voters

						Description
8.	Bk	D	Bl	L	329,000	New England Breckinridge voters One-half Mid-Atlantic, Midwest, Border, and Western Breckinridge voters One-fourth Southern Breckinridge voters
9.	Bk	D	L	Bl	104,000	One-half Mid-Atlantic and Midwest Breckinridge voters
10.	Bk	Bl	D	L	413,000	One-half Mid-Atlantic and Midwest Breckinridge voters Three-quarters Southern Breckinridge voters
11.	Bl	L	D	Bk	270,000	All New England, Mid-Atlantic, and Midwest Bell voters One-half Border and Western Bell voters One-third Southern Bell voters
12.	Bl	Bk	D	L	146,000	One-third Southern Bell voters One-sixth Border Bell voters One-quarter Western Bell voters
13.	Bl	Bk	L	D	31,000	One-sixth Border Bell voters One-quarter Western Bell voters
14.	Bl	D	Bk	L	28,000	One-sixth Border Bell voters
15.	Bl	D	L	Bk	114,000	One-third Southern Bell voters

Note. L = Lincoln. D = Douglas. Bl = Bell. Bk = Breckinridge.

because it alone proved able to split the persistent, winning Jeffersonian-Jacksonian coalition and thereby generate cycles in which anti-Jacksonians had a chance to win. The slavery issue thus survived by a natural selection that is always motivated by the drive for losers to win. A fortunate by-product of that process was the abolition of slavery, even though civil war was needed to achieve it.

10

Liberalism, Populism, and the Theory of Social Choice

In Chapter 9, I showed how a very large, apparent, popular majority was fractionated and replaced with a partially overlapping, partially contradictory one—an illustration of the fragility of even the strongest majority. This is a concrete instance of what I have previously shown by abstract argument—namely, that the outcomes of voting are not necessarily fair and true amalgamations of voters' values, that these outcomes may be meaningless, and that the majorities that make outcomes are themselves in flux. Having thus raised a variety of issues about the interpretation of voting, I will now return to the main problem raised in Chapter 1, the significance of the theory of social choice for the theory of democracy.

10.A. The Adequacy of Voting

In the democratic tradition, theorists have seldom raised questions about the reliability of the voting mechanism in amalgamating individual values into a social decision. Many writers have indeed feared tyranny by the majority. But their fear has rarely, so far as I can discover, led them to question the adequacy of the way majorities are made.

Fear of majority tyranny is a fear that the values of the "majority" may be morally scarce and that enforcement of them will deprive the "minority" of its values. This fear has led some writers (from gentle Christians like T. S. Eliot to modern tyrants like Lenin or Mao) to reject democracy altogether. Others have argued that, to minimize the danger, on the more important political issues an extraordinary majority ought to be required. And still others (following the lead of Madison) have defended democracy by showing that majorities are temporary, arguing that the majority is not likely to tyrannize over people who may themselves be on top after the next election.

Given the last argument, the most frequently uttered defense of democracy against the charge of majority tyranny, one would expect traditional theorists to recognize that majorities are at best temporary artifacts and therefore to wonder whether these artifacts are well or poorly made. Unfortunately, very little such speculation has occurred, except on the part of those, from A. V. Dicey to Anthony Downs, who have recognized that all majorities are themselves coalitions of minorities. And even those theorists have not systematically inquired into how such coalitions work.

That, however, is precisely the question of social choice theory. Its main interpretation is that the process of compounding individual choices into a social choice does not inspire confidence in the quality of majorities or similar amalgamations for decision. I will now summarize the conclusions of the previous chapters, setting forth the difficulties with amalgamation.

Conclusion 1. If there are more than two alternatives on any issue— as is almost always the case for any reasonably free, open, and fair political system—then there exist a wide variety of methods by which the values of members may be incorporated into the social decision. For convenience, I have grouped these methods into three categories—majoritarian, positional, and utilitarian—although methods in the same category are often quite different. Unfortunately, the numerous methods do not necessarily lead to the same social outcome with the same set of individual values. Not only do majoritarian methods, for example, typically lead to different social choices from positional and utilitarian methods, but also the methods in any one category do not typically lead to identical outcomes.

The difference in methods would not occasion much difficulty for democratic theory if one method were clearly technically or morally superior to others. Yet this is not the case. A good argument can be made for the fairness or efficiency or both of most of the majoritarian or positional methods and even of the utilitarian methods—which is indeed why methods in each category have been invented and recommended. The difference among the methods is simply that they are fair or efficient in different ways because they embody different ethical principles. Unfortunately, there seems to be no way to show that one such ethical principle is morally superior to another. Consequently, there is no fundamental reason of prudence or morality for preferring the amalgamation produced by one method to the amalgamation produced by another.

The moral and prudential standoff among methods would not in itself occasion difficulty for democratic theory if "most of the time" most methods led to the same social choice from a given profile of individual values. But this is not the case. Between any pair of methods there may be agreement on the choice from a large proportion of possible profiles.[1] But it is not enough to consider agreement between pairs of methods. One ought instead to compare outcomes among all commonly used and frequently proposed methods. So far as I know, no one has attempted such a comparison. But it seems a safe conjecture that, if such a comparison were made, the proportion of social profiles from which all the compared methods produced identical results would indeed be tiny. How, then, can it be said that any particular method truly amalgamates individual values when different methods—all with distinguishable but nevertheless justifiable claims to fairness—amalgamate quite differently?

Different methods produce different results, and usually we are ignorant of just how different the results are. For most of the methods in wide use, not enough information on preference orders is collected to reveal how the actual outcome differs from outcomes that might have been selected by another method. This means that, *even if some method produces a reasonably justifiable amalgamation, we do not know it.* Suppose, for example, that a profile contains one kind of "reasonably justifiable outcome," namely, a Condorcet winner, and that many methods of amalgamation would produce that alternative as the actual outcome. Since we lack full detail on profiles, however, we do not know whether that alternative has actually been chosen by some given method. Furthermore, we do not even know whether the actual choice is "close" to being a Condorcet winner, or whether it is, by this standard, a very bad choice indeed.

In section 9.E, in my reconstruction of the election of 1860, it appears that methods other than plurality voting would have produced winners other than the actual choice. But of course we do not know if my reconstruction is right or, if wrong, how or where it is wrong. In the absence of the collection of complete preference orders from all voters—an impossible task—we will always be in doubt about whether a particular method has produced an outcome regarded as fair by some a priori standard of fairness, *even if all usable methods would in fact have produced the same winner.*

Any particular outcome from voting may be regarded as partially the outcome of a previous historical event, the selection of a constitution. Since the amalgamation often depends as much on this antecedent choice as on the individual values, today's social decisions on substance reflect in part yesterday's social decisions on procedures. It is hard to believe that a social choice that depends in some unknown degree on the constitution that happens to exist and in some equally unknown degree on voters' values is a fair amalgamation of those values.

It is not that any particular method of voting is unfair, because every method is in some sense fair. Rather it is that the very idea of truly and accurately amalgamating values by voting is unfair because one does not know the effect of different methods on (usually) incompletely known profiles. The claim that voting produces a fair and accurate outcome simply cannot be sustained when the method of counting partially determines the outcome of counting.

This is, then, the first conclusion: Outcomes of voting cannot, in general, be regarded as accurate amalgamations of voters' values. Sometimes they may be accurate, sometimes not; but since we seldom know which situation exists, we cannot, in general, expect accuracy. Hence we cannot expect fairness either.

Conclusion 2. Suppose, however, that the people in a society have decided to use a particular method of voting and to define as fair the outcomes produced by that method. Because of the revelations from Arrow's theorem, from Gibbard's and Satterthwaite's theorems, and from Black and Newing's and Plott's and McKelvey's and Schofield's notions of equilibrium and related developments, there is no reason to suppose that one profile of individual values will always produce the same outcome with that method. Consequently, the alternative outcomes by a particular method on a particular profile cannot be said to be a fair or true amalgamation, even though the method itself is assumed to be fair. In that sense, we never know what an outcome means, whether it is a true expression of public opinion or not. Every reasonably fair method of voting can be manipulated in several ways. Since we cannot know whether manipulation has occurred, the truth and meaning of *all* outcomes is thereby rendered dubious.

One method of manipulation is strategic voting, wherein voters vote contrary to their true tastes in order to bring about an outcome more desirable than the outcome from voting truthfully. We know from Gibbard's theorem that all methods of voting are manipulable in this way. Since we can never be certain what "true tastes" are—all we ever know are revealed tastes—we can never be certain when voting is strategic. (Witness the difficulty in section 6.C of interpreting votes on the Powell amendment.) Yet if strategic voting occurs, it is hard to say that the outcome is a fair or true amalgamation of voters' values, especially when the successful manipulators are a small minority. It is possible, even probable, that strategic voting is commonplace in the real world, as evidenced by the frequency of allegations of, for example, vote-trading. If so, then *all* voting is rendered uninterpretable and meaningless. Manipulated outcomes are meaningless because they are manipulated, and unmanipulated outcomes are meaningless because they cannot be distinguished from manipulated ones.

Another method of manipulation is by control of the agenda to change the outcome from what it would be in the absence of such control. We know from the theorems about path independence that all nonoligarchic methods of voting are susceptible to changing outcomes by rearranging the agenda. Indeed, from McKelvey's and Schofield's theorems we know that, except in the rare and fragile instances of equilibrium, simple majority voting can, when the agenda is appropriately manipulated, lead to *any* possible outcome. Since we also know from a vast amount of conventional analysis of political institutions that much political dispute concerns control (and, presumably, manipulation) of the agenda, we can be fairly certain that this kind of manipulation is utterly commonplace. But of course we never know precisely when and how such manipulation occurs or succeeds. Since this manipulation is frequent but unidentified, again *all* outcomes of voting are rendered meaningless and uninterpretable.

A dynamic method of controlling the agenda is the introduction of new dimensions and issues in order to generate disequilibrium in which the previous kinds of manipulation are possible. Suppose that, by processes no individual person or oligarchy controls, the set of alternatives has been reduced to precisely two and that one of these always wins by a simple majority vote. This seems to be a stable equilibrium; yet it can be upset, dynamically, by the introduction of new dimensions and issues. If new issues result in situations vulnerable to strategic voting and manipulation of the agenda, then even stable equilibria are dynamically unstable. Again the meaning of outcomes is hard to interpret.

For most of the 60 years after 1800, Jeffersonian-Jacksonian agrarian expansionism with its implicit concomitants of slavery usually seemed to be a stable equilibrium. But it was upset and indeed repudiated in 1856 and 1860 over the issue of free soil. In 1860 it seems likely there was no Condorcet winner; but, if there were, it was almost certainly Douglas or Bell, not Lincoln. It is hard to say, then, that the most momentous election of American history was a fair or true amalgamation of individual values, mainly because the decision was thoroughly—and, as I showed in Chapter 9, deliberately—confused by the inclusion of several issues. The outcome probably was morally desirable, even though it involved a bloody civil war; but it is difficult to say that it was socially preferred. Slavery was not a false issue, as Polk believed. (Men in office always believe that new issues threatening them are "mischievous.") Rather, as a new issue it generated disequilibrium, the outcome of which could not be said to be a clear social choice. In this sense, *all* social decisions obtained by disrupting equilibria with new issues are not fair or true amalgamations of public opinion, even though the disruption may be socially and morally necessary and desirable.

This, then, is the second conclusion: Outcomes of any particular method of voting lack meaning because often they are manipulated amalgamations rather than fair and true amalgamations of voters' judgments and because we can never know for certain whether an amalgamation has in fact been manipulated.

10.B. The Rejection of Populism

The social amalgamations of individual values are, for reasons just summarized, often inadequate—indeed meaningless—interpretations of public opinion. Furthermore, we seldom know whether to assign any particular social choice to the inadequate category. Hence *all* choices can be suspected of inadequacy. What does this conclusion imply for the two views of voting in democracy set forth in Chapter 1? Can either populism or liberalism stand up?

Clearly populism cannot survive. The essence of populism is this pair of propositions:

1. What the people, as a corporate entity, want ought to be social policy.

2. The people are free when their wishes are law.

Since social choice theory is a device to analyze moral (and descriptive) propositions, not an ethical theory to choose among them, social choice theory cannot illuminate the question, implied in proposition 1, of what *ought* to be public policy. But, if the notion of the popular will is itself unclear, then what the people want cannot be social policy simply because we do not and cannot know what the people want. An election tells us at most which alternative wins; it does not tell us that the winner would also have been chosen over another feasible alternative that might itself have a better claim to be the social choice. Hence falls proposition 1. And if we do not know the people's wishes, then we cannot make them free by enacting their wishes. Thus falls proposition 2.

Populism as a moral imperative depends on the existence of a popular will discovered by voting. But if voting does not discover or reveal a will, then the moral imperative evaporates because there is nothing to be commanded. If the people speak in meaningless tongues, they cannot utter the law that makes them free. Populism fails, therefore, not because it is morally wrong, but merely because it is empty.

In the history of political ideas, a similar rejection of a moral imperative on the ground that it was uninterpretable occurred in the sixteenth and seventeenth centuries when religious directives on politics lost their presumed clarity. So long as the spiritual authority of the pope was unquestioned, he could state the political content of moral and divine law. With the success of the Reformation, however, there were many conflicting voices speaking for God, no one of which was more clearly vested with divine quality than another. Thus, even though no one seriously questioned the existence of the Divinity or the authority of divine direction of human politics, the direction nevertheless failed simply because no one could be sure what the Divinity said. Modern secular political thought begins with that uncertainty. Similarly I believe that in the next generation populist claims will be rejected simply because it will be realized that, however desirable they might be, they are based on a flawed technique that renders populism unworkable.

Perhaps it will be said in defense of populism that, although there is always doubt about the meaning of any particular electoral outcome, a series of elections over time establishes a rough guide to policy. Yet even that defense cannot be sustained. It is possible that alternative x (say, some political platform) repeatedly beats alternative y (another platform) so that one is fairly certain that x has a good majority over y. But suppose x wins only because z was eliminated earlier or was suppressed by the Constitution or by the method of counting or by manipulation. What then is the status of x? If x is as precise as a motion, then one can still be fairly sure that x at least beats y. But if x is as vague as an ideology, it is far from certain that a clear decision is ever made.

In the history of American presidential elections, three long-enduring clusters of ideas have repeatedly been more or less endorsed by the voters. From 1800 to 1856, the agrarian expansionism of Jefferson and Jackson won most of the time; indeed it was clearly beaten only in 1840. From 1860 to 1928, the Republican program of commercial development won most of the time; it was clearly beaten (in popular vote, but not in the election itself) only in 1876. From 1932 to the present, Democratic welfare statism won most of the time; it was clearly beaten only in 1952, 1956, 1972, and 1980. Can it not be said that these repeatedly endorsed clusters of ideas have been, though rather vague, the true and revealed popular will? In a very narrow sense they have indeed been approved because x (one of these three clusters) has beaten some y (not always the same y) a number of times, frequently in two-party contests. But x has never won over *all* relevant alternatives. No party program has ever been approved *in general*.

The Jefferson-Jackson program of agrarian expansion was approved two-thirds of the time from 1800 to 1856; but it failed to obtain a majority whenever it was effectively shown that agrarian expansion entailed approval of slavery: in 1840, 1844, 1848, 1856, and 1860. The election of 1852 and its aftermath are instructive. In 1852, Whigs, themselves in office, did not raise the slavery issue; the Free Soil party was weak; and the Democratic party, again united on its traditional economic platform, won by a clear majority. Democratic leaders, assuming they had a mandate, then produced the Kansas-Nebraska Act (1854), which, though ostensibly mere agrarian expansion and free soil at that, actually promoted the expansion and approval of slavery. Thereafter, and directly as a consequence, the Democratic party did not get a national majority for more than 20 years. Though this party with its policy of approval of slavery for the sake of expansion was apparently endorsed overwhelmingly in 1852, only a slight variation in its program resulted in savage repudiation in the next five elections. The point is clear: x (agrarian expansion and slavery) was approved against y (commercial development of Federalism and Whiggery) but lost by a huge margin to z (commercial development and free soil, ultimately the Republican combination).

In the next period, between 1860 and 1928, the Republican platform of commercial development usually triumphed against a dying agrarianism. But again, there was no general mandate for commercialism alone. Initially it succeeded (except in 1876, when, however, technically it did win) because it was associated with free soil; in its heyday it succeeded because, I believe, its commercial ideal was clearly linked to social welfare. When the welfare aspects were forgotten in an excess of commercialism (especially around the 1880s, when the old Democratic combination of agrarianism and repression of blacks was not yet fully rejected), the Republican party failed to maintain its majority: in 1876, 1880, 1884, 1888, 1892, 1912, and 1916. Notice that even the interlude of Wilson's presidency was occasioned by an internal Republican split that presumably reflected Theodore Roosevelt's distaste for Taft's pure emphasis on commerce. Thus the mandate often thought to be overwhelming was at best conditional on an appeal to interest wider than commerce alone.

Finally, in the third period, from 1932 to the present, welfare statism appeared to receive a huge mandate under Franklin Roosevelt and thereafter as long as welfare rather than statism was emphasized. But whenever statism dominated, as in the wars undertaken by Truman and Johnson—wars involving huge statist compulsion of citizens in unpopular causes—then welfare statism lost to a combination of commerce and civil liberties as expressed in Eisenhower's mitigation of the military draft and Nixon's elimination of it. As the statist component of welfare statism becomes increasingly apparent in other ways besides military adventures, it may well be that welfare statism as a whole will be rejected. The victory of Ronald Reagan in 1980 may well be the beginning of a more general rejection of welfare statism.

In all three periods, then, a dominant program has been dominant only when it has been tested in one dimension. When more than one dimension has been salient to voters, majorities have disappeared, even when the second dimension is closely related to the first. Voters rejected agrarian expansion when its slavery component was emphasized. They rejected commercial development when mere commerce was emphasized at the expense of development, and they rejected welfare statism when the statist feature of militarism exceeded the welfare component of redistribution. Throughout all three periods, one cluster of ideas was repeatedly endorsed; but there was no clear Condorcet winner, and indeed there were probably always covert, unrevealed cycles of popular values. The inference is clear: The popular will is defined only as long as the issue dimensions are restricted. Once issue dimensions multiply, the popular will is irresolute. Slight changes in dimensions induce disequilibrium. Thus it is indeed difficult to speak of a popular will so narrowly construed, and that is why populism is an empty interpretation of voting and why the populist ideal is literally unattainable.[2]

10.C. The Survival of Liberalism and Democracy

Given that social choice theory reveals populism to be inconsistent and absurd, how does the liberal interpretation of voting fare? For democracy, this is a crucial question. Since populism and liberalism, as I have defined them, exhaust the possibilities and since populism must be rejected, then, if liberalism cannot survive, democracy is indefensible. Fortunately, liberalism survives, although in a curious and convoluted way. Liberalism does not demand much from voting, and hence the restrictions placed on the justification of voting by social choice theory do not quite render the liberal ideal unattainable.

The essence of the liberal interpretation of voting is the notion that voting permits the rejection of candidates or officials who have offended so many voters that they cannot win an election. This is, of course, a negative ideal. It does *not* require that voting produce a clear, consistent, meaningful statement of the popular will. It requires only that voting produce a decisive result: that this official or this party is retained in office or rejected. This very restricted expectation about voting can, I believe, easily coexist with all the defects we have observed in the voting mechanism. If so, then liberalism survives.

Let us investigate systematically the relation between liberalism and the discoveries of social choice theory. To do so, I will begin by assuming the existence of what we already know does not exist—namely, a fair and accurate amalgamation of voters' values. That this assumption is unrealistic does not taint the analysis because I will use it only as an initial standard, not as an instrument of interpretation. With this initial assumption, let us then consider the following cases:

1. Suppose an official or candidate has not offended enough voters for them to reject him or her in a fair and true amalgamation of their values. If, in the actual voting under any particular method, the official or candidate is not rejected, then the method is working adequately in this case.

2. Suppose, however, that the actual voting does lead to the rejection of an unoffending official or candidate. Such rejection might occur in many ways. A Condorcet winner (assume him or her to be a "true winner") might lose in a plurality or approval or Borda election, or clever opponents might beat him or her by strategic voting or by manipulation of the agenda or by the introduction of additional, divisive candidates. If this happens, has the ideal of liberalism been violated? In our populistic era, even many liberals might say yes. Madison himself would have been troubled by this case. But if the liberal ideal is strictly interpreted, it has not been violated. First and foremost liberalism requires the rejection of the offending, not the retention of the unoffending. If a system admits rejection at all, then there is no a priori reason why it may not sometimes work imperfectly. One should expect, therefore, that some times an official or candidate will be rejected "wrongly."

This means that we must modify to some degree our expectations from liberalism. As originally stated in section 1.D, liberalism was said to mitigate the oppression caused by the failure of officials to act as agents of voters' participation. It is clear now, however, that the expectation of such an agency is a populist fantasy, not a tenet of liberalism (which is a wholly negative kind of control). This means that an official in a liberal regime may indeed abandon any effort to ensure voters' participation through reading the voters' will, not because the official is sophisticated enough to know that there is nothing there to read, but merely because he or she knows by experience that voters' rejection may be random. Such randomness, however, does not really matter for the liberal hope of preventing an official's abuse of office and authority. The threat of the next election retains its force. Indeed, an official who faces an electorate knowing that it sometimes works randomly and may "unfairly" reject him or her has a powerful motive to try even harder to avoid offending voters.

3. Suppose, on the other hand, that an official or candidate has—in our imaginary true and fair amalgamation—offended enough voters to be rejected. If he or she is in fact rejected, then, clearly, the voting method is working adequately.

4. But what if the offending official or candidate wins? This might happen because he or she successfully manipulates the agenda or invents additional issues or sets up spurious opponents. Has the ideal of liberalism then been violated? Again, most liberals in this populist era would say yes. I imagine that Madison would have believed this case impossible. But still, if the liberal ideal is strictly interpreted, there is no violation. Liberalism requires only that it be *possible* to reject a putatively offending official, not that the rejection actually occur. We know from social choice theory that those who should be winners in our imaginary true and fair amalgamation can be defeated. We also know that those who should be losers can also be defeated, as, of course, they should be. Consequently, the voting system does not prevent the rejection of offenders—and that is precisely the condition liberalism requires. Of course, it may happen that an uninformed or unsophisticated or well-manipulated electorate fails to operate the voting system as its members would wish. But the fact that in particular instances people fail to make the system work well does not alter the fact that they *can* make it work. And if success is even sometimes possible, then the liberal interpretation can be sustained.[3]

It seems worthwhile to point out just how little is contained in the liberal interpretation of voting. In some sense it is very close to the cynical view that counting heads is better than breaking heads to solve the problem of succession. Let me point out some of the things that the liberal interpretation is not, simply to show how easy it is for liberalism to survive the criticisms of social choice theory. For one thing, liberalism does not require that society itself act. In the liberal interpretation, society is an anthropomorphized entity that cannot order or choose anything either consistently or inconsistently. Rather it is thought that individual people in the society choose, and what they individually choose is whether to support or oppose candidates. The social amalgamation of these choices need not be fair or just. It may even be part of a social cycle. But if it results in a decision on candidates, it is, from the liberal point of view, adequate.

Since social decisions are not, in liberal theory, required to mean anything, liberals can cheerfully acknowledge that elections do not necessarily or even usually reveal popular will. All elections do or have to do is to permit people to get rid of rulers. The people who do this do not themselves need to have a coherent will. They can be—and often are—strange bedfellows. Voters on the far right and the far left, for example, can combine to throw out a ruler in the center. The liberal purpose is then accomplished, even though one could not make a coherent ideological statement about what these voters did and even though their majority might be cyclical. The Indian rejection of Indira Gandhi in 1977 was accomplished by just such a coalition, the Janata party, which was, however, so incoherent in its combination of right and left that Mrs. Gandhi was able to win again in 1979.

The liberal interpretation of voting thus allows elections to be useful and significant even in the presence of cycles, manipulation, and other kinds of "errors" in voting. Since it is precisely cycles, manipulation, and "error" that render populism meaningless, the fact that liberalism can tolerate them demonstrates that liberalism can survive the revelations of social choice theory, while populism cannot.

The kind of democracy that thus survives is not, however, popular rule, but rather an intermittent, sometimes random, even perverse, popular veto. Social choice theory forces us to recognize that the people cannot rule as a corporate body in the way that populists suppose. Instead, officials rule, and they do not represent some indefinable popular will. Hence they can easily be tyrants, either in their own names or in the name of some putative imaginary majority. Liberal democracy is simply the veto by which it is sometimes possible to restrain official tyranny.

This may seem a minimal sort of democracy, especially in comparison with the grandiose (though intellectually absurd) claims of populism. Still, modest though liberal democracy may be, it fully satisfies the definition of democracy offered in Chapter 1. To begin with, it necessarily involves popular participation. Though the participation is not the abstract self-direction of a corporate people, it is the concrete self-direction of individuals who vote and organize voting to make the democratic veto work. Furthermore, since the veto does exist—even when manipulated or cyclical—it has at least the potential of preventing tyranny and rendering officials responsive.

Since officials are not responsive to some imaginary popular will, this popular participation is not the act of making policy. At best officials are responsive to a (possibly random) threat of expulsion from office. But this *may* lead them to avoid gross offense to groups of citizens who can eject them from office. Participation in this sense is then the act of placing a curb on policy, a veto at the margin. Nevertheless it is participation. Furthermore, it can engender that self-direction and self-respect that democracy is supposed to provide because candidates, trying to construct winning platforms in the face of that potential veto, also try to generate majorities, at least momentary ones.

Furthermore, the liberal veto generates freedom because of the very fact that it is a curb on tyranny. Whether one thinks of freedom as the absence of restraint ("negative liberty" in Isaiah Berlin's terms) or as the ability to direct one's own life ("positive liberty"), it is apparent that oppression by rulers eliminates either kind of freedom. Suppose freedom is simply the absence of governmental restraint on individual action. Then the chance to engage in vetoing by rejecting officials and the chance that the rejection actually occur are the very essence of this freedom, which is substantially equivalent to liberal democracy. Suppose, however, freedom is defined as the ability to use government to work one's will—the populist expectation. The agent of this (imaginary) will is government—that is, rulers who can oppress both the minority and the very majority whose will they are supposed to work. An extreme example is socialist rulers who, in order to free workers from the supposed bondage to owners, subject them to the ownership of the state and the terrorism of the police. But conventional populists turned dictator (for example, Vargas, Gandhi, and Perón) are often just as oppressive. Liberal democracy, insofar as it allows people to restrain and reject, is the main sanction against this majoritarian oppression also.

Sometimes populists argue that the true meaning of democracy is not to be found in voting, party organization, and the like, but rather in the democratic ideals of civil liberties, tolerance, and humane concern for popular rights. As I emphasized in Chapter 1, no one doubts that these ideals are indeed truly central in democratic thought (although I suspect that efforts to distinguish them from voting are often the first step—à la Marx—to some kind of coercive enterprise). Still, these democratic ideals depend on a vigilant citizenry. What permits a citizenry to be vigilant is the liberal method of regular elections. In that sense liberal democracy is a necessary part of what populists claim to want.

In the same way, liberal democracy promotes a kind of equality. Equal chances to restrain, to reject, and to veto inhere in the very idea of using votes to control officials. This is the notion of the equality of the right of democratic participation, which is the essence of the idea of juristic equality. Equality has many other derived meanings, including notions such as equal shares of the national treasure and equality before the law (that is, in the courtroom). But equality in these derived senses cannot occur unless juristic equality exists. In that way, juristic equality is primary, and that is what liberal democracy provides.

So the liberal interpretation of voting, however much it admits of "unfair" voting methods, manipulation, cycles, and the like, still contains the essential elements of democracy. It may, from the populist view, be a minimal kind of democracy; but this is the only kind of democracy actually attainable. It is the kind of democracy we still have in the United States; and it is the kind of democracy so much admired by those who live in closed societies.

10.D. Are Liberal and Populist Interpretations Compatible?

To say that the populist interpretation of voting cannot survive criticism, but the liberal interpretation can, does not necessarily imply that the two interpretations are incompatible. It may be that if voting permits the rejection of officials (the liberal goal), then from the liberal point of view it makes no difference whether people attempt, however fruitlessly, to use voting to embody the supposed popular will in law (the populist goal). Since the populist method is not valid, it will usually fail. But it may sometimes succeed. And if its failure or success are irrelevant by liberal standards, then there is no necessary incompatibility between liberalism and populism.

The case can be put thus: Let liberal rejectability or LR stand for "citizens are able to reject some rulers," and let populist incorporability or PI stand for "citizens are able to embody popular will in law." Then, if we guarantee at least LR and sometimes also get PI, we have perhaps obtained an extra benefit. This happy result can occur, however, only if LR and PI are complementary. If they are inconsistent, if, for example, PI is equivalent to the negative of LR, then populism is certainly incompatible with liberalism. It is important to discover, then, whether *LR* and *PI* can be simultaneously affirmed.

In the view of liberalism set forth by Berlin (see section 1.F) populism transforms liberalism into tyranny when a coercive oligarchy claims to enforce an imaginary popular will. But that transformation assumes an oligarchy that refuses to submit to the liberal discipline of the next election. Suppose, however, that free and regular elections are preserved. Then, even though the populist ideal may be unattainable, populism need not destroy freedom. So the question really is: Can liberal institutions (that is, the ability to reject rulers) be maintained when the populist interpretation of voting and populist institutions are adopted?

To answer, I will first define briefly the institutions appropriate for each interpretation of voting.

Populist institutions. The populist ideal requires that rulers move swiftly and surely to embody in law the popular decision on an electoral platform. Constitutional restraints that retard this process are populistically intolerable. The appropriate institutions are those that facilitate speedy embodiment, and the simplest such institutions are so-called constitutional dictatorships, by which I mean dictatorial executives who submit to real elections or plebiscites but rule by decree or through a complaisant legislature. Latin American governments often have this form. Mexico is perhaps an example, though, since Mexican presidents never stand for reelection, the one-party plebiscites may not be real elections.

More complex populist institutions are those that develop out of parliamentary governments when they degenerate into a sovereign self-regenerating legislature run by a leader (who is also the executive) of a disciplined majority party. For the legislature to be sovereign, there cannot be external restraints like an externally selected executive and independent courts; nor can there be internal restraints such as multiple houses with different constituencies. For the legislature to be disciplined, members of the majority party dare not defy the party leader. Furthermore, at least one party must be a majority alone. With such arrangements the party leader can then ensure that party platforms are quickly adopted in true populist fashion. Finally, since the legislature is self-regenerating, this leader can manipulate the time and conditions of elections to facilitate his or her own continuance in office.

The closest current approximation to this ideal is Great Britain as it has developed over the last generation. External checks on the House of Commons have been removed. The House of Lords was effectively countered by the Parliament Act of 1911, and the last attempt at even personal freedom in the Crown was repulsed at the abdication of Edward VIII in 1937. Strong third parties, a characteristic feature of nineteenth-century Parliaments (for example, the Radicals, Irish, and Labour), were eliminated with the decline of Liberalism after the 1920s, though they may be reappearing in the new Liberalism or Social Democracy. The national leaders of the two main parties acquired control of nominations so that the members became disciplined. And finally the national leadership of the majority party was lodged in the prime minister, who, once in office, could usually control all factions of his or her party and, within wide limits, ensure his or her continuance in office. What has so far saved the British system from constitutional dictatorship is, I believe, a three-century-old liberal tradition of free and regular elections. But even that tradition now seems threatened. The ideal of new elections when the government loses in the House of Commons has degenerated into the government's selection of a propitious time within the limits of a five-year term. (And that term has twice been doubled with the excuse of war.) More significant evidence of the populist elimination of electoral restraint, however, is the confiscatory and truly oppressive taxation and inflation by which rulers have financed their reelection, thereby acting against the society that they are supposed to serve.

Liberal institutions. Liberalism, as here defined, simply requires regular elections that sometimes lead to the rejection of rulers. It is often thought that liberalism also involves additional constitutional restraints, and it is indeed historically true that liberal regimes have always had them. This association, however, may be no more than a historical accident, owing to the fact that liberal democracy developed out of the imposition of constitutional restraints on monarchies. Perhaps, in the abstract, liberal methods do not need to be supplemented with these restraints because liberalism has only one stipulated sanction on rulers—namely, the threat of the next election. Nevertheless, in practice, liberal democracy probably does not work without the additional restraints always heretofore associated with it—multicameral legislatures, decentralized parties, and so on.

Having defined populist and liberal institutions, it is now possible to investigate the main question: Is the liberal interpretation of voting compatible with populist institutions? The answer depends on whether rulers in a populist system can be expected to maintain the electoral arrangements essential for liberal democracy.

It is difficult, I believe, for rulers of any kind to maintain free elections. The function of an election is to put at stake the rulers' jobs, even their lives. In nations where the democratic tradition is fragile or externally imposed, it is common for rulers who have won office in elections to prohibit elections they might lose. Even adherents of the democratic ideal hesitate to hold elections when they fear the electorate may do something "foolish" or "wrong." Dictators from Cromwell to Perón, who have possibly genuinely regarded themselves as caretakers until democracy can be resumed, have always been reluctant to trust an electorate that might install an alternative demagogue.

In general, therefore, the electoral system is only precariously maintained. But in populist systems both the temptation and the ability to weaken the electoral sanction are especially strong. For one thing, with a populist interpretation of voting it is easy for rulers to believe their programs are the "true" will of the people and hence more precious than the constitution and free elections. Populism reinforces the normal arrogance of rulers with a built-in justification for tyranny, the contemporary version of the divine right of rulers.

The main threat to democracy from populism is not, however, the exceptional temptation to subvert elections but the exceptional ability to do so. Populist institutions depend on the elimination of constitutional restraints, and the populist interpretation of voting justifies this elimination. With the restraints removed, it is easy to change electoral arrangements, which is why populist democracies so often revert to autocracies. Perhaps the leaders of some future populism will be so thoroughly imbued with liberal ideals that they will never meddle with free elections. But since even in Britain, where liberal ideals originated, the populist elimination of constitutional limitations has begun to produce attacks on the integrity of elections, it seems unlikely that the liberal sanction can survive populist institutions. Indeed this empirical regularity suggests to me that there is a profound theoretical reason that populism induces rulers to ensconce themselves in office. At any rate, on the practical level at least, the answer is clearly negative to the main question of this section: Is liberal rejectability compatible with populist incorporability? No: because the constitutional restraints practically associated with liberalism *must* be destroyed to achieve populism.

10.E. The Preservation of Liberal Democracy

It seems clear to me that democracy cannot be preserved simply with the liberal interpretation of voting. Suppose one had a liberal regime without the constitutional limitations typically associated with liberalism. Would the regime long remain liberal? Would it not operate for all the world as if it were populist? Would it not move certainly toward some kind of oppression by rulers? I think the answers to these questions are yes and so did Madison. Although he argued that the necessary and sufficient condition for republicanism (that is, democracy) to *exist* was simply regular, popular elections, it is still true that he did not think this condition was sufficient to *preserve* the liberal system. Instead he argued the necessity of constitutional limitations. And the constitution he was justifying in *The Federalist* contained a variety of very real restraints that together have successfully kept rulers from subverting regular, popular elections for 200 years. These restraints have the effect of preventing any single ruler or any single party from getting enough power to subvert:

1. *A multicameral legislature* (really three "houses": the president, Senate, and House of Representatives) based on different divisions of the people into constituencies. The different constituencies have typically kept the interests of rulers separate and thus forestalled the fusion of their ability to rule into a tyranny.

2. *A division between legislative and executive authority.* Though constitutional interpreters from Montesquieu on have believed this a fundamental limitation, in the American system it is no more than an extension of the differing constituencies of the multicameral legislature.

3. *A division of authority between national and local governments.* This is the famous American federalism, copied over half of the world. The constitutional restraint is not, however, the legal division of duties between central and local governments but rather the resultant localization of political parties that renders national leadership of them impossible.

4. *An independent judiciary.* American lawyers have typically believed this to be the main limitation. Indeed, the separation of the judiciary from the rest of government does render blocking possible. But the judiciary has no independent constituency and so always loses in a crisis. Hence, this limitation is much less important than the multicameral legislature or the decentralized parties.

5. *Limited tenure and regular elections.* This is the fundamental restraint, but it is not a self-enforcing limitation. It depends rather on the force of tradition and on the other restraints previously listed.

About the only important restraint commonly found in other constitutional democracies and not included in this one is a system of more than two political parties so that no single party is ever a majority by itself. Something of that restraint, however, is provided in the American system by decentralized parties.

Madison was correct, I believe, in his assertion that constitutional limits preserve liberal democracy. Fortunately the limits he helped provide retain most of their original force. Yet in the American political tradition there has always been a strong strand of populism, usually expressed as the notion that the winners of an election ought to be able immediately to embody their platform in law and policy. This was, for example, the basis for the attack by Jacksonians on bureaucratic tenure, for the attack by populist political philosophers (such as Charles Beard and J. Allen Smith) on constitutional limitations of all sorts, for the persistent advocacy (described in section 3.G) of a rigid system of two disciplined political parties (thus allowing a "majority" immediately to enact its program), and finally in recent decades for the idealization of "presidential leadership"— a euphemism for transcending constitutional limitations by the domination of a populistically endorsed, quasi-monarchical president.

Along with the populist notion of an unfettered agent (whether party or president) of the popular will, there is also the notion that the popular will can express itself directly, as in legislation by referenda and even by public opinion polls. The device of referendum was developed in the progressive era—an epoch of the populist spirit—to provide a "truer" expression of the popular will than statutes produced by legislatures, which were, it was argued, merely distorting intermediaries of the popular will. Since that time there has been considerable disillusionment with referenda because they have produced both inconsistent and bizarre legislation. Still, the populist belief in direct democracy dies hard, even though it can in no wise escape the defects of manipulation. So now there is considerable enthusiasm for using cable television to conduct elections on the content of statutes and even of administrative policy. Presumably citizens will listen to debate and then vote by push button, supplanting thereby the need for any kind of legislature.

Many current proposals for institutional reform are populistically intended to nullify constitutional limitations. In spite of disasters with the "imperial" presidencies of Johnson and Nixon, people continue to search for ways to enhance presidential leadership—by tightening presidential control of the bureaucracy and by elaborating presidential influence in the party. The decentralization of political parties, the fundamental restraint in federalism, is under constant attack with proposals for frequent policy-making conventions to be dominated by national leaders and proposals for centralized national financing of campaigns. While at the moment proposals to eliminate legislatures with direct law-making over cable television or to substitute (à la Marcus Raskin, as cited in section 1.G) instructions from grand juries for legislative judgment seem bizarre, I have no doubt that, as technology and opportunity combine, such populist proposals will be taken seriously.

The present situation in the United States is, therefore, that, although the fundamental constitutional limitations remain, populists persistently seek to undermine them. Since the twentieth century is a populist era worldwide, our homegrown populists may well succeed.

Populism puts democracy at risk. Democracy requires control of rulers by electoral santions; the spirit of populism and populist institutions allows rulers to tamper with this sanction, thereby rendering it a weak defense against the tyranny of officials. The maintenance of democracy requires therefore the minimization of the risk in populism.

How can we minimize the risk? This is the great question of political prudence forced on us by the revelations of social choice theory. I will conclude this survey with some remarks on this practical problem.

The main defense against populist excesses is the maintenance of the constitutional limitations inherited from eighteenth-century Whiggery. It would probably help also to have a citizenry aware of the emptiness of the populist interpretation of voting. And surely a wide dissemination of the discoveries of social choice theory is a desirable additional defense. But the dissemination of a rather arcane theory is a task for generations. (It took me a score of years of reflection on Black's and Arrow's discoveries to reject the populism I had initially espoused.) Consequently, the fundamental method to preserve liberty is to preserve ardently our traditional constitutional restraints—decentralized parties and multicameral government.

Almost everyone who has written about American politics has emphasized its peculiar style. Except for the one great disaster of the Civil War, the nastiest features of political scarcity have seldom flourished. One group has not persistently tried to do in another, probably because political coalitions are always shifting and constitutional restraints make it difficult to organize zero-sum situations. Consequently, there are no elaborately rationalized ideologies that carry with them a logically clear and intricately arranged set of public policies. Instead, political leaders are almost always engaged in constructing petty and pragmatic compromises for marginal adjustments in policy. Only in a few great crises have great leaders emerged, and great leaders have always disappeared as the crises have subsided.

The reason for this style is, I believe, the existence of constitutional limitations. In his famous defense in *The Federalist,* No. 51, of the notion of the separation of powers, Madison remarked:

A dependence on the people [by which he meant democracy, or regular elections and limited tenure of office] is, no doubt, the primary control on the government; but experience has taught mankind the necessity of auxilliary precautions [by which he meant precisely the constitutional restraints here enumerated].

The experience of the subsequent two centuries has reinforced the teaching to which Madison referred. And the reason is this: Liberal democracy almost guarantees some circulation of leadership so that great power is usually fleeting and no vested interest lasts forever. The constitutional restraints have always reinforced this style. Multicameralism and federalism have enforced localism in parties, and this in turn has forced rulers to persuade rather than to control. The total effect is that policy does not change either rapidly or sharply enough to hurt anyone very badly, which is why we have usually—except in the Civil War—avoided the worst features of political scarcity. That the system has worked in this moderate way is due partly to luck; but it also is due to that happy mixture of liberal democracy and constitutional restraints that has so far preserved us from the hatreds and oppression implicit in populism.

Notes

Chapter 1

[1]Duncan Black, *The Theory of Committees and Elections* (Cambridge, England: Cambridge University Press, 1958).

[2]Kenneth Arrow, *Social Choice and Individual Values,* 2nd ed. (New Haven: Yale University Press, 1963); originally published in 1951.

[3]Robin Farquharson, *Theory of Voting* (New Haven: Yale University Press, 1969); accepted as a doctoral dissertation in 1958.

[4]See, for example, Dennis F. Thompson, *The Democratic Citizen* (Cambridge, England: Cambridge University Press, 1970), p. 43. Thompson recognizes that the theory of collective choice "remains a serious difficulty for any democratic theory," but he avoids dealing with it because he is concerned with individual actions.

[5]Robert Dahl, *A Preface to Democratic Theory* (Chicago: University of Chicago Press, 1956), pp. 42–44.

[6]William H. Riker, *Democracy in the United States,* 2nd ed. (New York: Macmillan, 1964), chap. 1. The documents were Pericles' Funeral Oration, the Agreement of the People, the Declaration of Independence, the Declaration of the Rights of Man and Citizen, and Lincoln's Gettysburg Address.

[7]The words "Madisonian" and "populist" are used in Dahl, *A Preface to Democratic Theory;* my usage, however, is quite different.

[8]James Madison, *The Federalist,* No. 39. That "democracy" and "republic" meant about the same thing in Madison's day is indicated by Thomas Nugent's translation (1750) of Montesquieu's *Spirit of the Laws,* Bk. II, chap. 2: "When the body of the people in a republic are possessed of supreme power, this is called a democracy." Adrienne Koch, in her preface to *Madison's Notes of Debates in the Federal Convention of 1787* (New York: Norton, 1966), p. xix, argues that by "republic" Madison meant "representative democracy."

[9]Robert Sherwood, *Roosevelt and Hopkins* (New York: Harper and Row, 1948), p. 127; see also p. 102 for the controversy over Hopkins' remark, mentioned subsequently in the text.

[10]Madison, *The Federalist,* No. 51. See also No. 10.

[11]Dahl, in *A Preface to Democratic Theory,* so interprets it. In my terms, Dahl turns out to be a liberal and Madisonian; his "polyarchal" democracy is very similar to my interpretation of Madison.

[12]Jean Jacques Rousseau, *Social Contract,* Bk. I, chap. 8.

[13]Isaiah Berlin, *Two Concepts of Liberty* (Oxford, England: Oxford University Press, 1958), later revised in *Four Essays on Liberty* (Oxford, England: Oxford University Press, 1969).

[14]C. B. MacPherson, *Democratic Theory* (Oxford, England: Oxford University Press, 1973), pp. 108–109. I have added the words in brackets.

[15]Willmoore Kendall, *John Locke and the Doctrine of Majority Rule* (Urbana: University of Illinois Press, 1941).

[16]Ibid., p. 135.

[17]The distinction I have drawn between liberalism and populism can also be found under the names "liberalism" and "radicalism" in Samuel H. Beer, "New Structures of Democracy," in *Democracy in the Mid-Twentieth Century,* ed. William N. Chambers and Robert H. Salisbury (St. Louis: Washington University Press, 1960), pp. 32–33. In discussing the rise of popular government out of the medieval corporativism of "estates" and "orders," Beer points out that liberals such as Macauley and Madison "remained committed to parliamentarianism," but the object

represented ceased to be corporate bodies and became individuals, "based on the rational, independent man." On the other hand, radicals such as Bentham "would make government the instrument of the 'will of the people,' a unified and authoritative force in which he found the only sovereign of the polity and for which the majority spoke." Beer goes on to show that the radical tradition, superficially individualistic, went full circle to the collectivist and corporativist notions of, especially, the Labour party, which is of course precisely Berlin's development of coercion out of positive liberty or the necessity, as I have shown, of self-mastery becoming coercion in the presence of populist voting.

[18]William A. Rusher, *The Making of the New Majority Party* (New York: Sheed and Ward, 1975); Marcus Raskin, *Notes on the Old System: To Transform American Politics* (New York: McKay, 1974). Since Rusher describes himself as a conservative and often denounces liberalism, I should, in fairness to him and the reader, explain why I call him a liberal. Originally "liberal" described independence from government (negative liberty, following Berlin). In this century it came to mean first positive liberty and then, by the transformation Berlin described, coercion, statism, and dependence on government, in effect exactly the reverse of the earlier meaning. My usage preserves the original sense, while Rusher as an antistatist has used the word "conservative" as a new name for antistatism. (It is probably not a good choice because the Tory is also a statist.) Nevertheless, Rusher seems to me to represent one extreme version of the Madisonian tradition, so I will continue to call him a liberal. Raskin, on the other hand, condemns all brands of liberalism. As a collectivist he is against Madisonian liberalism, and as a radical he is against the statism of positive liberalism. So I think it fair to call him a populist.

[19]Raskin, p. 153, quoting from Martin Buber, "The Gods of the Nations and God," in *Israel and the World* (New York: Schocken Books, 1948), p. 210.

Chapter 2

[1]To define proportional representation formally: For $1, 2, \ldots, m$ parties, let v_i be the number of votes for party i, and s_i be the number of seats for party i. Then the total vote is $V = \sum_{i=1}^{m} v_i$, and the number of seats is

$S = \Sigma_{i=1}^{m} s_i$, where V and S refer to the district or the nation as the case may be. Then proportional representation is the situation in which

$$\frac{s_i}{S} / \frac{v_i}{V} = 1, \qquad \text{for all } i$$

[2]See Douglas Rae, *The Political Consequences of Electoral Laws* (New Haven: Yale University Press, 1971), pp. 28–39, for detail on the effects of the two methods. Briefly, the effects can be explained in this way: In the highest-average method, an average, a_i, is calculated for each party, i; thus:

$$a_i = v_i/(s_i + 1)$$

where v_i and s_i are defined as in note 1. (Initially, $s_i = 0$; so $a_i = v_i$.) The party with the highest a_i is assigned the first seat; a_i is recalculated for that party; again the party with the highest a_i is assigned a seat; a_i is recalculated for that party; and so forth until all seats are assigned.

In the largest-remainder method, a quota, q, or the "price" of a seat, is calculated thus, using V and S as defined in note 1: $q = V/S$, or $q = V/(S + 1)$, depending on the method used in various countries. Each party, i, is initially assigned s_i seats, where

$$s_i = [v_i/q]$$

and where $[v_i/q]$ is the largest integer contained in the number v_i/q. (Of course, if the largest integer is zero, the party is initially assigned zero seats.) After the initial allocation, a remainder, r_i, is calculated for each party, i,

$$r_i = v_i - (s_i q)$$

The next seat is assigned to the party with the largest r_i, and the process is repeated until all the seats are assigned.

It is probably not readily apparent to ordinary citizens, but it is immediately obvious to contriving politicians, that the highest-average method varies from true proportionality in favor of the larger parties and the largest-remainder method varies from true proportionality in ways that do not systematically favor either large or small parties. Consider a stage in an election at which some seats have been assigned, others not. In the highest-average method, the size of the original vote (v_i) is just as relevant at this stage as initially. Hence large parties are more likely than small ones to get the next seat. But in the largest-remainder method, the size of the original vote ceases to be relevant after the initial assignment of seats. Hence at this stage the next seat is equally likely to go to a large or to a small party.

As can be seen in Display N2-1, the Gaullists (with most votes) get the first, third, fifth, and tenth seats by the highest-average formula, but only the first, third, and seventh seats by the largest-remainder formula. Notice that the two parties with the most votes get the first four seats by both methods, but the highest average allocates the fifth seat to the party with the most votes (because the initial number of votes dominates the calculation) while the largest remainder allocates that same seat to a small party (because the initial number of votes is no longer relevant).

Let us define the proportionality, p, of a party, i, as

$$p_i = \frac{s_i}{S} / \frac{v_i}{V}$$

This formula was used in note 1 to define the objective of proportional representation as a system as one in which $p_i = 1$ for all i. The degree to which $p_i < 1$ represents the advantage of party i. It is apparent that, since the highest-average method tends to give more seats to large parties, the p_i's for large parties will be significantly smaller (and significantly more advantageous) than for small parties. Since the largest-remainder method is indifferent among parties of various sizes, p_i's under this method will not be related to party size.

[3]James S. Dyer and Ralph E. Miles, Jr., "An Actual Application of Collective Choice Theory to the Selection of Trajectories for the Mariner Jupiter/Saturn 1977 Project," *Operations Research,* Vol. 24 (March 1976), pp. 220–244.

[4]This method was the Von Neumann–Morgenstern experiment described in section 4.F.

[5]Dyer and Miles, p. 228.

[6]My colleague Richard Niemi, however, has examined the actual ballots for 22 elections, mostly by proportional representation, at the University of Rochester. He found that in 11 elections, some of the elected candidates could not beat all the losers in a head-to-head vote and thus would

Display N2-1

Values of p_i with Alternative Calculations of Seats (Based Approximately on the Constituency of Paris, First, 1951, with Ten Seats)

Parties	Highest-average method						Largest-remainder method				
	$a_i = v_i$	$v_i/2$	$v_i/3$	$v_i/4$	p_i	Σs_i	$r_i = v_i$	$v_i - q$	$v_i - 2q$	p_i	Σs_i
Radicals	27				*	—	27 (IX)			.675	1
Socialists	37 (VI)				.925	1	37 (V)			.925	1
MRP	35 (VII)				.875	1	35 (VI)			.875	1
Communists	103 (II)	51.5 (IV)	34.3 (VIII)		.858	3	103 (II)	63 (IV)	23 (X)	.858	3
Gaullists	114 (I)	57 (III)	38 (V)	28.5 (X)	.713	4	114 (I)	74 (III)	34 (VII)	.950	3
Rightists	33 (IX)				.825	1	33 (VIII)			.825	1
Misc. parties	15, 10, 9				*	—	15, 10, 9	$q = \dfrac{V}{S} = \dfrac{400}{10} = 40$		*	—
	7, 5, 5						7, 5, 5				
	400					10	400				10

Note. Roman numerals in parentheses indicate the order (I, first; II, second; etc.) in which seats are assigned during the calculation. In the highest-average method, it is the case that, except for the Rightists, the two large parties have smaller p_i's than the smaller parties. In the largest-remainder method, one large party has the largest p_i (nearly 1), while the other large party has a medium-sized p_i.

*p_i is undefined because $s_i = 0$.

not have been elected by the Condorcet method. See Richard Niemi, "The Occurrence of the Paradox of Voting in University Elections," *Public Choice,* Vol. 7 (Spring 1970), pp. 91–100.

Chapter 3

[1] Here and in subsequent sections, I rely heavily on that elegant presentation of the whole field, Peter C. Fishburn, *The Theory of Social Choice* (Princeton: Princeton University Press, 1973).

[2] That is, of the three possible relations, $x \, P_i \, y$, $x \, I_i \, y$, and $y \, P_i \, x$, the relation, R_i, includes the two former and excludes the latter.

[3] Using the symbolism $\Sigma_{i=1}^{n} D_i$ to mean "the sum of D_i where $i = 1, 2, \ldots, n$" (that is, $D_1 + D_2 + \ldots + D_n$), then F is a *simple majority decision rule* if and only if

$$\sum_{i=1}^{n} D_i \begin{cases} > 0 \text{ means } F(D) = 1 & (x \text{ wins}) \\ = 0 \text{ means } F(D) = 0 & (x \text{ and } y \text{ tie}) \\ < 0 \text{ means } F(D) = -1 & (y \text{ wins}) \end{cases} \qquad \text{(N3-1)}$$

[4] Kenneth O. May, "A Set of Independent Necessary and Sufficient Conditions for Simple Majority Decision," *Econometrica,* Vol. 20 (October 1952), pp. 680–684.

[5] Formally, an F is *monotonic* (or *non-negatively responsive*) if and only if,

for all D and D' in D, it is true that, for all i, $D_i \geq D'_i$
implies $F(D) \geq F(D')$ (N3-2)

[6] F is the *jury function* if and only if,

for $\sum_{i=1}^{n} D_i = t,$

$$\text{where } \begin{cases} t = n & \text{means } F(D) = 1 & (\text{conviction}) \\ -n < t < n & \text{means } F(D) = 0 & (\text{a hung jury}) \\ t = -n & \text{means } F(D) = -1 & (\text{acquittal}) \end{cases} \qquad \text{(N3-3)}$$

[7] An F is *strongly monotonic* (or *positively responsive*) if and only if F is monotonic and, for all D and D' in D, and if, for all i, $D_i \geq D'_i$,

if $F(D') = 0$ and if, for some i, $D_i > D'_i$, then $F(D) = 1$

if $F(D) = 0$ and if, for some i, $D_i > D'_i$, then $F(D') = -1$

$$(\text{N3-4})$$

[8]An F is *unanimous* if and only if, when $D = (1, 1, \ldots, 1)$,

$$F(D) = 1, \text{ and, when } D = (-1, -1, \ldots, -1), F(D) = -1$$

$$(\text{N3-5})$$

An F is *weakly unanimous* if and only if, when $D = (1, 1, \ldots, 1)$,

$$F(D) \neq -1, \text{ and, when } D = (-1, -1, \ldots, -1), F(D) \neq 1$$

$$(\text{N3-6})$$

[9]This function was brought to my attention by Robert Freeman, dean of the Eastman School of Music of the University of Rochester. Its peculiar properties were discovered and analyzed by Bradford Chaney. Of course, D_i must be redefined in terms of points and $F(D)$ in terms of point totals (like weighted voting in equation [N3-7] in note 13).

[10]John H. Smith, "Aggregation of Preferences with Variable Electorate," *Econometrica,* Vol. 51 (November 1973), pp. 1027–1041.

[11]This is the so-called Hare system, which John Stuart Mill praised so highly in *Considerations on Representative Government* (1862).

[12]Gideon Doron and Richard Kronick, "Single Transferable Vote: An Example of a Perverse Social Choice Function," *American Journal of Political Science,* Vol. 21 (May 1977), pp. 303–311.

[13]An F is *weighted majority voting* if and only if, for $\Sigma_{i=1}^{n} w_i = W$:

$$\sum_{i=1}^{n} w_i D_i \begin{cases} > 0 \text{ means } F(D) = 1 \\ = 0 \text{ means } F(D) = 0 \\ < 0 \text{ means } F(D) = -1 \end{cases} \qquad (\text{N3-7})$$

[14]Lloyd Shapley and Martin Shubik, "A Method of Evaluating Power in a Committee System," *American Political Science Review,* Vol. 48 (September 1954), pp. 787–792; John F. Banzhaf III, "Weighted Voting Doesn't Work: A Mathematical Analysis," *Rutgers Law Review,* Vol. 19 (Winter 1965), pp. 317–343; John Deegan and E. W. Packel, "A New

Index of Power for Simple *n*-Person Games," *International Journal of Game Theory,* Vol. 7, No. 2 (1978), pp. 113–123; H. P. Young, *Lobbying and Campaigning with Application to the Measure of Power* (Laxenburg, Austria: International Institute for Applied Systems Analysis, 1977).

[15]See Philip Straffin, "Homogeneity, Independence, and Power Indices," *Public Choice,* Vol. 30 (Summer 1977), pp. 107–118, wherein it is shown that the Shapley-Shubik and Banzhaf indices give quite different interpretations of a proposed Canadian constitution because the former assume voters have homogeneous standards of judgment and the latter assumes that each voter's judgment is independent of each other voter's judgment. Since one does not know ahead of time which assumption is appropriate, it turns out to be impossible to translate fairly and accurately rules distinguishing voters into a weighted voting scheme.

[16]An *F* is *undifferentiated* if and only if, for all *D* in *D*, and for all permutations,

$$F(D_1, D_2, \ldots, D_n) = F(D_{\sigma(1)}, D_{\sigma(2)}, \ldots, D_{\sigma(n)}) \tag{N3-8}$$

[17]T. Nicholaus Tideman and Gordon Tullock, "A New and Superior Process for Making Social Choices," *Journal of Political Economy,* Vol. 84 (December 1976), pp. 1145–1159. A special issue of *Public Choice,* Vol. 22, (Supplement to Spring 1977) is devoted to papers on the demand-revealing process, although only the papers by Tideman and Tullock seriously suggest its use in popular elections. Tideman incidentally remarks, in "Ethical Foundations of the Demand Revealing Process" (p. 73), that it "contributes practically nothing to equality" and "has a potential for increasing inequality." Difficulties arising from the absence of undifferentiatedness are discussed in William H. Riker, "Is 'A New and Superior Process' Really Superior?" *Journal of Political Economy,* Vol. 87 (August 1979), pp. 875–890.

[18]The alert reader doubtless observes that, if there is more than one voter on each side and if the voters favoring the loser, *y*, know S_x, then they can make *y* win tax-free by offering $m_i > S_x$ for all *i* who prefer *y* to *x*. Then the formula for the tax is $[S_x - (S_y - m_i)]$, because *y* is now the winner; and the tax formula is negative for all such *i*. In the example in the text, if persons 1 and 4 each offer \$16 for *y* and persons 2 and 3 do not change their offers, then *y* wins tax-free (i.e., $15 - (32 - 16) = -1$). Generally, if $S_x > S_y$ and if, for all *i* such that $x P_i y$, the number of *i* is ≥ 2, and if $m_i > S_y$, then $[S_y - (S_x - m_i)]$ is negative, and so *x* wins tax-free.

[19]To express all this precisely, let each person reverse his or her judgments:

If $D_i = 1$ (i.e., $x\,P_i\,y$), then $-D_i = -1$ (i.e., $y\,P_i\,x$).

If $D_i = 0$ (i.e., $x\,I_i\,y$), then $-D_i = 0$ (i.e., $y\,I_i\,x$).

If $D_i = -1$ (i.e., $y\,P_i\,x$), then $-D_i = 1$ (i.e., $x\,P_i\,y$).

For $D = (D_1, D_2, \ldots, D_n)$, the *reverse* or *dual* of D is $-D = (-D_1, -D_2, \ldots, -D_n)$. Neutrality is the condition that a reversed profile of preferences leads to reversed results. This means that, if $F(D) = 1$ (or -1), then $F(-D) = -1$ (or 1), and, if $F(D) = 0$, then $F(-D) = 0$. An F is *dual* (or *neutral*) if and only if,

for all D in D, $F(-D) = -F(D)$.　　　　　(N3-9)

[20]Vocabulary necessary to state the condition formally is: D_i is an ordering by person i, $i = 1, 2, \ldots, n$, of the m alternatives in $X = (x_1, x_2, \ldots, x_m)$. So $D_i = (x_h R_i x_j R_i \ldots R_i x_k)$ or, briefly, $x_h x_j \ldots x_k$, which is a permutation of X where each of $h, j, \ldots, k$ is a different element of $\{1, 2, \ldots, m\}$. As before, the social profile is $D = (D_1, D_2, \ldots, D_n)$, D is the set of all possible D, and $F_g(D, X)$ is the social choice from X, given some rule g and some particular profile D. If X is permuted, we get $[\sigma(x_1), \sigma(x_2), \ldots, \sigma(x_m)]$, where $\sigma(x_i)$ is the replacement for x_i. The associated orders, profile, and social choice are D_i^σ, D^σ, and $F_g(D^\sigma, X)$. Finally, a permutation of $F_g(D, X)$ is $\sigma[F_g(D, X)]$.

Here is an example, with three voters, three alternatives (x_1, x_2, x_3), the Condorcet rule that the winning alternative is that which can beat all others in a head-to-head vote, and the permutation $[\sigma(x_1) = x_1,$ $\sigma(x_2) = x_3, \sigma(x_3) = x_2]$:

D		D^σ	
D_1:	$x_1\,x_2\,x_3$	D_1^σ:	$x_1\,x_3\,x_2$
D_2:	$x_2\,x_1\,x_3$	D_2^σ:	$x_3\,x_1\,x_2$
D_3:	$x_3\,x_2\,x_1$	D_3^σ:	$x_2\,x_3\,x_1$

$F_c(D, X) = x_2$ (because in D, x_2 beats x_1 and x_3)

$F_c(D^\sigma, X) = x_3$ (because in D^σ, x_3 beats x_1 and x_2)

$\sigma[F_c(D, X)] = x_3$ (because $\sigma(x_2) = x_3$)

Definition: An *F* is *neutral* if, for all *D* in **D**,

$$F(D^\sigma, X) = \sigma[F(D, X)]. \qquad\qquad (N3\text{-}10)$$

Since F_c satisfies neutrality,

$$F(D^\sigma, X) = x_3 = \sigma[F_c(D, X)]$$

which means that the choice from a permuted *X* is equivalent to the same permutation of the choice set.

[21]The history of this tradition is well told in Austin Ranney, *The Doctrine of Responsible Party Government* (Urbana: University of Illinois Press, 1954). The first book in the tradition is Woodrow Wilson, *Congressional Government* (Boston: Houghton Mifflin, 1885); the report of the American Political Science Association's Committee on Political Parties is *Toward a More Responsible Two-Party System* (New York: Holt, Rinehart and Winston, 1950).

[22]Wilson, p. 93.

[23]A. Lawrence Lowell, "The Influence of Party upon Legislation," *Annual Report of the American Historical Association for the Year 1901,* Vol. 1 (1901), pp. 321–542.

[24]Pendleton Herring, *The Politics of Democracy* (New York: Holt, Rinehart and Winston, 1940); David Truman, *The Governmental Process* (New York: Knopf, 1951); Arthur F. Bentley, *The Process of Government* (Chicago: University of Chicago Press, 1908).

[25]Robert Dahl, *A Preface to Democratic Theory* (Chicago: University of Chicago Press, 1956), p. 146.

[26]Anthony Downs, *An Economic Theory of Democracy* (New York: Harper and Row, 1956).

[27]Peter C. Ordeshook, "Extensions of a Model of the Electoral Process and Implications for the Theory of Responsible Parties," *Midwest Journal of Political Science,* Vol. 14 (February 1970), pp. 43–70.

[28]Richard D. McKelvey, "Policy Related Voting and Electoral Equilibrium," *Econometrica,* Vol. 43 (September 1975), pp. 815–843, at p. 835.

Chapter 4

[1]The main argument against transitivity is that, in many laboratory experiments, some subjects (often regularly) reveal intransitive preferences. See Amos Tversky, "Intransitivity of Preferences," *Psychological Review,* Vol. 76 (January 1969), pp. 31–48, where intransitivity is induced by forcing subjects to judge by two or more standards. The main argument for transitivity is that it is a fundamental condition of consistency and that people prefer to be consistent. The revealed intransitivities from experiments are explained away as the result of confusion on the part of subjects and trickery on the part of experimenters. (Presumably most people will reject inconsistency if it is pointed out, especially with something like the extreme example of the Money Pump: Person 1 arranges his judgments intransitively: xy, yz, zx. To begin, person 1 possesses z; but since he likes y better than z, he is willing to trade, giving z and some money—say, one dollar—for y. Now person 1 has y, but since he likes x better than y, he trades y and one dollar for x. Now person 1 has x, but since he likes z better than x, he trades x and one dollar for z. Now person 1 is back where he started—with z—but he has lost three dollars. Presumably, this process could be repeated until person 1's money is exhausted.) On the other hand, there are good examples suggesting that indifference need not be transitive: If $x_0, x_1, x_2, \ldots, x_m$ are grains of salt, then some person, i, might be indifferent between x_j and x_{j-1} grains on potatoes, but prefer x_0 grains to x_m grains: $x_m I_i x_{m-1}, x_{m-1} I_i x_{m-2}, \ldots, x_1 I_i x_0$, and $x_0 P_i x_m$.

[2]Using $|i: x P_i y|$ to mean "the number of persons, i, who prefer x to y," then

$$x M y \text{ means } |i: x P_i y| > |i: y P_i x| \qquad (\text{N4-1})$$

Similar definitions, comparable to the individual relations of I and R are

$$x T y \text{ means } |i: x P_i y| = |i: y P_i x| \qquad (\text{N4-2})$$

$$x MT y \text{ means } |i: x R_i y| \geq |i: y R_i x| \qquad (\text{N4-3})$$

[3]Actually, typical American procedure provides for this final step only in the most attenuated form because often several sets X are collected together (as a report from the committee of the whole) and step 5 for all these sets is contained in the motion to adopt the report. American procedure is therefore logically less adequate than the procedure outlined (which is equivalent to Duncan Black's procedure α; see his *The Theory*

of *Committees and Elections* [Cambridge, England: Cambridge University Press, 1958], p. 21). See William H. Riker, "The Paradox of Voting and Congressional Rules for Voting on Amendments," *American Political Science Review,* Vol. 52 (June 1958), pp. 349–366.

[4]This example is based on the dominated winner paradox in Peter C. Fishburn, "Paradoxes of Voting," *American Political Science Review,* Vol. 68 (June 1974), pp. 537–546. One can easily obtain examples of a substantive winner that loses to a rejected motion with just four alternatives; but, since s is fixed as the last alternative, it takes five alternatives to create an example in which a rejected motion is *unanimously* preferred to the winner.

[5]Specifically: $c(x) = |y$ in $X: x \, M \, y| - |y$ in $X: y \, M \, x|$.

[6]Peter C. Fishburn, *The Theory of Social Choice* (Princeton: Princeton University Press, 1973), p. 170.

[7]Thomas Schwartz, "Rationality and the Myth of the Maximum," *Noûs,* Vol. 6 (May 1972), pp. 97–117.

[8]John Kemeny, "Mathematics Without Numbers," *Daedalus,* Vol. 88 (Fall 1959), pp. 577–591. See also Arthur Levenglick, "Fair and Reasonable Election Systems," *Behavioral Science,* Vol. 20 (January 1975), pp. 34–46. That the Copeland, Schwartz, and Kemeny rules produce different results may be seen in this example:

D		
D_1:	$y\,a\,b\,c\,d\,e\,x$	$F_{\text{Copeland}}(X, D) = x$
D_2:	$b\,x\,y\,c\,d\,e\,a$	
D_3:	$x\,c\,d\,e\,a\,b\,y$	$F_{\text{Schwartz}}(X, D) = x\,y\,a\,b\,c\,d\,e$
D_4:	$x\,d\,e\,a\,b\,c\,y$	
D_5:	$y\,e\,a\,b\,c\,d\,x$	$F_{\text{Kemeny}}(X, D) = b$

A number of other interesting but unused rules have been devised. These are reviewed in Peter C. Fishburn, "Condorcet Social Choice Functions," *SIAM Journal of Applied Mathematics,* Vol. 33 (November 1977), pp. 469–489. A particularly difficult Condorcet extension was devised by Charles Dodgson (Lewis Carroll), for which see Black, pp. 224–230; for

Black's own proposal see p. 66; for a proposal by Condorcet see pp. 175–176; and for one by Nanson see p. 187.

[9]Notice that in the Dyer and Miles study, described in section 2.B, the Borda method was, for convenience, operated in reverse: one point for first place ... m points for last place, with the alternative with the lowest points the winner.

[10]Fishburn, *The Theory of Social Choice,* p. 147.

[11]See Black, pp. 176–177.

[12]For an alternative, if $r(x, y, D)$ is the number of orders D_i in D in which x precedes y, then

$$s(x) = \sum_{\substack{y \text{ in } x \\ y \neq x}} [r(x, y, D) - r(y, x, D)] \qquad \text{(N4-4)}$$

[13]To illustrate the calculation with $s(y)$:

For y and x, 2 yx (in D_2, D_5) − 3 xy (in D_1, D_3, D_4) = −1

For y and a, 5 ya (in D_1, D_2, D_3, D_4, D_5) − 0 ay = 5

For y and b, 5 yb (in D_1, D_2, D_3, D_4, D_5) − 0 by = 5

For y and c, 4 yc (in D_1, D_2, D_4, D_5) − 1 cy (in D_3) =   3

$s(y) = $ 12

[14]See Black, p. 216; Fishburn, *The Theory of Social Choice,* p. 150.

[15]The logic of this dynamic effect of the plurality system is examined in William H. Riker, "The Number of Political Parties: A Re-examination of Duverger's Law," Vol. 9, *Comparative Politics* (October 1976), pp. 93–106.

[16]Steven J. Brams and Peter C. Fishburn, "Approval Voting," *American Political Science Review,* Vol. 72 (September 1978), pp. 831–847.

[17]Black, pp. 65–66.

[18]Fishburn, "Paradoxes of Voting."

[9]See, for example, Robert Dahl, *A Preface to Democratic Theory* (Chicago: University of Chicago Press, 1956); and James Buchanan and Gordon Tullock, *The Calculus of Consent* (Ann Arbor: University of Michigan Press, 1962).

[0]See John Von Neumann and Oskar Morgenstern, *The Theory of Games and Economic Behavior,* 3rd ed. (Princeton: Princeton University Press, 1953). A simpler introduction is to be found in William H. Riker and Peter C. Ordeshook, *An Introduction to Positive Political Theory* (Englewood Cliffs, N.J.: Prentice-Hall, 1973), chap. 2.

[1]*Bentham's Political Thought,* ed. Bhikhu Parekh (London: Croom Helm, 1973), pp. 114–127, 40, 16–17, 309–310.

[2]An interesting application of this rule involves locating voters in a space by measuring their judgments on several scales and then choosing the candidate whose location minimizes the sum of the distances from the voters' judgments. See I. J. Good and T. Nicholaus Tideman, "From Individual to Collective Ordering Through Multidimensional Attribute Space," *Proceedings of the Royal Society,* Vol. A-347 (1976), pp. 371–385. Since this method ultimately rests on some kind of utility measurement, it is essentially a summation technique.

[23]T. Nicholaus Tideman and Gordon Tullock, "A New and Superior Process for Making Social Choices," *Journal of Political Economy,* Vol. 84 (December 1976), pp. 1145–1159.

[24]J. F. Nash, "The Bargaining Problem," *Econometrica,* Vol. 18 (April 1950), pp. 155–162.

[25]An *F* is *undifferentiated* if and only if, for all *D* in *D*, and for any permutation of *N*,

$$F[X, (D_1, D_2, \ldots, D_n)] = F[X, (D_{\sigma(1)}, D_{\sigma(2)}, \ldots, D_{\sigma(n)})] \qquad \text{(N4-5)}$$

[26]An *F* is *neutral* if and only if, for all *D* in *D*, and for any permutation of *X* such that x_j is replaced by $\sigma(x_j)$, for x_j belonging to *X*,

$$F(X, D^\sigma) = \sigma F(X, D) \qquad \text{(N4-6)}$$

where these terms are defined as in Chapter 3, note 20.

[27]An F is *monotonic* if and only if, for all i in N and all D, D' in $\mathbf{D}$,

where $D'_j = D_j$, for all $j \neq i$

where D'_i on $(X - \{x\}) = D_i$ on $(X - \{x\})$ (N4-7)

and where, if $x\,P'_i\,y$ implies $x\,P_i\,y$ and $x\,I'_i\,y$ implies $x\,R_i\,y$, for all y in $(X - \{x\})$, then, if x is in $F(X, D')$, x is in $F(X, D)$; and if $y\,P'_i\,x$ implies $y\,P_i\,x$ and $y\,I'_i\,x$ implies $y\,R_i\,x$, for all y in $(X - \{x\})$, then, if x is not in $F(X, D')$, x is not in $F(X, D)$.

[28]An F is *unanimous* if and only if, for y such that

$(x : x$ in X, $x\,P_i\,y$, for all i in $N)$, y is not in $F(X, D)$ (N4-8)

This kind of unanimity is often called *Pareto optimality*. Originally this sense of optimality meant that an outcome was socially optimal if any change from it made someone worse off. Clearly, if everybody dislikes y and y is not the social choice, then to include y in the social choice would surely make some people worse off.

[29]An F is *Condorcet* if and only if $F(X, D)$ includes the set

$\{x : x\,MT\,y$, for all y in $X\}$.   (N4-9)

[30]An F is *consistent* if and only if, when N is divided into disjoint sets N^1 and N^2 and D^1 is a profile on N^1 and D^2 is a profile on N^2,

if $F(X, D^1) \cap F(X, D^2) \neq \emptyset$,

then $F(X, D^1 + D^2) \subseteq F(X, D^1) \cap F(X, D^2)$ (N4-10)

(Note: The symbol $\cap$ is to be read "the intersection of sets S and T" and means those elements that are in both S and T; the symbol $\emptyset$ means "the empty set"; and the symbol $\subseteq$ means "the set on the left contains or equals the set on the right."

[31]An F is *independent from irrelevant alternatives* if and only if,

for S included in X, $D = D'$ on S, then $F(S, D) = F(S, D')$

                                                       (N4-11)

[32]The main reason for the dispute is, I believe, the fact that, when it was first presented in Kenneth Arrow, *Social Choice and Individual Values,* 2nd ed. (New Haven: Yale University Press, 1963), it was discussed (but not used) as if it forbade variations in orderings of alternatives outside the set of alternatives being considered. Thereby it was made into a consistency condition on the way choices from various subsets of alternatives were nested inside each other, a condition that will be discussed in Chapter 5. It is, however, not a consistency condition on choices from sets of different sizes, but simply a consistency condition on the rule, F, of choice. In that sense it is also a condition of equity, as noted in sections 4.I and 5.D.

[33]A simple example, due to Fishburn, *The Theory of Social Choice,* p. 89, is:

$$D \text{ (where } y \, M \, x \, M \, w \, M \, z \, M \, y)$$

D_1:	$x \, w \, z \, y$
D_2:	$y \, x \, w \, z$
D_3:	$z \, y \, x \, w$

so $F_{\text{Schwartz}}(X, D) = w, x, y, z$, although, for all i, $x \, P_i \, w$.

[34]H. P. Young, "An Axiomatization of Borda's Rule," *Journal of Economic Theory,* Vol. 9 (September 1974), pp. 43–52; H. P. Young, "Social Choice Scoring Functions," *SIAM Journal of Applied Mathematics,* Vol. 28 (June 1975), pp. 824–838. Levenglick asserts that Kenemy's function satisfies consistency, but Fishburn, in "Condorcet Social Choice Functions," provides a counterexample. Approval voting, not considered by Young, clearly satisfies the criterion: If N^1 has $1 \ldots k$ voters and N^2 has $k + 1 \ldots n$ voters, if x has $j \leq k$ votes and y has $g \leq j$ votes in N^1, and if x has $f \leq (n - k)$ votes and y has $h \leq f$ votes in N^2, then in $N = N^1 \cup N^2$, $g + h \leq j + f$. So if x with $j + f$ votes is in $F_{\text{approval}}(X, D^1) \cap F(X, D^2)$, then x is in $F_{\text{approval}}(X, D^1 + D^2)$.

[35]Gideon Doron, "The Hare Voting System is Inconsistent," *Political Studies,* Vol. 27 (June 1979), pp. 283–286. In this paper Doron offers an example in which, with the single transferable vote, as used in the government of Ireland and in many private societies, one alternative may win in two districts separately and another may win in these districts together (see section 3.C for the rules of this voting method). Doron's example is set forth in Display N4-1.

Display N4-1

Violation of Consistency
Under the Hare System

One candidate is to be elected in N^1, in N^2, and in $N^1 + N^2$.

D^1 (for N^1)	
D_1–D_8:	w x y z
D_9–D_{12}:	x y z w
D_{13}–D_{15}:	y w z x
D_{16}–D_{21}:	z y x w

Note $N^1 = 21$;
quota $= 11$.

D^2 (for N^2)	
D_{22}–D_{29}:	w x y z
D_{30}–D_{33}:	x y z w
D_{34}–D_{39}:	y w z x
D_{40}–D_{42}:	z w x y

Note $N^2 = 21$;
quota $= 11$.

For N^1, no candidate has the quota; so the candidate, y, with fewest first-place votes is eliminated, and the votes are transferred to w, who then wins. For N^2, where again no candidate has the quota, candidate z is eliminated, and the votes are again transferred to w, who then wins. So w wins in N^1 and in N^2, but in $N^1 + N^2$, as follows, w loses:

$D^1 + D^2$ (for $N^1 + N^2$)	
D_1–D_8, D_{22}–D_{29}:	w x y z (16 voters)
D_9–D_{12}, D_{30}–D_{33}:	x y z w (8 voters)
D_{13}–D_{15}, D_{34}–D_{39}:	y w z x (9 voters)
D_{16}–D_{21}:	z y x w (6 voters)
D_{40}–D_{42}:	z w x y (3 voters)

Note $N^1 + N^2 = 42$; quota $= 22$

For $N^1 + N^2$, again no candidate has the quota; so first x is eliminated with the votes transferred to y (who then has 17 votes); then z is eliminated with the 9 votes transferred, 6 to y and 3 to w. Hence y has 23 votes and is elected—in clear violation of consistency, which requires that the winner (here w) in N^1 and N^2 also win in $N^1 + N^2$.

[36]George H. Haynes, *The Senate of the United States,* Vol. 1 (Boston: Houghton Mifflin, 1938), pp. 81–95.

[37]To exempt approval voting from this defect, it is sometimes said that ballots rather than preference orders are permuted. All definitions of anonymity (undifferentiatedness) known to me, however, state that preference orders (D_i with $x R_i y$ or $y R_i x$) are permuted, not ballots (with $C_i(xy) = x$ or y or (xy)).

[38]Tideman and Tullock attempt to satisfy independence by fixing cardinal relations. The technique of Good and Tideman violates independence because the social choice between two alternatives depends on the spatial location of a third.

Chapter 5

[1]William H. Riker, "Voting and the Summation of Preferences," *American Polical Science Review,* Vol. 55 (December 1961), pp. 900–911.

[2]Since many proofs are easily available to those who wish to follow up the subject, I will not reiterate the proof here. For Arrow's proof, as revised by Julian Blau, see Kenneth Arrow, *Social Choice and Individual Values,* 2nd ed. (New Haven: Yale University Press, 1963), pp. 96–100. A refined form of Arrow's proof is to be found in Amartya K. Sen, *Collective Choice and Social Welfare* (San Francisco: Holden-Day, 1970), chap. 3. See also Peter C. Fishburn, *The Theory of Social Choice* (Princeton: Princeton University Press, 1973), p. 206. Bengt Hansson, "The Existence of Group Preference Functions," *Public Choice,* Vol. 28 (Winter 1976), pp. 89–98, contains a topological proof. An informal sketch of Arrow's proof is contained in William H. Riker and Peter C. Ordeshook, *An Introduction to Positive Political Theory* (Englewood Cliffs, N.J.: Prentice-Hall, 1973), pp. 92–94.

[3]See Duncan Black, *The Theory of Committees and Elections* (Cambridge, England: Cambridge University Press, 1958), pp. 50–51, where the calculation was first proposed. Calculations are set forth in Richard Niemi and Herbert Weisberg, "A Mathematical Solution for the Prob-

ability of the Paradox of Voting," *Behavioral Science,* Vol. 13 (July 1968), pp. 317–323; Mark Gorman and Morton Kamien, "The Paradox of Voting: Probability Calculations," *Behavioral Science,* Vol. 13 (July 1968), pp. 306–316; Frank DeMeyer and Charles Plott, "The Probability of a Cyclical Majority," *Econometrica,* Vol. 38 (March 1970), pp. 345–354. See also R. M. May, "Some Mathematical Remarks on the Paradox of Voting," *Behavioral Science,* Vol. 16 (March 1971), pp. 143–151; Peter C. Fishburn and William V. Gehrlein, "An Analysis of Simple Two-Stage Voting Systems," *Behavioral Science,* Vol. 21 (January 1976), pp. 1–12; Fishburn and Gehrlein, "An Analysis of Voting Procedure with Nonranked Voting," *Behavioral Science,* Vol. 22 (May 1977), pp. 178–185; Gehrlein and Fishburn, "The Probability of the Paradox of Voting," *Journal of Economic Theory,* Vol. 13 (August 1976), pp. 14–25; and the papers cited in note 8 of this chapter.

[4]Duncan Black, "On the Rationale of Group Decision Making," *Journal of Political Economy,* Vol. 56 (February 1948), pp. 23–34; Black, *The Theory of Committees and Elections,* chaps. 4 and 5.

[5]Fishburn, *The Theory of Social Choice,* p. 105.

[6]Black, *The Theory of Committees and Elections,* chap. 4.

[7]Fishburn, *The Theory of Social Choice,* pp. 111–144. See also Sen, pp. 166–186. A somewhat different kind of condition for transitivity (not involving restrictions on D_i) has been identified by Rubin Saposnik, "On Transitivity of the Social Preference Relation Under Simple Majority Rule," *Journal of Economic Theory,* Vol. 10 (January 1975), pp. 1–7, where it is shown that, if the number of voters in D having orders constituting the forward cycle is equal to the number constituting the backward cycle, then the social order is transitive. Saposnik calls this condition, which must be extremely rare in the real world, "cyclical balance."

[8]Richard Niemi, "Majority Decision Making with Partial Unidimensionality," *American Political Science Review,* Vol. 63 (June 1969), pp. 489–497. Similar results with somewhat different methods are found in D. Jamieson and E. Luce, "Social Homogeneity and the Probability of Intransitive Majority Rule," *Journal of Economic Theory,* Vol. 5 (August 1972), pp. 79–87; and Peter C. Fishburn, "Voter Concordance, Simple Majorities, and Group Decision Methods," *Behavioral Science,* Vol. 18 (September 1973), pp. 364–373.

[9]Bengt Hansson, "The Independence Condition in the Theory of Social Choice," *Theory and Decision,* Vol. 4 (September 1973), pp. 25–49.

[10]Hansson's independence condition (see note 9) allows for just the variability that Arrow's prohibits, but it has not attracted adherents precisely because it seems arbitrary.

[11]James Buchanan, "Individual Choice in Voting and the Market," *Journal of Political Economy,* Vol. 62 (August 1954), pp. 334–343.

[12]This means, of course, that there may be either no best alternative or more than one best alternative, which is grammatically dubious but entirely understandable if we define a *best alternative* formally thus: For a set S, let x be a best alternative in S if and only if, for all y in S, $x \, R \, y$. The set of all best alternatives in S is the choice set, $C(S)$, for some relation, R. For example, let two persons have preferences $x \, y \, z$ and $y \, z \, x$. Clearly y is in the choice set because socially $y \, P \, z$ (inasmuch as $y \, P_1 \, z$ and $y \, P_2 \, z$) and socially $y \, I \, x$ (inasmuch as $x \, P_1 \, y$ and $y \, P_2 \, x$). So also is x in the choice set because $x \, I \, y$ and $x \, I \, z$. But z is not in $C(S)$, because it is false that $z \, R \, y$ (inasmuch as both persons have $y \, P_i \, z$).

[13]Heretofore I used $F_g(X, D)$ to refer to a social choice by some voting rule. To generalize and thus to avoid the particularism of a specific rule, I now use $C(X)$ to mean simply the social choice from X.

[14]Formally, for $X = (x_1, x_2, \ldots, x_n)$, if $x_1 \, P \, x_2$, $x_2 \, P \, x_3$, $\ldots$, $x_{n-1} \, P \, x_n$, it is not true that $x_n \, P \, x_1$. This means $x_1 \, R \, x_n$, so that no cycle of any size exists. Acyclicity requires less than quasi-transitivity for two reasons. First, acyclicity requires only that the consequent be $x_1 \, R \, x_n$, which admits either $x_1 \, P \, x_n$ or $x_1 \, I \, x_n$. Quasi-transitivity, on the other hand, requires (in the sentence "If $x_1 \, P \, x_2$ and if $x_2 \, P \, x_3$, then $x_1 \, P \, x_3$.") that the consequent be $x_1 \, P \, x_3$ only. So acyclicity admits a more general consequent. Acyclicity also requires less than quasi-transitivity in the sense that quasi-transitivity is a property of every triple in X, while acyclicity is a property of X as a whole. Indeed it is possible for every triple in X to be acyclic, but for X itself to be cyclic, as seen in Display N5-1, which is based on Sen, p. 16.

[15]Sen, pp. 48, 52–53.

[16]This was proved by Allen Gibbard in an unpublished paper (1969), and a proof is found in Fishburn, *The Theory of Social Choice,* pp. 209–210.

Display N5-1

A Cyclic Set with Acyclic Triples

	D
D_1:	w x y z
D_2:	x y z w
D_3:	y z w x
D_4:	z w x y

**Number of Votes for the Alternative
in the Row When Placed in Contest
Against the Alternative in the Column**

	w	x	y	z
w	—	3	2	1
x	1	—	3	2
y	2	1	—	3
z	3	2	1	—

Notice that each alternative beats one other, ties with one other, and loses to one other.

All triples are acyclic:

w x y:	wPx,	xPy,	wIy
w x z:	zPw,	wPx,	zIx
w y z:	yPz,	zPw,	wIy
x y z:	xPy,	yPz,	xIz

Yet the entire set, X, is in a cycle: wPx, xPy, yPz, and zPw.

An oligarchy, which may be any subset of the set N of choosers, including N itself, is a subset, O, such that, if *everyone* in O prefers x to y, then the social choice is x and if *any* person in O prefers x to y, then the social choice is not y. Thus, if the oligarchy agrees, it can impose a choice; and every member of the oligarchy has a veto.

[17]Fishburn, *The Theory of Social Choice,* p. 208.

[18]Donald Brown, "Acyclic Choice" (Cowles Foundation Discussion Paper, Yale University, 1973); Brown, "An Approximate Solution to Arrow's Problem," *Journal of Economic Theory,* Vol. 9 (December 1974), pp. 375–383. As John A. Ferejohn has pointed out, in "Brown's Theory of Collective Choice" (Social Science Working Paper, California Institute of Technology, March 1976), Brown's collegia are almost imperceptibly different from oligarchies, so that no real gain occurs in substituting acyclicity for transitivity.

[19]Andrew Mas-Colell and Hugo Sonnenschein, "General Possibility Theorem for Group Decision," *Review of Economic Studies,* Vol. 39 (April 1972), pp. 185–192.

[20]Arrow, p. 120.

[21]Sen's conditions are set forth in *Collective Choice and Social Welfare,* chap. 4, and reviewed in detail in a review article, A. K. Sen, "Social Choice Theory: A Re-examination," *Econometrica,* Vol. 45 (January 1977), pp. 53–88. Sen's article is an excellent review of the technical literature. Plott's condition is set forth in Charles Plott, "Path Independence, Rationality, and Social Choice," *Econometrica,* Vol. 41 (October 1973), pp. 1075–1091. Plott's interpretation of the whole problem is set forth in an excellent review for political scientists, Charles Plott, "Axiomatic Social Choice Theory," *American Journal of Political Science,* Vol. 20 (August 1976), pp. 511–596.

[22]Since F is "irrelevant" to the choice between B and C, property α or the Weak Axiom of Revealed Preference (WARP) is sometimes called "independence from irrelevant alternatives," though it is quite different from Arrow's Condition I. One can, of course, imagine situations in which the third alternative is relevant: Let T be {Republican, Democrat, Independent} and S be {Republican, Democrat}. Then an electorate might choose R from T and D from S by plurality voting. But it is precisely because of both of these possibilities that many political scientists and social choice theorists criticize plurality voting—and that criticism constitutes a justification of property α.

[23]Plott, "Path Independence, Rationality, and Social Choice," pp. 1079–1080.

[24]Formally, $C(S \cup T) = C[C(S) \cup C(T)]$.

[25]Formally, PI^*: $C(S \cup T) \subseteq C[C(S) \cup C(T)]$

and $^*PI$: $C[C(S) \cup C(T)] \subseteq C(S \cup T)$

Manifestly, if $\subseteq$ holds in each direction, then $C(S \cup T)$ is equivalent to $C[C(S) \cup C(T)]$, which is PI itself. So: $PI^* + {}^*PI = PI$.

[26]This fact was proved by R. E. Parks in an unpublished paper cited in Plott, "Path Independence, Rationality, and Social Choice."

[27]G. Bordes, "Alpha Rationality and Social Choice," an unpublished paper cited in Sen, "Social Choice Theory: A Re-examination."

[28]See Sen, ibid.

[29]John A. Ferejohn and David M. Grether, "Weak Path Independence," *Journal of Economic Theory,* Vol. 14 (January 1977), pp. 19–31.

[30]Ibid.

Chapter 6

[1]Duncan Black, *The Theory of Committees and Elections* (Cambridge, England: Cambridge University Press, 1958), p. 21, calls a method with this ultimate step "procedure α" and says it is "almost universally used." It is true that α is used in the British House of Commons; but, in the Committee of the Whole in the U.S. House of Representatives, it appears in a form so attenuated that it is equivalent to the procedure described in the text. See William H. Riker, "The Paradox of Voting and Congressional Rules for Voting on Amendments," *American Political Science Review,* Vol. 52 (June 1958), pp. 349–366.

[2]Duncan Black, "On the Rationale of Group Decision Making," *Journal of Political Economy,* Vol. 56 (February 1948), p. 29; Kenneth Arrow, *Social Choice and Individual Values,* 2nd ed. (New Haven: Yale Univer-

sity Press, 1963), pp. 80–81; Topas Majundar, "Choice and Revealed Preference," *Econometrica,* Vol. 24 (January 1956), pp. 71–73; William Vickery, "Utility, Strategy, and Social Decision Rules," *Quarterly Journal of Economics,* Vol. 74 (November 1960), pp. 507–535; Michael Dummet and Robin Farquharson, "Stability in Voting," *Econometrica,* Vol. 29 (January 1961), pp. 33–42; William H. Riker, "Arrow's Theorem and Some Examples of the Paradox of Voting," in *Mathematical Applications in Political Science,* ed. J. Claunch (Dallas: Arnold Foundation, Southern Methodist University, 1965), pp. 41–69; Robin Farquharson, *Theory of Voting* (New Haven: Yale University Press, 1969).

[3]Allan Gibbard, "Manipulation of Voting Schemes: A General Result," *Econometrica,* Vol. 41 (July 1973), pp. 587–601; Mark Satterthwaite, "Strategy Proofness and Arrow's Conditions," *Journal of Economic Theory,* Vol. 10 (October 1975), pp. 187–217. See also Peter Gärdenfors, "A Concise Proof of a Theorem on Manipulation of Social Choice Functions," *Public Choice,* Vol. 32 (Winter 1977), pp. 137–140.

[4]To express this fact formally, let D_i be an ordering of X by strict preference, P, and let D be a profile of such orderings. An outcome, $F(X, D)$, of a voting method is a function, g, of strategies of voting, s_i, chosen by each person, i, given i's D_i. Thus, $F(X, D) = g[s_1(D_1), \ldots, s_n(D_n)]$. Let $\sigma_i(D_i)$ be that particular strategy in which a voter votes exactly in accord with the preferences in D_i. (For example, if $a\, P_i\, b\, P_i\, c$, then, if on a vote between b and c, i votes for b, i is following $\sigma_i(D_i)$). Hence $g[\sigma_1(D_1), \ldots, \sigma_n(D_n)]$ is the outcome if all i vote according to their true tastes. A voting method is manipulable by strategic voting if, for some i, for $F(X, D) = g[\sigma_1(D_1), \ldots, \sigma_i(D_i), \ldots, \sigma_n(D_n)]$ and for some $F(X, D') = g[\sigma_1(D_1), \ldots, s_i(D_i), \ldots, \sigma_n(D_n)]$, where $s_i(D_i) \neq \sigma_i(D_i)$, voter i prefers $F(X, D')$ to $F(X, D)$. That is, i prefers the outcome with personal dissimulation to that without dissimulation.

[5]Jerry S. Kelly, "Strategy-Proofness and Social Choice Functions Without Singlevaluedness," *Econometrica,* Vol. 45 (March 1977), pp. 439–446, shows that methods of amalgamation that allow the choice of *all* Pareto optimal outcomes, which may be many, may indeed be immune to manipulation. Peter Gärdenfors, "Manipulation of Social Choice Functions," *Journal of Economic Theory,* Vol. 13 (October 1976), pp. 217–228, offers a specific example of such a method: Given that all D_i in D are strong orders (that is, no indifference is allowed), then define $F(X, D)$ thus: $F(X, D) = x_j$ if there is an absolute majority of voters who place x_j first in their preference orders, and $F(X, D) = X$ otherwise. That is, an F is not manipulable that chooses either that x_j for which there is an abso-

lute majority or the whole set of alternatives if no x_j has an absolute majority. Of course, this rules out the most interesting cases—for example, where D has a Condorcet winner without an absolute majority or when D has a cycle under majority rule.

It is true, however, that, if there is enough similarity in voters' preference orders, many voting systems are strategy-proof. For example, if everyone has the same ordering, manipulation is impossible under majority rule. For an investigation of conditions of similarity that ensure strategy-proofness, see Joseph Greenberg, "Consistent Majority Rules over Compact Sets of Alternatives," *Econometrica,* Vol. 47 (May 1979), pp. 627–636; and Bezalel Peleg, "Consistent Voting Systems," *Econometrica,* Vol. 46 (January 1978), pp. 153–161.

[6]Furthermore, Allan Gibbard has shown, in "Manipulation of Schemes That Mix Voting with Chance," *Econometrica,* Vol. 45 (April 1977), pp. 665–679, that in social choices by lotteries—based on probabilities determined by individual ballot marking in which voters rank lotteries by their cardinal utilities for outcomes—if voters can advantageously mark ballots strategically, the social choice is manipulable and, if manipulable, either dictatorial or imposed, à la Arrow. For other proofs that manipulation is possible with some chance mechanisms, see Gärdenfors, "Manipulation of Social Choice Functions."

[7]P. K. Pattanaik, "Counter Threats and Strategic Manipulation Under Voting Schemes," *Review of Economic Studies,* Vol. 43 (February 1976), pp. 11–18, extends Gibbard's result to situations in which i's strategic voting can be countered by the strategic voting of others. Pattanaik shows that, even then, all voting methods admit of situations in which it is still to i's advantage to vote strategically. So strategic voting cannot be eliminated by opposition.

[8]Most examples of strategic voting involve the commonly used methods—plurality voting or the amendment procedure. But in theory the Borda method is equally manipulable. See Duncan Black, "Partial Justification of the Borda Count," *Public Choice,* Vol. 28 (Winter 1976), pp. 1–15; and William G. Ludwin, "Strategic Voting and the Borda Method," *Public Choice,* Vol. 33, No. 1 (1978), pp. 85–90.

[9]Douglas Rae, *The Political Consequences of Electoral Laws* (New Haven: Yale University Press, 1971), p. 93; William H. Riker, "The Number of Political Parties: A Re-examination of Duverger's Law," *Comparative Politics,* Vol. 9 (October 1976), pp. 93–106. It may be, however, that relatively few voters really vote strategically because, as has often been pointed out, individual voters cannot expect to have much influence over

the outcome of elections. (See Anthony Downs, *An Economic Theory of Democracy* [New York: Harper and Row, 1967], pp. 260–276; William H. Riker and Peter C. Ordeshook, "A Theory of the Calculus of Voting," *American Political Science Review,* Vol. 62 [March 1968], pp. 25–42; Paul E. Meehl, "The Selfish Voter Paradox and the Thrown-Away Vote Argument," *American Political Science Review,* Vol. 71 [March 1977], pp. 11–30.) If so, then the motive for the Duverger result is the reluctance of politicians to expose themselves to strategic voting. That is, third-party leaders, fearing that their supporters will strategically desert them and assuming therefore that they cannot win, simply abandon the effort, thus generating a two-party system. In this view, the mere *possibility* of strategic voting has profound consequences.

[10]The expected utility, *Eu*, of an action, a_i, is calculated thus:

$$Eu(a_i) = \sum_{i=1}^{n} p_i(O_i)u_i(O_i)$$

[11]Howard Rosenthal, "Game Theoretic Models of Bloc Voting Under Proportional Representation," *Public Choice,* Vol. 18 (Summer 1974), pp. 1–23.

[12]This is based on Riker, "Arrow's Theorem and Some Examples of the Paradox of Voting."

[13]*Congressional Quarterly Almanac, 1956,* pp. 806–807. These numbers include live pairs and thus differ slightly from numbers in the *Congressional Record.*

[14]*Congressional Record,* Vol. 102, Part 9 (85th Cong., 2nd sess.), p. 11758.

[15]Of course, not all strategic voting is successful. Bo Bjurulf and Richard Niemi, "Strategic Voting in Scandinavian Parliaments," *Scandinavian Political Studies,* Vol. 1, New Series (1978), pp. 5–22, describe, among other things, an instance in which strategic voting backfired so that the *least*-desired alternative was chosen.

[16]Richard D. McKelvey and Richard Niemi, "A Multistage Game Representation of Sophisticated Voting for Binary Procedures," *Journal of Economic Theory,* Vol. 18 (January 1978), pp. 1–22.

[17]Robin Farquharson, "Sophisticated Voting and an Example Due to M. Kreweras," in *La Decision,* ed. G. Th. Guilbaud (Paris: Editions du Centre Nationale de la Recherche Scientifique, 1969), pp. 115–122, of-

fers the following example in which sincere and strategic voting lead to different results:

$$D_{1-33}: \quad x \, y \, z$$
$$D_{34-51}: \quad y \, x \, z$$
$$D_{52-63}: \quad y \, z \, x$$
$$D_{64-100}: \quad z \, y \, x$$

The Condorcet winner (always found with binary procedures whether sincere or strategic voting occurs) and the Borda winner is y. Runoff elections between the two highest candidates in the first round give x with sincere voting and y with strategic voting. Plurality elections never get to y, however. Under plurality, sincere voting produces z and strategic voting produces x. Which is better? Since x has a sincere majority over z, x may seem better, but since z has more sincere Borda points than x, z may seem better. All we can say for sure is that they are different.

[18]In terms of choice, cyclicity is: $C(xy, \bar{x}y) = xy$, $C(\bar{x}y, x\bar{y}) = \bar{x}y, \ldots,$ $C(xy, \bar{x}\bar{y}) = \bar{x}\bar{y}$.

[19]Thomas Schwartz, "Collective Choice, Separation of Issues and Vote Trading," *American Political Science Review,* Vol. 71 (September 1977), pp. 999–1010, from which I have adopted the notation of q_x, Q^*, and Q.

[20]James Enelow, "A Game Theoretic Model of Legislative Vote Trading" (Ph.D. diss., University of Rochester, 1977), and Enelow, "Non-Cooperative Counterthreats to Vote Trading," *American Journal of Political Science,* Vol. 23 (February 1979), pp. 121–128.

[21]Since demand-revealing voting admits blackmail and bribery of one individual by another, it even induces individual strategic voting in the potential blackmailer and bribee.

[22]This example is drawn from William H. Riker, "Is A 'New and Superior Process' Really Superior?" *Journal of Political Economy,* Vol. 87 (August 1979), pp. 875–890.

[23]Schwartz, p. 1010.

[24]William H. Riker and Steven J. Brams, "The Paradox of Vote Trading," *American Political Science Review,* Vol. 67 (December 1973), pp. 1235–1247.

[25]Richard McKelvey and Peter Ordeshook, "Vote Trading: An Experimental Study," mimeographed (Pittsburgh: Carnegie Mellon University, 1978), report such coalitions occurring (along with the worst possible outcomes) in three- and five-person laboratory groups in which all the motions were known before bargaining began.

[26]See McKelvey and Niemi, and Schwartz.

[27]Black, *The Theory of Committees and Elections,* p. 182.

[28]Ibid., pp. 232–233.

Chapter 7

[1]Recall that a method of voting is path independent if $C(X) = C[C(S) \cup C(T)]$, where S and T are any subsets that disjointly partition X.

[2]So at least I read the last sentence of letter 14 of book 7, to Titus Aristo, as guided by the translation of Betty Radice, Pliny, *Letters,* Vol. 2 (Cambridge, Mass.: Harvard University Press, 1969), pp. 33–47. Farquharson, who had only a bad seventeenth-century translation in which this sentence is ambiguous, carefully avoided mention of the outcome.

[3]Charles Plott and Michael Levine, "A Model of Agenda Influence on Committee Decisions," *American Economic Review,* Vol. 68 (March 1978), pp. 146–160; Levine and Plott, "Agenda Influence and Its Implications," *Virginia Law Review,* Vol. 63 (May 1977), pp. 561–604.

[4]Kenneth Arrow, *Social Choice and Individual Values,* 2nd ed. (New Haven: Yale University Press, 1963), p. 17.

[5]Anthony Downs, *An Economic Theory of Democracy* (New York: Harper and Row, 1956), pp. 114–120.

[6]See, among others, Otto A. Davis and Melvin J. Hinich, "A Mathematical Model of Policy Formation in a Democratic Society," in *Mathematical Applications in Political Science,* Vol. 2, ed. J. A. Bernd (Dallas: Southern Methodist University Press, 1966), pp. 175–208; Otto A. Davis,

Melvin J. Hinich, and Peter C. Ordeshook, "An Expository Development of a Mathematical Model of the Electoral Process," *American Political Science Review,* Vol. 64 (June 1970), pp. 426–449; William H. Riker and Peter C. Ordeshook, *An Introduction to Positive Political Theory* (Englewood Cliffs, N.J.: Prentice-Hall, 1973), pp. 307–375. Davis and Hinich introduce the notion of a multidimensional median, which McKelvey and Schofield carry about as far as it can go (see notes 11, 12, and 15).

[7]Duncan Black and R. A. Newing, *Committee Decisions with Complementary Valuation* (Edinburgh: William Hodge, 1951), pp. 19–28. See also Duncan Black, *The Theory of Committees and Elections* (Cambridge, England: Cambridge University Press, 1958), chap. 16.

[8]Gerald H. Kramer, "On a Class of Equilibrium Conditions for Majority Rule," *Econometrica,* Vol. 41 (March 1973), pp. 285–297.

[9]Charles Plott, "A Notion of Equilibrium and Its Possibility Under Majority Rule," *American Economic Review,* Vol. 57 (September 1967), pp. 787–806.

[10]Richard D. McKelvey and Richard E. Wendell, "Voting Equilibria in Multidimensional Choice Spaces," *Mathematics of Operations Research,* Vol. 1 (May 1976), pp. 144–158.

[11]In n dimensions, single-peaked is defined with respect to ideal points, x^*, of individuals, i. A line is single-peaked if it is always sloping away from an individual's ideal point, x_i^*. That is, a line connecting some y and some z is single-peaked if, for all x in X on the line such that $x \neq x_i^*$,

$$u_i[\alpha x + (1 - \alpha)x_i^*] > u_i[\beta x + (1 - \beta)x_i^*]$$

where $0 \leq \alpha < \beta \leq 1$.

[12]Richard D. McKelvey, "Intransitivities in Multidimensional Voting Models and Some Implication for Agenda Control," *Journal of Economic Theory,* Vol. 12 (June 1976), pp. 472–482 (emphasis in original). See also McKelvey, "General Conditions for Global Intransitivities in Formal Voting Bodies," mimeographed (Pittsburgh: Carnegie Mellon University, 1977).

[13]That is, for any y in $P(x)$, y beats x_n, x_n beats x_{n-1}, . . . , x_o beats x.

[14]Linda Cohen and Steven Matthews, "Constrained Plott Equilibria, Directional Equilibria, and Global Cycling Sets," Social Science Working Paper, California Institute of Technology, 1977; see also Linda Cohen, "Cyclic Sets in Multidimensional Voting Models," *Journal of Economic Theory*, Vol. 20 (February 1979), pp. 1–12.

[15]Norman Schofield, "Instability of Simple Dynamic Games," *Review of Economic Studies*, Vol. 45 (October 1978), pp. 575–594.

[16]Kenneth Shepsle, "Institutional Arrangements and Equilibrium in Multidimensional Voting Models," *American Journal of Political Science*, Vol. 23 (February 1979), pp. 27–59.

[17]Gerald H. Kramer, "A Dynamical Model of Political Equilibrium," *Journal of Economic Theory*, Vol. 16 (December 1977), pp. 310–334; and Kramer, "Some Extensions of a Dynamical Model of Electoral Competition," mimeographed (July 1977).

[18]That is, $v(x) = \max_{y} n(x, y)$.

[19]That is, $n^* = \min_{x} v(x)$. Of course, more than one x may share the same minmax number.

[20]The notion that candidates, parties, and so on seek to minimize, rather than maximize, the size of winning coalitions is one application of the so-called size principle. According to this principle, in situations in which opponents are completely opposed (that is, situations that are zero-sum so that what one wins, the other loses) and information is perfect, coalitions tend toward minimal winning size. Elections and binary votes on motions are one of the few places in the political world in which the zero-sum condition can be realized. The size principle was defined, described, and defended in William H. Riker, *The Theory of Political Coalitions* (New Haven: Yale University Press, 1963). Subsequently much empirical work has shown that, despite ideological concerns that encourage larger than minimal winning coalitions in such matters as cabinet formation (compare Abram DeSwaan, *Coalition Theories and Cabinet Formation* [San Francisco: Jossey-Bass, 1973], which rejects the size principle; and Michael Leiserson, "Factions and Coalitions in One-Party Japan," *American Political Science Review*, Vol. 62 [September 1968], pp. 710–737,

and Robert Axelrod, *Conflict of Interest* [Chicago: Markham, 1970], which accept a version of the size principle modified to account for ideology), still the force of the principle can be observed in such facts as that coalitions in the U.S. Senate tend to be minimal *constitutional* majorities (that is, just over half of the membership rather than just over half of those voting) (compare David Koehler, "Legislative Coalition Formation: The Meaning of Minimal Winning Size with Uncertain Participation," *American Journal of Political Science,* Vol. 19 [February 1975], pp. 27–39), and that minimal winning cabinet coalitions tend to last much longer than either oversized or undersized coalitions (compare Lawrence C. Dodd, *Coalitions in Parliamentary Government* [Princeton, Princeton University Press, 1976]). The issue of the theoretical validity of the size principle has also been much discussed. In Robert Butterworth, "A Research Note on the Size of Winning Coalitions," *American Political Science Review,* Vol. 65 (September 1971), pp. 741–745, and Russell Hardin, "Hollow Victory: The Minimum Winning Coalition," *American Political Science Review,* Vol. 70 (December 1976), pp. 1202–1214, supposed counterexamples to the size principle are mistakenly presented. The errors in these supposed examples are pointed out in William H. Riker, "Comment on Butterworth," *American Political Science Review,* Vol. 65 (September 1971), pp. 745–747, and William H. Riker, "Communication on Hardin," *American Political Science Review,* Vol. 71 (September 1977), pp. 1056–1059. In Kenneth Shepsle, "The Size of Winning Coalitions," *American Political Science Review,* Vol. 68 (June 1974), pp. 505–518, the size principle is deduced from concepts for solutions of *n*-person games. In Richard McKelvey and Richard Smith, "Internal Stability and the Size Principle," mimeographed (Pittsburgh: Carnegie Mellon University, 1974), in Riker, "Communication on Hardin," and, with great mathematical elegance, in Norman Schofield, "Generalized Bargaining Sets for Cooperative Games," *International Journal of Game Theory,* Vol. 7, No. 3–4 (1978), pp. 183–199, the size principle is deduced from the notion of the so-called bargaining set as a solution for *n*-person games. (For the definition of the *bargaining set,* see R. J. Aumann and Michael Maschler, "The Bargaining Set for Cooperative Games," in *Advances in Game Theory, Annals of Mathematics Study No. 52,* ed. M. Drescher, L. S. Shapley, and A. W. Tucker (Princeton: Princeton University Press, 1964).

[21]William H. Riker, "Arrow's Theorem and Some Examples of the Paradox of Voting," in *Mathematical Applications in Political Science,* ed. J. Claunch (Dallas: Arnold Foundation, Southern Methodist University, 1965), pp. 57–59.

[22]*Congressional Record,* Vol. 35 (1902), p. 5953.

[23]But in June 1911, the Democrats had a clear majority and defeated the Sutherland amendment, so the constitutional amendment passed. Thus the cycle was broken, but it had lasted more than ten years.

[24]Residents of countries (like Britain) with rigidly disciplined two parties often believe that such contrivances as the DePew amendment must be rare because they seem to depend on the remarkable ingenuity of men like DePew. But whenever there are more than two parties or factions, it often happens that the mere offering of alternative motions expressing the true values of each faction presents an opportunity for agenda control. This is what happened in the case of the Powell amendment. Bo Bjurulf and Richard Niemi found similar instances in Scandinavian parliaments during periods of minority coalitions. See Bjurulf and Niemi, "Strategic Voting in Scandinavian Parliaments," *Scandinavian Political Studies,* Vol. 1, New Series (1978), pp. 5–22. In such cases agenda control is obtained not by introducing new alternatives, but by exploiting alternatives naturally in the agenda.

Chapter 8

[1]J. M. Keynes, *The General Theory of Employment Interest and Money* (New York: Harcourt Brace Jovanovich, 1937), p. 383.

[2]To define a *core,* let N be the set of all participants, $N = (1, 2, \ldots, n)$. Let x be a vector in R^n of payment to participants, $x = (x_1, x_2, \ldots, x_n)$. Let K be the set of all possible coalitions, C, of participants. Conventionally, K is the power set of N, that is, $P(N)$. Hence $K = (C_1, C_2, \ldots, C_{2^n})$ and includes all coalitions of a single individual. Let the value of C_j be $v(C_j)$; and let $v(C_j) = k_j$, where $j = 1, 2, \ldots, 2^n$, and k_j is the amount the jth coalition can assure itself by itself. Then the core is defined as an allocation such that

$$\sum_{i \text{ in } C_j} x_i \geq k_j \qquad \text{for all } C_j \text{ in } K$$

[3]In terms of the definition in note 2, the k_j for some j is partially determined by j's initial endowments. If k_j is low, then, although j cannot be worse off in the core, still j may not satisfy his or her dreams.

[4]An example is the declaration of war by the United States on December 8, 1941. Only one member of Congress was opposed. Hence effective unanimity existed. But clearly the political decision had in fact been made the day before the voting occurred.

[5]William H. Riker, "A Method of Determining the Significance of Roll Calls in Voting Bodies," in *Legislative Behavior,* ed. John Wahlke and Heinz Eulau (Chicago: Free Press, 1959), pp. 377–384.

[6]David Easton, *The Political System: An Inquiry into the State of Political Science* (New York: Knopf, 1953), pp. 129–134.

[7]William H. Riker, "The Future of a Science of Politics," *The American Behavioral Scientist,* Vol. 21 (September 1977), pp. 11–38.

Chapter 9

[1]One previous effort along similar lines is the notion of critical elections, first set forth by V. O. Key, Jr., "A Theory of Critical Elections," *Journal of Politics,* Vol. 17 (February 1955), pp. 3–18. The goal of Key's analysis was to identify, by looking at the distribution of votes among parties, certain crucial turning points in national politics. The identification of crucial times also involved some identification of crucial issues. From this analysis one gets a picture of a new issue, coming from nowhere, abruptly breaking up a previously winning coalition. This interpretation simply cannot be sustained, as is elegantly demonstrated in Allan J. Lichtman, "Critical Election Theory and the Reality of American Presidential Politics, 1916–40," *American Historical Review,* Vol. 81 (April 1976), pp. 317–357.

The picture I offer here is quite different. Key and his successors were never able to identify critical elections precisely. Which election from 1852 to 1868 or from 1888 to 1900 or from 1928 to 1940 was "critical"? The very question reveals the inadequacy of the notion, for it turns out that the fundamental and underlying change is not in election results but in political agendas. Thus my approach is to describe the change in agendas, which in national politics is a temporally long process. One therefore expects not critical elections but rather constant experimentation by losers to find an issue that cleaves the winners. When found, it is exploited until elections begin to go the other way. Consequently, what I offer is not an identification of critical elections but rather a theory about the way that the forces of partisan interest bring about a change in national agendas.

²Such an inquiry is pointless anyway, for it is impossible to specify the cause of a huge event like a war. A cause is a necessary and sufficient condition; and for a temporal event, a unique necessary and sufficient condition is the just-preceding event with the same spatial boundaries and the same movers and actors. (See William H. Riker, "Events and Situations" and "The Causes of Events," *Journal of Philosophy,* Vol. 54 [January 31, 1957], pp. 57–69, and Vol. 55 [March 27, 1958], pp. 281–290.) The cause of a war is thus the entire state of the warring parties just before the war. Such states cannot, of course, be fully or even roughly specified.

³One must not attribute too much prescience to the prophets of civil war. Threats of secession had been a continuing feature of political life throughout the first generation of the Republic. One of the main motives for the constitutional convention of 1787 was the fear of western secession (to join Spain). The Virginia and Kentucky resolutions of 1798 had been Jefferson's threat of secession, and at the Hartford Convention of 1814 a rump of Federalists had threatened a separate peace. Of course, none of those who, before 1861, wrote so easily of civil war had the slightest comprehension of how awful that war would be. Blithe predictions of disunion were not predictions of the catastrophe that actually occurred.

⁴Glover Moore, *The Missouri Controversy, 1819–1821* (Lexington: University of Kentucky Press, 1953), pp. 36–37.

⁵Cecil B. Egerton, "Rufus King and the Missouri Question" (Ph.D. diss., Claremont Graduate School, 1967, University Microfilms), pp. 220, 222.

⁶This is an elegant application of the size principle, because Jackson was reducing internal strains in his own coalition. See William H. Riker, *The Theory of Political Coalitions* (New Haven: Yale University Press, 1963), passim.

⁷Lee Benson, *Toward the Scientific Study of History* (Philadelphia: Lippincott, 1972), pp. 225–339.

⁸Louis Filler, *The Crusade Against Slavery, 1830–1860* (New York: Harper and Row, 1960), p. 145.

[9]Gilbert H. Barnes, *The Anti-Slavery Impulse, 1830–1844* (New York: Appleton, Century, 1933), p. 256, reports a count of petitions by presenters, showing that Whigs presented 95 percent.

[10]Barnes, p. 118, remarks: "In 1835, . . . 'The Whig minority was tyrannized over and they were naturally in a refractory, restless and perturbed condition, and if they could not be heard orderly, they would do so disorderly.' To raise disorder, no better weapon than abolition petitions could have been devised."

[11]Ibid., p. 189.

[12]James K. Polk, *Diary,* 4 vols., ed. Milo M. Quaife (Chicago: McClurg, 1910).

[13]Charles B. Going, *David Wilmot: Free Soiler* (New York: Appleton, 1929), pp. 16, 24, 27.

[14]Filler, p. 187. Going, p. 499, quotes Wilmot's platform as Republican candidate for governor in 1857: "Slavery is the deadly enemy of free labor."

[15]Polk, Vol. 2, p. 76: "Mexico is indebted to the U.S. in a large sum, which she is unable to pay. . . . When peace is made the only indemnity which the U.S. can have will be a cession of territory. . . . No Government [i.e. of Mexico], however, . . . is strong enough to make a treaty ceding territory and long maintain power unless they could receive . . . money enough to support the army. Whatever party can keep the army in its support can hold the power."

[16]*Congressional Globe,* 29th Cong., 1st sess., p. 1218.

[17]Polk, Vol. 2, p. 77, August 10, 1846.

[18]Ibid.

Chapter 10

[1]See, for example, the calculation in Peter C. Fishburn, *The Theory of Social Choice* (Princeton: Princeton University Press, 1973), p. 172, showing similar results for the Borda and Copeland methods.

[2]It probably ought to be pointed out here that the notion of a public interest, so cherished by populist propagandists, is not, technically speaking, rendered meaningless simply because the populist interpretation of voting is meaningless. A public interest is an interest attached to the collective body of the society; and as long as a society exists, it has, presumably, some purposes, which are its common or public interests. (See Brian Barry, *Political Argument* [New York: Humanities Press, 1965], passim.) By definition, however, a common or public interest is held in common, so voting is unnecessary to reveal it: Any randomly chosen member of the society can articulate public interest as well as any other, provided he or she thinks about the interest of the society rather than his or her own private interest. This fact reveals the emptiness of the populist interpretation of the public interest. No public interest can be defined in practice if people must count heads to discover it. A public interest may even exist when people do not agree. There may really be an objectively right but not indisputably evident policy for the society—and of course every man and woman is then free to offer his or her interpretation. But when people have to vote on which interpretation is correct, then clearly the true public interest will not be revealed, without substantial unanimity. Either Ralph Nader or George Wallace might state the public interest correctly, but voting will not tell us which one has the right vision. Indeed they both may be simply opportunistic and malicious. So what is implied by the emptiness of populism is not the absence of a public interest but rather that the public interest cannot be revealed by nonunanimous voting. This means, of course, that all politicians and publicists who claim to explicate the public interest from an election are merely interpreting election results in a nonauthoritative way, although they have just as much or as little right as anyone else to state their interpretation.

[3]It may seem to some that I have applied an easier test to liberalism than to populism. I allow liberalism to survive provided it works occasionally, but I do not admit the survival of populism if it fails at all. These different standards are imposed because of the difference in the claims made in the two interpretations. Populism is supposed to reveal a substantive will, a proposition with content. Yet if voting can fail to reveal such propositions accurately and if we do not and cannot know in any particular instance whether failure has occurred, then none of the propositions supposedly revealed can be believed. Liberalism on the other hand asks only for a workable procedure—namely, that voting eliminate some offenders—and if it works sometimes, that is enough.

Glossary

Acyclicity A property of a set of alternatives such that the alternatives are not arranged in a cycle (by an individual or by a social choice function).

Anonymity A property of a social choice function such that undifferentiated voters are not individually identified.

Approval voting A social choice function such that the social choice has the largest number of votes when voters are permitted to cast one vote for as many alternatives as they wish.

Arrow's theorem, or the General Possibility Theorem The proposition that, if a social choice function satisfies universal admissibility, unanimity (or monotonicity and citizens' sovereignty), independence from irrelevant alternatives, and nondictatorship, then the social choice may not satisfy transitivity.

Bentham criterion See *Utilitarian social choice function.*

Borda rule A social choice function such that the social choice for a preference profile is the alternative with the largest sum of rank scores across all voters' preference orders, where, for each voter, the highest score is given to the alternative in first place, the next highest score is given to the alternative in second place, and so on down to the lowest score given to the alternative in last place.

Citizens' sovereignty, or nonimposition A property of a social choice function such that it is not the case that a particular alternative is chosen from any preference profile. This is one of the fairness conditions in Arrow's theorem.

Condorcet rule A social choice function such that the social choice beats or ties all other alternatives in paired comparisons.

Condorcet winner The alternative selected by the Condorcet social choice function.

Consistency conditions on choice from a set and its subsets:

Property α *(Weak Axiom of Revealed Preference)*   The condition that, if the choice from a set is in a subset, then that choice is the choice from the subset.

Property β   The condition that, if a choice from a set is a member of a subset, then all choices from the subset are choices from the set.

Consistency criterion   A property of a social choice function such that, if the voters are divided into two groups and if one alternative is a social choice in both groups, then that alternative is chosen from the voters in the group as a whole.

Copeland rule   A social choice function such that the social choice for a preference profile is chosen the largest net number of times by simple majority decision over pairs of alternatives (where "net" means the number of times chosen less the number of times not chosen).

Cycle of alternatives   An arrangement of alternatives compared by the relation (*R*) of preference and indifference combined such that one alternative is ahead of a second, a second is ahead of a third, and so on until the last is ahead of the first.

Demand-revealing rule (also known as the Groves-Ledyard rule or the Tideman-Tullock rule)   A utilitarian (Benthamite additive utility) social choice function such that voters are putatively encouraged to reveal their true cardinal utilities by reason of the Clarke tax, which is a tax on a voter's contribution, if it exists, to the margin of victory for an alternative.

Democracy   A form of government consisting of a political ideal of freedom, equality, and self-control (that is, government, at least partially, by oneself as distinguished from government by others), and a political method of free and equal participation in government.

Duverger's law   The proposition that the simple majority, single ballot system favors the two-party system.

Equilibrium   The state toward which internal forces propel a process and at which a process remains stable. For majority voting, a strong equilibrium occurs when one alternative simultaneously defeats all others and a weak equilibrium occurs when there is a Condorcet winner.

Hare method of proportional representation   See *Single transferable vote.*

Independence from irrelevant alternatives   A property of a social choice function such that, if two preference profiles are identical with respect to some subset of alternatives, then the social choice from each profile is the same from that subset. This is one of the fairness conditions in Arrow's theorem.

Indifference relation (I)   A relation imposed by an individual on two alternatives placing one the same as the other in terms of desirability.

Highest-average method   A method of counting votes under proportional representation such that each seat is assigned to the party with the highest ratio of votes received to the number of seats already assigned plus one.

Largest-remainder method   A method of counting votes under proportional representation such that, given a quota for a seat (which is approximately the ratio of total votes to total seats), each seat is assigned to the party for which the remaining votes are largest, after subtracting from its original votes the product of the quota and the number of seats already assigned to that party.

Monotonicity   A property of a social choice function such that, if an individual raises the socially chosen alternative in his or her preference order and other individuals do not change their orders, then the function continues to select that social choice, and, if an individual lowers an alternative not socially chosen and others do not change their orders, then the function continues not to select the losing alternative. Monotonicity is one of the fairness conditions in Arrow's theorem.

Neutrality   A property of a social choice function such that, if alternatives are permuted the same way in all preference orders of a preference profile, the social choice function selects from the permuted profile the alternative that is the transformation of the alternative selected from the unpermuted profile.

Nondictatorship   A property of a social choice function such that it is not the case that, if one individual prefers one alternative to another, the preferred alternative is the social choice. This is one of the fairness conditions in Arrow's theorem.

Paradox of voting   The situation in which the preference profile of a society is such that each individual has a preference order (that is, a transitive and complete arrangement of alternatives), while the arrangement of alternatives produced by simple majority decision on pairs of alternatives is not an ordering (that is, is not transitive).

Path independence   A property of a social choice function such that the choice from a union of two sets is the same as the choice from the union of the choices from the two sets.

Plurality rule   A social choice function such that the social choice is the alternative with the largest number of first places in preference orders in a preference profile.

Preference and indifference relation (R)   A relation imposed by an individual on two alternatives placing one ahead of or the same as the other in terms of desirability.

Preference order   A transitive and complete arrangement of alternatives by an individual in terms of the relation R of preference and indifference combined. A preference order is a permutation of n alternatives.

Preference profile   A set of preference orders, one for each member of society.

Preference relation (P)   A relation imposed by an individual on two alternatives placing one ahead of the other in terms of desirability.

Proportional representation (PR) for governing bodies   An electoral system in which, insofar as is arithmetically possible, seats are assigned to a party in proportion to the votes cast for it. Ideally, for each constituency, the ratio of the votes cast for a particular political party to the total votes cast equals the ratio of the number of seats for that party to the total number of seats in the body.

Quasi-transitivity   A property of a set of alternatives such that the alternatives are arranged (by an individual or by a social choice function) according to the relation P of preference but not according to the relation R of preference and indifference combined.

Runoff election   A two-stage social choice function with majority rule such that the alternative with over half of the votes is selected at the first stage, but, if no such alternative exists, the two alternatives with the most votes are subjected to simple majority decision at the second stage.

Schwartz rule   A social choice function such that the social choice is the Condorcet winner or, if none exists, the alternatives in the top cycle, which is a cycle of the alternatives that beat all alternatives not in the cycle.

Self-control in democratic theory   The ability of the individual to control his or her environment and future by participation in the government of a society.

Simple majority decision   A social choice function for exactly two alternatives by the rule that the social choice is the alternative for which more than half (or, in case of a tie, half) of the votes are cast.

Single-peakedness   A condition on a preference profile such that the profile contains a Condorcet winner when every curve representing a preference order (with alternatives on the horizontal axis and degree of preference on the vertical axis) is single-peaked.

Single-member district system An electoral system in which, in each constituency, one and only one official is chosen for a governing body.

Single transferable vote A kind of proportional representation and a method of vote-counting such that, given a quota to elect a candidate, an individual's vote is used in whole or in part for her or his first choice (until that candidate is elected by receiving the requisite quota of votes, or eliminated by receiving the fewest votes when no candidate has the quota) and then for the second choice, and so on, until her or his vote is used up.

Social choice function A rule, operating on the preference profile of a group, to select one (or more) alternatives out of a set of alternatives.

Sophisticated voting A kind of strategic voting in which the voter eliminates, for all participants, all strategies (that is, complete choices of alternatives to support) that are dominated by (that is, are worse or no better than) an alternative strategy and then votes according to one of his or her remaining strategies.

Strategic voting Voting not in accord with the voter's true preference order, with the intent of bringing about a social choice more desired by the voter than the social choice that would result, other things being equal, from voting in accord with the voter's true preference order.

Transitivity A condition of logical arrangement such that, if one alternative is related in a particular way to a second and if a second is related in the same way to a third, then the first is related in that way to the third.

Unanimity A property of a social choice function such that, if all individuals in a group prefer one alternative to another, the social choice is the alternative thus preferred. This is one of the fairness conditions in Arrow's theorem.

Undifferentiatedness A property of a social choice function such that, if preference orders of alternatives are permuted among individuals in a group, the function chooses the same alternative. By this property (usually but inaccurately called "anonymity"), the social choice function treats all individuals the same.

Universal admissibility A property of a social choice function such that the function accepts any possible preference order by an individual. This is one of the fairness conditions in Arrow's theorem.

Utilitarian social choice function   A rule for selection of a social choice such that the winning alternative has, over the set of all voters, the largest sum (Bentham) or the largest product (Nash) of voters' cardinal utility numbers.

Utility   A measure of preference among alternatives. Ordinal utility is based on an ordinal scale of measurement. Cardinal utility is based on a cardinal scale of measurement.

Von Neumann–Morgenstern utility measurement   A method of transforming ordinal utility for an ordered set of alternatives to cardinal utility.

Vote-trading   A kind of strategic voting such that each trader receives vote support on his or her more-preferred alternative from trading partners, who vote contrary to their true preference orders, in return for which each trader, by voting contrary to his or her own true preference order on his or her less-preferred alternative, gives vote support to trading partners on that alternative, which is their more-preferred alternative.

Weighted voting   A class of voting rules (such as weighted majority voting) such that each voter is assigned a specified number of votes.

Bibliography

American Political Science Association, Committee on Political Parties. *Toward a More Responsible Two-Party System*. New York: Holt, Rinehart and Winston, 1950.

Arrow, Kenneth. *Social Choice and Individual Values*. 2nd ed. New Haven: Yale University Press, 1963.

Aumann, R. J., and Michael Maschler. "The Bargaining Set for Cooperative Games." In *Advances in Game Theory*, edited by M. Dresher, L. S. Shapley, and A. W. Tucker, pp. 443–476. Annals of Mathematics Study, no. 52. Princeton, N. J.: Princeton University Press, 1964.

Banzhaf, John F., III. "Weighted Voting Doesn't Work: A Mathematical Analysis." *Rutgers Law Review*. Vol. 19 (Winter 1965), pp. 317–343.

Barnes, Gilbert H. *The Anti Slavery Impulse, 1830–1844*. New York: Appleton-Century, 1933.

Barry, Brian. *Political Argument*. New York: Humanities Press, 1965.

Beer, Samuel H. "New Structures of Democracy." In *Democracy in the Mid-Twentieth Century*, edited by William N. Chambers and Robert H. Salisbury, pp. 30–59. St. Louis: Washington University Press, 1960.

Berlin, Isaiah. *Two Concepts of Liberty*. Oxford, England: Oxford University Press, 1958.

Bjurulf, Bo, and Richard Niemi. "Strategic Voting in Scandinavian Parliaments." *Scandinavian Political Studies*. Vol. 1 (new series, 1978), pp. 5–22.

Black, Duncan. "On the Rationale of Group Decision Making." *Journal of Political Economy*. Vol. 56 (February 1948), pp. 23–34.

———. *The Theory of Committees and Elections*. Cambridge, England: Cambridge University Press, 1958.

———. "Partial Justification of the Borda Count." *Public Choice*. Vol. 28 (Winter 1976), pp. 1–15.

Black, Duncan, and R. A. Newing. *Committee Decisions with Complementary Valuation*. Edinburgh: William Hodge, 1951.

Brams, Stephen J., and Peter C. Fishburn. "Approval Voting." *American Political Science Review*. Vol. 72 (September 1978), pp. 831–847.

Brown, Donald. "Acyclic Choice." Cowles Foundation Discussion Paper. New Haven: Yale University, 1973.

———. "An Approximate Solution to Arrow's Problem." *Journal of Economic Theory*. Vol. 9 (December 1974), pp. 375–383.

Buchanan, James. "Individual Choice in Voting and the Market." *Journal of Political Economy*. Vol. 62 (August 1954), pp. 334–343.

Buchanan, James, and Gordon Tullock. *The Calculus of Consent*. Ann Arbor: University of Michigan Press, 1962.

Cohen, Linda. "Cyclic Sets in Multidimensional Voting Models." *Journal of Economic Theory*. Vol. 20 (February 1979), pp. 1–12.

Cohen, Linda, and Steven Matthews. "Constrained Plott Equilibria, Directional Equilibria, and Global Cycling Sets." Social Science Working Paper. Pasadena: California Institute of Technology, 1977.

Dahl, Robert. *A Preface to Democratic Theory*. Chicago: University of Chicago Press, 1956.

Davis, Otto A., and Melvin J. Hinich. "A Mathematical Model of Policy Formation in a Democratic Society." In *Mathematical Applications in Political Science II,* edited by J. A. Bernd, pp. 175–208. Dallas: Southern Methodist University Press, 1966.

Davis, Otto A., Melvin J. Hinich, and Peter C. Ordeshook. "An Expository Development of a Mathematical Model of the Electoral Process." *American Political Science Review*. Vol. 64 (June 1970), pp. 426–449.

Deegan, John, and E. W. Packel. "A New Index of Power for Simple n-Person Games." *International Journal of Game Theory*. Vol. 7, No. 2 (1978), pp. 113–123.

DeMeyer, Frank, and Charles Plott. "The Probability of a Cyclical Majority." *Econometrica*. Vol. 38 (March 1970), pp. 345–354.

Dodd, Lawrence. *Coalitions in Parliamentary Government*. Princeton: Princeton University Press, 1976.

Doron, Gideon. "The Hare Voting System Is Inconsistent." *Political Studies*. Vol. 27 (June 1979), pp. 283–286.

Doron, Gideon, and Richard Kronick. "Single Transferable Vote: An Example of a Perverse Social Choice Function." *American Journal of Political Science*. Vol. 21 (May 1977), pp. 303–311.

Downs, Anthony. *An Economic Theory of Democracy*. New York: Harper and Row, 1956.

Dummet, Michael, and Robin Farquharson. "Stability in Voting." *Econometrica*. Vol. 29 (January 1961), pp. 33–42.

Dyer, James S., and Ralph E. Miles, Jr. "An Actual Application of Collective Choice Theory to the Selection of Trajectories for the Mariner Jupiter/Saturn 1977 Project." *Operations Research*. Vol. 24 (March 1976), pp. 220–244.

Egerton, Cecil B. *Rufus King and the Missouri Question*. Ph.D. dissertation, Claremont Graduate School, 1967. University Microfilms.

Enelow, James. "Non-cooperative Counterthreats to Vote Trading." *American Journal of Political Science*. Vol. 23 (February 1979), pp. 121–138.

———. *A Game Theoretic Model of Legislative Vote Trading*. Ph.D. dissertation, University of Rochester, 1977.

Farquharson, Robin. *Theory of Voting.* New Haven: Yale University Press, 1969.

———. "Sophisticated Voting and an Example Due to M. Kreweras." In *La Decision,* edited by G. Th. Guilbaud, pp. 115–122. Paris: Editions du Centre Nationale de la Recherche Scientifique, 1969.

Ferejohn, John A. "Brown's Theory of Collective Choice." Social Science Working Paper. Pasadena: California Institute of Technology, March 1976.

Ferejohn, John A., and David M. Grether. "Weak Path Independence." *Journal of Economic Theory.* Vol. 14 (January 1977), pp. 19–31.

Fishburn, Peter C. *The Theory of Social Choice.* Princeton: Princeton University Press, 1973.

———. "Voter Concordance, Simple Majorities and Group Decision Methods." *Behavioral Science.* Vol. 18 (September 1973), pp. 364–376.

———. "Paradoxes of Voting." *American Political Science Review.* Vol. 68 (June 1974), pp. 537–546.

———. "Condorcet Social Choice Functions." *SIAM Journal of Applied Mathematics.* Vol. 33 (November 1977), pp. 469–489.

Gärdenfors, Peter. "Manipulation of Social Choice Functions." *Journal of Economic Theory.* Vol. 13 (October 1976), pp. 217–228.

———. "A Concise Proof of a Theorem on Manipulation of Social Choice Functions." *Public Choice.* Vol. 32 (Winter 1977), pp. 137–140.

Gehrlein, William V., and Peter C. Fishburn. "The Probability of the Paradox of Voting." *Journal of Economic Theory.* Vol. 13 (August 1976), pp. 14–25.

Gibbard, Allan. "Manipulation of Voting Schemes: A General Result." *Econometrica.* Vol. 41 (July 1973), pp. 587–601.

———. "Manipulation of Voting Schemes That Mix Voting with Chance." *Econometrica.* Vol. 45 (April 1977), pp. 665–679.

Good, I. J., and T. Nicholaus Tideman. "From Individual to Collective Ordering Through Multidimensional Attribute Space." *Proceedings of the Royal Society.* Vol. A-347 (1976), pp. 371–385.

Gorman, Mark, and Morton Kamien. "The Paradox of Voting: Probability Calculations." *Behavioral Science.* Vol. 13 (July 1968), pp. 306–316.

Greenberg, Joseph. "Consistent Majority Rules over Compact Sets of Alternatives." *Econometrica.* Vol. 47 (May 1979), pp. 627–636.

Hansson, Bengt. "The Existence of Group Preference Functions." *Public Choice.* Vol. 28 (Winter 1976), pp. 89–98.

———. "The Independence Condition in the Theory of Social Choice." *Theory and Decision.* Vol. 4 (September 1973), pp. 25–49.

Jamieson, D., and E. Luce. "Social Homogeneity and the Probability of Intransitive Majority Rule." *Journal of Economic Theory.* Vol. 5 (August 1972), pp. 79–87.

Kelly, Jerry S. "Strategy-Proofness and Social Choice Functions Without Single Valuedness." *Econometrica.* Vol. 45 (March 1977), pp. 439–446.

Kemeny, John. "Mathematics Without Numbers." *Daedalus.* Vol. 88 (Fall 1959), pp. 577–591.

Kendall, Willmoore. *John Locke and the Doctrine of Majority Rule.* Urbana: University of Illinois Press, 1941.

Key, V. O., Jr. "A Theory of Critical Elections." *Journal of Politics*. Vol. 17 (February 1955), pp. 3–18.

Koehler, David. "Legislative Coalition Formation: The Meaning of Minimal Winning Size with Uncertain Participation." *American Journal of Political Science*. Vol. 19 (February 1975), pp. 27–39.

Kramer, Gerald A. "A Dynamical Model of Political Equilibrium." *Journal of Economic Theory*. Vol. 16 (December 1977), pp. 310–334.

———. "On a Class of Equilibrium Conditions for Majority Rule." *Econometrica*. Vol. 41 (March 1973), pp. 285–297.

Levenglick, Arthur. "Fair and Reasonable Election Systems." *Behavioral Science*. Vol. 20 (January 1975), pp. 34–46.

Levine, Michael, and Charles Plott. "Agenda Influence and Its Implications." *Virginia Law Review*. Vol. 63 (May 1977), pp. 561–604.

Lichtman, Allan J. "Critical Election Theory and the Reality of American Presidential Politics, 1916–40." *American Historical Review*. Vol. 81 (April 1976), pp. 317–351.

Lowell, A. Lawrence. "The Influence of Party upon Legislation." *Annual Report of the American Historical Association for the Year 1901*. Vol. 1 (1901) pp. 321–542.

Ludwin, William G. "Strategic Voting and the Borda Method." *Public Choice*. Vol. 33, No. 1 (1978), pp. 85–90.

McKelvey, Richard D. "Policy Related Voting and Electoral Equilibrium." *Econometrica*. Vol. 43 (September 1975), pp. 815–843.

———. "Intransitivities in Multi-dimensional Voting Models and Some Implications for Agenda Control." *Journal of Economic Theory*. Vol. 12 (June 1976) pp. 472–482.

McKelvey, Richard D., and Richard Niemi. "A Multistage Game Representation of Sophisticated Voting for Binary Procedures." *Journal of Economic Theory*. Vol. 18 (January 1978), pp. 1–22.

McKelvey, Richard D., and Peter C. Ordeshook. "Vote Trading: An Experimental Study." Mimeographed. Pittsburgh: Carnegie Mellon University, 1978.

McKelvey, Richard D., and Richard E. Wendell. "Voting Equilibria in Multidimensional Choice Spaces." *Mathematics of Operations Research*. Vol. 1 (May 1976), pp. 144–158.

MacPherson, C. B. *Democratic Theory*. Oxford, England: Oxford University Press, 1973.

Majundar, Topas. "Choice and Revealed Preference." *Econometrica*. Vol. 24 (January 1956), pp. 71–73.

Mas-Colell, Andrew, and Hugo Sonnenschein. "General Possibility Theorem for Group Decision." *Review of Economic Studies*. Vol. 39 (April 1972), pp. 185–192.

May, Kenneth O. "A Set of Independent Necessary and Sufficient Conditions for Simple Majority Decision." *Econometrica*. Vol. 20 (October 1952), pp. 680–684.

Meehl, Paul E. "The Selfish Voter Paradox and the Thrown-Away Vote Argument." *American Political Science Review*. Vol. 70 (March 1977), pp. 11–30.

Moore, Glover. *The Missouri Controversy, 1819–1821*. Lexington: University of Kentucky Press, 1953.

Nash, J. F. "The Bargaining Problem." *Econometrica.* Vol. 18 (April 1950), pp. 155–162.

Niemi, Richard. "Majority Decision Making with Partial Unidimensionality." *American Political Science Review.* Vol. 63 (June 1969), pp. 489–497.

———. "The Occurrence of the Paradox of Voting in University Elections." *Public Choice.* Vol. 7 (Spring 1970), pp. 91–100.

Niemi, Richard, and Herbert Weisberg. "A Mathematical Solution for the Probability of the Paradox of Voting." *Behavioral Science.* Vol. 13 (July 1968), pp. 317–323.

Ordeshook, Peter C. "Extensions of a Model of the Electoral Process and Implications for the Theory of Responsible Parties." *Midwest Journal of Political Science.* Vol. 14 (February 1970), pp. 43–70.

Parekh, Bhikhu, ed. *Bentham's Political Thought.* London: Croom Helm, 1973.

Pattanaik, P. K. "Counter Threats and Strategic Manipulation." *Review of Economic Studies.* Vol. 43 (February 1976), pp. 11–18.

Peleg, Bezalel. "Constant Voting Systems." *Econometrica.* Vol. 46 (January 1978), pp. 153–161.

Plott, Charles. "Axiomatic Social Choice Theory." *American Journal of Political Science.* Vol. 20 (August 1976), pp. 511–596.

———. "Path Independence, Rationality, and Social Choice." *Econometrica.* Vol. 41 (October 1973), pp. 1075–1091.

———. "A Notion of Equilibrium and Its Possibility Under Majority Rule." *American Economic Review.* Vol. 57 (September 1967), pp. 787–806.

Plott, Charles, and Michael Levine. "A Model of Agenda Influence on Committee Decisions." *American Economic Review.* Vol. 68 (March 1978), pp. 146–160.

Rae, Douglas. *The Political Consequences of Electoral Laws.* New Haven: Yale University Press, 1971.

Ranney, Austin. *The Doctrine of Responsible Party Government.* Urbana: University of Illinois Press, 1954.

Raskin, Marcus. *Notes on the Old System: To Transform American Politics.* New York: McKay, 1974.

Riker, William H. "Events and Situations." *Journal of Philosophy.* Vol. 54 (January 31, 1957), pp. 57–69.

———. "The Causes of Events." *Journal of Philosophy.* Vol. 55 (March 27, 1958), pp. 281–290.

———. "The Paradox of Voting and Congressional Rules for Voting on Amendments." *American Political Science Review.* Vol. 52 (June 1958), pp. 349–366.

———. "A Method of Determining the Significance of Roll Calls in Voting Bodies." In *Legislative Behavior,* edited by John Wahlke and Heinz Eulau, pp. 377–384. Chicago: Free Press, 1959.

———. "Voting and the Summation of Preferences." *American Political Science Review.* Vol. 55 (December 1961), pp. 900–911.

———. *The Theory of Political Coalitions.* New Haven: Yale University Press, 1963.

———. *Democracy in the United States.* 2nd ed. New York: Macmillan, 1964.

———. "Arrow's Theorem and Some Examples of the Paradox of Voting." In *Mathematical Applications in Political Science,* Vol. 1, edited by John

Claunch, pp. 41–69. Dallas: Arnold Foundation, Southern Methodist University, 1965.

―――. "The Number of Political Parties: A Re-examination of Duverger's Law." *Comparative Politics*. Vol. 9 (October 1976), pp. 93–106.

―――. "The Future of a Science of Politics." *The American Behavioral Scientist*. Vol. 21 (September 1977), pp. 11–38.

―――. "Is 'A New and Superior Process' Really Superior?" *Journal of Political Economy*. Vol. 87 (August 1979), pp. 875–890.

―――. "Implications from the Disequilibrium of Majority Rule for the Study of Institutions." *American Political Science Review*. Vol. 74 (June 1980), pp. 432–446.

Riker, William H., and Steven J. Brams. "The Paradox of Vote Trading." *American Political Science Review*. Vol. 67 (December 1973), pp. 1235–1247.

Riker, William H., and Peter C. Ordeshook. "A Theory of the Calculus of Voting." *American Political Science Review*. Vol. 62 (March 1968), pp. 25–42.

―――. *An Introduction to Positive Political Theory*. Englewood Cliffs, N. J.: Prentice-Hall, 1973.

Rosenthal, Howard. "Game Theoretic Models of Bloc Voting Under Proportional Representation." *Public Choice*. Vol. 18 (Summer 1974), pp. 1–23.

Rusher, William A. *The Making of the New Majority Party*. New York: Sheed and Ward, 1975.

Saposnik, Rubin. "On the Transitivity of the Social Preference Relation Under Simple Majority Rule." *Journal of Economic Theory*. Vol. 10 (January 1975), pp. 1–7.

Satterthwaite, Mark. "Strategy Proofness and Arrow's Conditions." *Journal of Economic Theory*. Vol. 10 (October 1975), pp. 187–217.

Schofield, Norman. "Generalized Bargaining Sets for Cooperative Games." *International Journal of Game Theory*. Vol. 7, No. 3–4 (1978), pp. 183–199.

―――. "Instability of Simple Dynamic Games." *Review of Economic Studies*. Vol. 45 (October 1978), pp. 575–594.

Schwartz, Thomas. "Rationality and the Myth of the Maximum." *Noûs*. Vol. 6 (May 1972), pp. 97–117.

―――. "Collective Choice, Separation of Issues and Vote Trading." *American Political Science Review*. Vol. 71 (September 1977), pp. 999–1010.

Sen, Amartya K. *Collective Choice and Social Welfare*. San Francisco: Holden-Day, 1970.

―――. "Social Choice Theory: A Re-examination." *Econometrica*. Vol. 45 (January 1977), pp. 53–88.

Shapley, Lloyd, and Martin Shubik. "A Method of Evaluating Power in a Committee System." *American Political Science Review*. Vol. 48 (September 1954), pp. 787–792.

Shepsle, Kenneth. "Institutional Arrangements and Equilibrium in Multidimensional Voting Models." *American Journal of Political Science*. Vol.23 (February 1979), pp. 27–59.

Smith, John H. "The Aggregation of Preferences with Variable Electorate." *Econometrica*. Vol. 51 (November 1973), pp. 1027–1041.

Straffin, Philip. "Homogeneity, Independence, and Power Indices." *Public Choice*. Vol. 30 (Summer 1977), pp. 107–118.

Tideman, T. Nicholaus. "Ethical Foundations of the Demand Revealing Process." *Public Choice.* Vol. 29 (Special Supplement to Spring 1977), pp. 71–78.

Tideman, T. Nicholaus, and Gordon Tullock. "A New and Superior Process for Making Social Choices." *Journal of Political Economy.* Vol. 84 (December 1976), pp. 1145–1159.

Tversky, Amos. "Intransitivity of Preferences." *Psychological Review.* Vol. 76 (January 1969), pp. 31–48.

Vickery, William. "Utility, Strategy, and Social Decision Rules." *Quarterly Journal of Economics.* Vol. 74 (November 1960), pp. 507–535.

Von Neumann, John, and Oskar Morgenstern. *The Theory of Games and Economic Behavior.* 3rd ed. Princeton: Princeton University Press, 1953.

Young, H. P. "An Axiomatization of Borda's Rule." *Journal of Economic Theory.* Vol. 9 (September 1974), pp. 43–52.

————. "Social Choice Scoring Functions." *SIAM Journal of Applied Mathematics.* Vol. 28 (June 1975), pp. 824–838.

————. *Lobbying and Campaigning with Application to the Measure of Power.* Laxenburg, Austria: International Institute for Applied Systems Analysis, 1977.

Index